THE LOYAL LIEUTENANT

GEORGE HINCAPIE

THE LOYAL LIEUTENANT

MY STORY

Leading Out Lance and Pushing Through the Pain on the Rocky Road to Paris

GEORGE HINCAPIE AND CRAIG HUMMER

HarperSport
An Imprint of HarperCollins*Publishers*

HarperSport
An Imprint of HarperCollins*Publishers*
77–85 Fulham Palace Road,
Hammersmith, London W6 8JB

www.harpercollins.co.uk

First published in the US by William Morrow,
an imprint of HarperCollins*Publishers* 2014
This edition published 2014

Designed by Jamie Lynn Kerner

1 3 5 7 9 10 8 6 4 2

© George Hincapie and Craig Hummer 2014

All photographs are courtesy of the author, unless otherwise indicated.

While every effort has been made to trace the owners of copyright material
reproduced herein and secure permissions, the publishers would like to
apologise for any omissions and will be pleased to incorporate missing
acknowledgements in any future edition of this book.

George Hincapie and Craig Hummer assert the moral
right to be identified as the authors of this work

A catalogue record of this book
is available from the British Library

HB ISBN 978-0-00-754955-9
PB ISBN 978-0-00-754957-3

Printed and bound in Great Britain by
Clays Ltd, St Ives plc

All rights reserved. No part of this publication may be
reproduced, stored in a retrieval system, or transmitted,
in any form or by any means, electronic, mechanical,
photocopying, recording or otherwise, without the prior
written permission of the publishers.

MIX
Paper from
responsible sources
FSC
www.fsc.org   FSC° C007454

FSC™ is a non-profit international organisation established to promote
the responsible management of the world's forests. Products carrying the
FSC label are independently certified to assure consumers that they come
from forests that are managed to meet the social, economic and
ecological needs of present and future generations,
and other controlled sources.

Find out more about HarperCollins and the environment at
www.harpercollins.co.uk/green

To my mom and dad. For the endless support—I can only hope to be as good as a parent to my children as you have been to me.

To Melanie, Julia, Enzo, and baby on the way. You are my raison d'être—I love you each more than words can say.

—GH

To my wife, Jennifer, who usually makes me laugh and always dares me to dream.

—CH

COAUTHOR'S NOTE

I SET OUT TO write a story with a man who just happened to be a cyclist.

George is many things to many people—son, sibling, friend, teammate, rival, cheater, mentor, and hero. The last moniker is the tricky one—rarely can "heroes" live up to the hype. Their status is a projection of perfection, which for 99.99 percent of athletes is an unattainable illusion, created by a fan base that chooses to be blind to the faults that make ANY hero, at his or her core, human.

What made George such a great subject of study for me was that his passion for everything he does is matched by his fans' fervor. His unique path through the labyrinth of life provides a motivational, and at times cautionary, tale of what can be attained through dedication, through an almost surreal singular focus.

We now know that George, like so many other cyclists of his generation, succumbed to the temptation of performance-enhancing drugs. Some people who read this book will be unable to look past that transgression. But what I would hope, and what George and I have tried in these pages to show, is that George's story is much more than that decision.

The sum of any of us is more than just one event, one choice, one path. George has ridden on many roads, and as divergent, varied, smooth, or troublesome as they have been, they have all led here. In that sense, he's no different than you, the reader.

For all of us, each moment is a chance for greatness.

FOREWORD

BY LANCE ARMSTRONG

GEORGE AND I GO back a long way: we've been friends for over twenty-five years now. *Domestique* was a word thrown around cycling a lot, referring to someone who operated as a helper or worker. I don't even know how much that term is really used anymore in cycling, but I do know it should never be used to describe George Hincapie. He was always so much more than that. George was always capable of being a champion in any race he entered. In the tours we raced together, George put all personal ambition aside in the interest of the team. He was always the most consistent ally, dependable teammate, and loyal friend you could ever have. It wasn't in his character to ever flinch or budge an inch on that. I'm proud that he's been one of my closest friends for twenty-five years. George was a little bit like cycling's answer to Scottie Pippen. Like Pippen in basketball, while George may always be remembered in a supporting role on championship teams, everyone in his sport knew he was one of the best men in history to ever compete.

The first time we met, George and I were just kids training at the Olympic Training Center. He was fifteen, while my seventeenth birthday was just around the corner. Before I even had a chance to meet George, I'd *heard* about him. Back then there were weekly and monthly cycling magazines out there—pretty primitive little things that came in the mail—and George was already being written about with a buzz around him. He was living outside New York City and they had these weekly races inside Central Park where George made a name for himself kicking everybody's ass. He had heard of me and I had heard of him. I saw this huge goofy kid with even bigger hair after I showed up from Plano, Texas, driving my IROC-Z with my bike on top. We immediately hit it off. Looking back, that was unusual for me. At that time, being the punk sixteen-year-old kid that I was, whenever I heard about another young, hotshot kid to look out for, I usually didn't warm to them all that quickly. I was already feuding with a few other hotshots. But something about George was different, not only for me but for everybody. He puts you at ease. We went from that Olympic Training Center to the Olympic team and then basically spent our entire professional careers together. I turned pro a little earlier and went to Motorola, and when he was available we recruited him to come to Motorola. I won the world championships in 1993 and he turned pro in 1994. We spent all the next few years together. We really got to know each other living in Como, Italy, with the rest of the team.

And then, of course, you can't not talk about that decision that we were all forced to make, when the majority of the peloton was in the process of going from low-octane to high-octane doping. There it was. When we as a group made that decision to play ball, George and I, along with the others on the team, crossed over that threshold together. But none of those kids who threw their legs over those bikes and made that decision were savages or robots or machines; all of us made that decision as human beings. Drugs were so prevalent in that era that the decision itself, as our team saw it, was either play ball with everyone else or go home. And now the world knows what George and I chose and we have to live with the consequences for the rest of our lives.

I got my diagnosis in the fall of 1996. Up until then, competition for me had always been about winning or losing, but suddenly it was about survival or death. Motorola went away that same year. George switched over to the U.S. Postal team in 1997. I took that year off to focus on my health and recovery, but George continued to be a constant force in my life and a great friend to me through that difficult time. I reunited with George on the Postal team in 1998 after I decided to return to racing. That year was a mixed bag for me, and I wasn't entirely sure I was even ready to race again. George and I weren't racing much together that year. After a couple races, one day I was getting my ass kicked in some frigid crosswinds and found myself thinking, What the fuck am I doing here? I pulled off to the side of the road, got in the team car, went back to the hotel, and told everybody I was going home. It was a hard time, but I ended up getting my shit together and finishing the season. I decided to race the 1999 season, which was where George and I were truly reunited. We won the tour seven times after that year.

The last two years for George and me have obviously been the most difficult, with everything that's happened and gone on around us. Nothing ever tested our friendship like what's gone on for both of us over that time. I wasn't sure we would get it back, but I'm very fortunate that we did and that George is still a very close friend of mine. We talk weekly, do fund-raisers together, ride our bikes together, and talk about our children. He makes fun of my newfound passion for golf as much as I make fun of his newfound passion for tennis.

A big problem with me is that I've always taken things too far. It helped me immensely on the bike and it badly hurt me off the bike. After I was diagnosed with cancer, competition for me literally became existential. I take responsibility for my mistakes. I realize them now, but I didn't then. For too long I viewed any confrontation in cycling as an attempt to steal my yellow jersey. Bottom line: I could have used a lot more of George Hincapie's DNA at that time.

I'm sure this book was not easy for George to write. George, unlike some, has never looked for attention or to cash in. George was always content being George Hincapie, a great friend and teammate, veteran of the most tours ever ridden and finished, a good husband and loving father of two (soon to be three) children, living a quiet life in Greenville, South Carolina. I'm aware there have been a lot of attempts to explore the time George and I shared together, to examine my own story, and to get to the bottom of what did and didn't happen during that period. There have been *a lot* of attempts at that. One man was there for all of it and knows the story better than anyone. That man was the best teammate I ever knew. That man is George Hincapie.

THE LOYAL LIEUTENANT

PROLOGUE

ON SOME LEVEL, TO be a professional cyclist is to embrace a life of loneliness. You spend countless hours on the road, with nothing but your thoughts, your insatiable drive, and the irrefutable fact that time in the saddle, more often than not, equates to success. It can become a maddening descent into a race against yourself—a no-win endgame where there are just not enough hours in the day to achieve your goals. Most pros learn at an early age to embrace not only the pain and suffering, but also the solitude. That was never a problem for me. From the formation of my earliest memories, I was as driven as anyone I had ever met. The way I looked at it, boiled down to its essence, cycling could be simplified to an equation of who could train the longest and the hardest, and once in a race, who could best withstand the intensity of the pain.

But cycling is a sport centered on preparation. You learn how to train, what to eat, when to rest, when to work with maximum effort, who to focus on, and what wheels to follow. If the desired results aren't achieved, any and all parts of the preparation equation are tinkered with and adjusted. Part of that omnipresent need for organization, the postrace period is one of rest, recuperation, and to a large degree, reconnection with the outside world.

After being on a bike for the better part of six hours, riders grasp for a return to the normalcy of everyday life. Ask any teenager, and they'll tell you they don't have a life without their cell phone. The pro peloton is no different, and at the end of a race, most of us reach for that electronic connection as if our lives depended on it. But if loneliness largely characterized my life as a cyclist, I never felt it as profoundly as when I received that voice mail after Stage 5 of the 2010 Amgen Tour of California.

The fifth edition of the race, the first to be run in May after the previous four were conducted in February, started in Nevada City and was to end in Agoura Hills, eight stages covering a total length of 810 miles. I'd just joined BMC Racing and was in charge of marshaling the team's other eight riders, made up of mostly Swiss and Americans. I knew my job—I was one of the top domestiques in the business—but even though my responsibility was to my new teammates, I had previously won three stages since the race's inception in 2006, and I had it in me to win some more.

I had no such luck through Stage 5, from Visalia to Bakersfield, which was won by the young superstar Peter Sagan, but the next stage was being called the toughest in the race's young history, finishing on a climb at Big Bear Lake, and I knew I could compete.

I spun my way over to the team bus to grab my phone in the hope of messages from my family on my voice mail. Hearing the voices of my wife and daughter has always been a balm for the mental anguish that comes with the rigors of my profession. But the voice that greeted me that afternoon belonged to Jeff Novitzky from the Food and Drug Administration.

Part pit bull, part bloodhound, Novitzky was a modern-day Eliot Ness, and his reputation for investigating drug use in sports was legendary. And though his message was a nonchalant request for me to give him a call—emphasizing that I was not under investigation but that the feds would very much like to talk to me—even years later, I have not forgotten the sickening feeling that my world was about to be turned upside down.

I honestly felt I would never have to deal with my drug use. Four years prior, I had made a very conscious and concerted decision to stop doping. It was before the 2006 Dauphiné Libéré (now called the Critérium du Dauphiné), and after narrowly missing an out-of-competition test where I felt I would have been caught, I decided using performance-enhancing drugs (PEDs) was no longer worth the price. At that time, I reached out to select team members to tell them of my decision and that I planned on becoming an advocate for clean racing.

So in 2010, my hope and honest belief was that I would never have to look over my shoulder again—that my part in the sordid PED tale was a thing of the past.

But a recent development had sent a shiver through the peloton. An article appearing in the *Wall Street Journal,* highlighted by quotes from Floyd Landis—the 2006 Tour de France champion eventually disqualified for drug use—proclaimed that the sport of cycling was rife with performance-enhancing drugs. Floyd's barbs were directed specifically at riders with whom he had formerly raced— Lance Armstrong, David Zabriskie, Levi Leipheimer, and me, in particular. Previously, in multiple e-mails to USA Cycling and the International Cycling Union (UCI), Floyd had sworn to expose the sport and the individuals involved. When confronted, I didn't deny involvement, but like a skilled politician I danced around the questions. Other, bigger names in the sport of cycling had managed to stay completely under the radar, not only while they were racing but *after* their careers on the bike ended, so I figured my name would be added to that list of those who had been spared media suspicion—let alone indictment.

My thoughts turned to my family. My children. My wife. My
mother and father. Then my scope got bigger. Being a witness to
a federal investigation. What did that mean? I'd only heard about
scenarios like this in movies. Then there was my legacy (even "Big
George" has an ego).

More immediately, would I be racing *tomorrow*? I didn't know
who else was aware I had received Novitzky's call or whether or not
the news would break during the stage race.

It wasn't a restful night, by any means. I confided in my friend,
and fellow pro, Dave Zabriskie, who was also taking part in the
race. Dave would eventually admit and take responsibility for his
PED use, but on that night back in May 2010, the subject during
the hours we spent talking in the hallway was me.

We touched on the decisions that had led us to this point. We
laughed, we cried, but ultimately I was left with no more answers
than I had had before I sat down. Eventually, I slowly ambled off
to bed and tried to find a way to drift off to sleep. But sleep never
came that night, and the restless hours only exacerbated the issue.
As the sun broke through the horizon on that sixth day of racing
in California, I knew one thing—it was going to be a long and
winding road ahead.

CHAPTER 1

I LOVED CARTOONS. WHAT KID doesn't? It didn't matter what superhero was blowing up buildings or saving the world: I loved them all. And in perhaps a Freudian prelude to my later life, I especially liked *Tom and Jerry*. I spent countless hours staring at the television dreaming of being a superhero myself. One of the few recurring skirmishes I had with my father, and it happened on a weekly basis, was when he'd pull me and my big brother, Rich, away from the TV on weekends for a morning bike ride.

Originally from Colombia, my father, Ricardo, had moved to the United States in 1964, sending for my mom, Martha, a year later. They brought few things with them except their hope for a better life and my dad's enthusiasm for cycling.

Since 1951, the Vuelta a Colombia (Tour of Colombia) had captivated that country every August. In the 1960s, one of the riders to garner heavy public support was Martín Emilio "Cochise" Rodríguez, who got his nickname because he was a great admirer of the Apache chief from the 1800s known for bravely resisting American intrusions onto Apache soil. *Cochise* (in Apache *Cheis*) means "having the quality or strength of oak."

It was the strength of this modern-day Colombian cycling warrior that my dad admired and wanted to instill in Rich and me. So as you can imagine, while these weekend rides were a way to combine his loves of cycling and family, they were not leisurely rides, and as we got older and more experienced, he was also primed to give us a taste of competitive cycling to expose us, in a small way, to the effort we would have to exert to be successful at anything we did in life.

Funnily enough, it was my sister, Clara, who provided me with my earliest memory on the bike, when, on a sidewalk in Queens, I graduated from training wheels . . . on her bike.

CLARA HINCAPIE BALTRUSITIS, GEORGE'S SISTER

It's fun to remember that moment. My bike had a banana seat, and a basket on the front. While he was learning, I'd run behind him as we went around the block. But on that day, he just took off! I was so excited to see him so happy.

RICARDO HINCAPIE, GEORGE'S FATHER

I grew up in love with the bike. I dreamed of sharing my passion with my sons. The first time I ever took George out, for a proper ride of about an hour and a half, he was five or six years old. Rich was much stronger than George, and as we hit a slight uphill, Rich raced through a light that was green, but by the time George, who was desperately trying to keep up, got there, it had turned red. I watched in horror and amazement as he shot through the intersection. He never hesitated, he was so focused on

catching Rich. I knew right then that he had the
focus to become a bike racer.

Once I got over being ripped away from *Tom and Jerry,* what I
remember most about those early rides is the fun I had alongside
my dad and brother.

TOM SPUHLER, CHILDHOOD FRIEND
George's family moved from Queens to Farming-
dale in the second grade, and our houses were back-
to-back. We'd always say, "I live up the hill, he lives
down the hill." We hit it off immediately, since we
were both athletes, but George was better than me
at everything. Except hitting a baseball! But we all
knew, even then, that George was destined to be
great in whatever sport he chose. He loved three
things: clothes, girls, and competition. He'd compete in anything, the girls went crazy for him, and
he'd take the bus to the flea market just to get jeans!

I'm the first to admit, I was an average student. School wasn't
hard because I didn't make it so. I was more than happy skimming
along just beneath the surface of academic excellence. Even though
I was fluent in Spanish, I took the subject in high school so I'd have
a free period to daydream of biking.

But my focus on the bike only added to my outsider status
during my years in school. I was a shy kid—I'm *still* shy—and I was
happiest sharing time and conversation on two wheels.

RANDOLPH SCOTT, CHILDHOOD FRIEND
I was a senior in high school and I'd just started
racing that spring. Each Sunday, at the spring series

races in Central Park, we'd race against some of the
best talent in the country. There would be former
Eastern Bloc riders who lived in the city, national
team members, and national champions, all there to
test their early-season form. I remember seeing this
kid named George who looked my age and acted
quite maturely, and we struck up a conversation.
The next week, I found out he was twelve!

Very few kids my age were into biking. I was living a real-life
version of the 1979 movie *Breaking Away,* where Dennis Chris-
topher's character, Dave Stoller, finds himself struggling to fit in,
unable to deny the joy and passion he has for the bicycle.

I spent the hour a day I was allowed to ride memorizing every
inch of the twenty-mile loop I circumnavigated near my home. I
would attack the pavement twenty to thirty, sometimes even forty,
times during the ride. Sprinting as hard as I could, I visualized
myself as one of my cycling heroes, Eddy Merckx or Bernard Hinault, able to win races at will. I never felt any pain, only intense
joy and freedom.

RANDOLPH SCOTT

Since I had a car, a beat-up, stick-shift Volkswagen GTI,
and was the only friend George and Rich knew who
had a license, Mr. Hincapie, after I met him, asked if I
could drive his sons home after a race. A part of me was
scared to take on the responsibility, but the other part,
which won out, thought, This could be a lot of fun! We
became an inseparable trio that spring and summer.

It didn't matter to me that I was the youngest, often by years,
kid in the peloton (literally "little ball" or "platoon" in French, but

more commonly used to mean the entire field or a group of bikers bunched together during a race). I was around peers, no matter what their birth certificates read. At thirteen or fourteen, my skills elevated me into races against men who had been shaving for years. And more often than not, I didn't see someone cross the finish line in front of me.

RANDOLPH SCOTT

George was just this dopey, friendly kid. Winning races to him was like the rest of us reaching into the fridge for a gallon of milk. It took very little effort at all. It was so easy for him. We would go to weekends where he would race in the twelve-to-thirteen-year-old age group, and win. Then he'd do the fourteen-to-fifteen, the sixteen-to-seventeen, and finally the Category 4 race. He'd win or place in all of them, and since every race had prize money, paid in cash, he'd come home each weekend with his pockets overflowing.

TOM SPUHLER

These weren't chump races he was winning. They were some of the best events on the eastern racing calendar. After George would lap the kids in his age group, then enter and usually beat the older ones, the race organizers would come and complain to Mr. Hincapie. Mr. H. would win the argument.

I was an adrenaline junkie. Nothing felt as good as soaring down a hill at sixty miles per hour, but it felt even better to know how to properly set my line in a turn, or to put myself in the perfect position within the peloton. It was a high that no drug could produce. I was so dialed in that what men decades older had a hard time convincing themselves to do, I did without even thinking, and with each passing race, that fearlessness transformed itself into experience. And the more experience I gained, the gutsier I became, and the wins piled on. After feeling myself to be average for as long as I could remember, here was something that I not only enjoyed but excelled at. Out on the road, shifting through gears with what seemed like a sixth sense, the road spoke to me through my saddle. A hyperawareness took hold as I caressed the handlebars. My pedals were the contact point for painless pistons. I had found my calling.

CHAPTER 2

For the Hincapies, cycling was a family affair. After my dad put in a monster amount of work with United Airlines during the week, he seamlessly transitioned into the role of mechanic, soigneur (French for "caretaker," "attendant," or "facilitator"—in the cycling community, someone who helps take care of the riders in all aspects), and chauffeur on the weekends.

RICARDO

I knew George might have a chance to be great from his very first race. I'd brought him to Nutley, New Jersey, and he got thrown into the Midget category (seven- to eleven-year-olds). There were about twenty kids entered and when the gun went off, George shot forward like he'd been launched out of a cannon. He won. Easily. And he continued to win, week after week.

As a father who shuttles children to and from athletic endeavors, I have begun to understand the sacrifice my parents, and my father in particular, made during those years. But he never complained or betrayed any sense that he was being inconvenienced.

TOM SPUHLER

Their family is so special. I didn't have a father around, but they treated me like their own. George's mom would feed me, and I'd usually pile into the car with them for the big races. They'd throw four bikes on the top of their little white Honda, and find a way to fit me in too.

All three Hincapie men, for a while, raced in our respective divisions. Eventually my dad sat on the sidelines more and more to coach both me and Rich, shouting out instructions lap after lap of whatever critérium (a race in which multiple laps are completed on the same course) we were taking part in.

RICARDO

I couldn't wait to take them to races. I used to get *Velo News,* and since this was before the Internet, the only way to enter a bike race was to tear out the entry form, or copy it, and send it in immediately after you saw it in the magazine. The races up and down the East Coast filled up fast, and I wanted to make sure Rich and George had the chance to test their skills against the best.

RANDOLPH SCOTT

Mr. Hincapie was very traditional, very serious, but 100 percent cycling crazy. When it came to biking, he was one of the boys, like a third brother to George and Rich. On the bike, it was easy to see where both sons got their fun-loving personality.

I knew my dad worked hard, saving to make sure Rich or I could have a new bike or get to a race. I saw how much he toiled to provide for my family and how much he loved his kids, and his unwavering support made me want to succeed.

While the men of the family raced, I remember my mom, Martha, not being a huge fan of the sport, but because her "boys" were completely devoted, she supported us any way she could.

MARTHA HINCAPIE, GEORGE'S MOM

It was our whole life. I didn't care at all about bike racing, but it was what Ricardo and the boys liked to do, so I wanted to support them. Every weekend, we'd be up at 4 a.m., and I'd take something to do while I sat and watched the races.

I recall my sister, Clara, the oldest of the Hincapie siblings, being very studious—always bringing her books to the races.

CLARA

It was just what our family did. I grew up watching first my dad, then Rich, and finally George. My dad had a full-time job, but in his spare time, he trained like he was a professional bike rider. Every day. My mom used to joke she'd have to plan her death around cycling. They were so proud of both my brothers. I loved being at the races too. It was fun to watch all three of them and their teammates. They taught me how to love the sport.

RICH HINCAPIE, GEORGE'S BROTHER

We were a family totally devoted to cycling. My mom did everything for us in terms of cooking, serving us (she'd even get up from the table to get us drinks), laundry . . . she made sure we could concentrate solely on bike riding. Part of it may have been, being from Colombia, she came from a culture, at least at that time, where the women served the men. That was obviously generational as well. But it went deeper than that. My mom genuinely loved seeing us excel. She had three men who were devoted to the sport, so her devotion to us took the form of doing everything outside of racing. It was just a "perfect storm" of how all the pieces of our family fit together. As George got better, we all played a part in allowing him to focus on being a better biker. And we were all extremely happy to do it.

Weekend after weekend the script remained the same. Rich and I raced, my dad cajoled us from the fringe of the crowd, and my mom and Clara occupied the time; then we would all load up into the Buick Regal to drive home and count the days until we would start the process all over again.

For motivation, my dad always had cycling magazines lying around the house. I would read about faraway races like Paris–Roubaix, or the most impressive race of all, the Tour de France. I also knew about the Vuelta a Colombia, since my father had witnessed it firsthand for so many years, and occasionally we had Colombian cyclists stay at the house. One such cyclist was Cochise Rodríguez, who stayed with us for a few days. I can't remember if it was a bigger deal for my father or for me.

But though my dad was a fan, he never put cycling's stars on a pedestal. It wasn't my father's way to be enamored with one cyclist or another. He respected their accomplishments and marveled at their ability, but he knew where that came from—dedication and hard work. I grasped that as well. It's what I credit my father most with passing on to me: a tangible respect for the amount of effort it takes to get good at anything.

So though I entertained dreams of being a professional cyclist, at that moment, my reality consisted of only a measured number of miles every day. Rich was older and had started cycling earlier, so he was already attending training camps and taking international trips as I began to explore my pedaling parameters. Every time Rich would travel, I would be happy for my brother but also envious of the experience he was getting. I used that angst to fuel my workouts and to expedite my conditioning.

After Rich returned from one such adventure, when I was thirteen and he was seventeen, the two of us headed out for a ride. I was eager to show off the form I had been refining in his absence. It was a pivotal moment in our relationship, as I beat my brother more than once in the designated sprints during that ride. But rather than making excuses to diminish my accomplishment, as a less supportive older brother might, Rich embraced the level I had reached. He was genuinely happy for me.

CLARA

It seems weird now, but back then, it was just the way they were. They ALWAYS got along. In the beginning, George was kind of lazy. My dad and Rich definitely trained harder, but George had more natural talent. Keep in mind, cycling was Rich's sport first. But I never saw Rich be jealous of George.

They were inseparable as they shared both the highs and lows.

Rich is my confidant, my alter ego, my sounding board for everything substantial. It's simplistic to say he is my best friend, but it's true.

RICH

It's funny, I can't really remember a time we didn't get along, or I wasn't genuinely happy for him and his successes. Well, except once. We were out doing stupid stuff, what typical teenage boys do, and George was with his group of friends, and they decided it would be funny to chase me through the woods and tie me to a tree. I put up a good fight, kicking and screaming, but eventually they succeeded, and they left me there for a couple hours. He came back and before he untied me, he put his BB gun up to my thigh and shot me—at point-blank range. I wanted to kill him. Looking back on it, I can't remember another instance I ever got mad at him.

RANDOLPH SCOTT

George, even though he was four years younger, almost seemed the bigger brother. That said, Rich was the serious one. He never picked on George. It was the exact opposite; he was always looking out for him. George, more often than not, was the one looking to have fun, and he picked on Rich every chance he got. But they were 100 percent best friends. I never saw them get in a real fight. They did, however, have a little ring time one afternoon. I got an excited call telling me to hurry over to their house; they'd purchased boxing gloves and wanted to try them out. Twenty minutes later I arrived, and a grinning George answered the door. He blurted out, "I KO'd Rich!" I looked past the giddy younger brother through the doorway. Off to the left, sitting on the staircase was Rich, definitely looking dazed and groggy. He lifted his head and feebly tried to defend his honor verbally, since he hadn't done it too well physically. "It was a lucky punch."

I credit Rich with helping me achieve everything that I have accomplished, and along the way, I have eagerly shared my success with my older brother.

Early on we shared more than a room. Within those four walls, we shared our hopes, our dreams, and our plans on how we would become better—not just better cyclists, but also better men, like our father. It was a bond that helped shape me and continues to keep me grounded. The Hincapie ideal of "family first" is very much a cornerstone of our lives, impressed upon us right from the beginning.

CHAPTER 3

WHILE I'M HARD PRESSED to remember a time in my youth where I worried about my biking, I distinctly remember watching my dad struggle in a Cat 1 race in New York. (Amateurs race in Categories 1 through 5; 5 is for beginners, 1 for the most experienced racers, one notch below the pros.) He crossed the line completely exhausted, just happy to hang on to the back of the pack and finish with the group.

He would never have made excuses—that wasn't his way—but the demands of my father's job and regularly alternating shifts prevented him from the training required to compete with semipros. That day, it started to become clear to me the time commitment required to finish *in front,* and I began to mentally build my life around this goal. I imagined myself bringing what I assumed had been my father's dream to fruition.

My father worked all the time, but it was clear we were never far from his mind. Sometimes his shift went from 4 a.m. to 2 p.m., but at least that meant my dad was around for late lunches, when we came home from school, and dinners. He also made it a habit to call twice a day to check in to see how everyone was doing, as well as to find out my progress on the bike during my afternoon rides. On the weekends, my dad would apply the knowledge he gleaned from those conversations, as well as his own brand of coaching, to the races in which Rich and I took part.

My dad emphasized *focus* above all else. This meant staying out of trouble in the group and concentrating only on my own ride, what *I* was doing, not worrying about others. My dad would hammer home that lesson: hold your position and keep your eye on the prize.

RICH

George definitely learned dedication from our father. Our dad came over to the U.S. with nothing, started working at a diner, and eventually worked at United Airlines for thirty years. He built our family's life in America from zero. George learned through my father's success that it's worth taking a chance and jumping in with both feet. Also, George absorbed the ideal that the harder you work, the better the rewards. Cycling was a sport founded on that principle.

He'd monitor my training closely and then, after a particular race, ask me how I felt and how I could use what happened to do better the next time. He based a lot of his ideas on how I felt in previous situations and what I was *thinking* during the race *tactically*. To advise accordingly, he became a local cycling encyclopedia, carefully considering the course opportunities in upcoming races and evaluating the competition.

Over the years, the strategy worked—time and time again. A normal race day consisted of my father finding a place on the side of the course, shouting instructions each time I passed. The commands changed depending on the lap, and were determined by how the race was developing. The usual outcome was me standing on the top step of the podium, but eventually my father admitted I had outgrown his skills.

RICARDO

George won almost everything, but he always dreamed of winning more. His personality never changed, because he realized there was always going to be somebody better out there, somebody he could use as a target. He'd continually ask me about strategy and for more ways to improve. He stayed humble because, even as a boy, he was wise enough to know everyone can always learn something new.

RICH

The first time I realized George had the potential to be not just good but great was when he was fifteen and we went to New Jersey to take part in the series of races around the Tour of Somerville (one of the oldest bike races in the U.S.). It was two days before the big race, but there were plenty of pros and Category 1 riders who were there to use this particular race as a warm-up for the event in two days' time. George attacked from the gun, and while most everyone chalked it up to exuberance, plenty of riders had to have been thinking, Who the F is this guy?! Eventually they caught him, but with about ten miles to go, George decided he was going to attack again. Nobody saw him until the finish. People definitely took notice.

The first person to help my career *not* named Hincapie was Gaylen "Lenny" Preheim. He was a New York City cycling guru who was the first person to talk to me about organized, structured training. Lenny was co-owner of the Toga Bike Shop on the West Side. He was famous for taking young athletes under his guidance and not just teaching them skills and strategy, but also instilling in them the discipline needed to create their own structure. Lenny believed it wasn't about taking things from a book or aping what others were doing; he urged his riders to make their training their own.

He was an aficionado, and took great pride in having the best team in the city. Early on, one of his star students had been former New York bike messenger Nelson Vails, the 1984 Olympic silver medalist in the one-thousand-meter match sprint competition.

Lenny started shaping young New York riders in 1975. Kenny Sloan, a rider on his team and later the manager of his shop, once said, "Lenny believed he had glasses that saw into the future," and it showed. In the cycling world at the time, Team Toga were the 1990s Dallas Cowboys—it wasn't *if* they were going to win, it was *how*.

He was always scouting for talent. He wore a green blazer and cowboy boots, and his flamboyant style was impossible to miss in Central Park. Lenny had seen me racing for weeks before he approached my dad, telling him that he would not only train me but give me a bike and other racing gear, which alone was a huge cost-saving measure. I was well aware that my dad did everything he could to help me, but there were times when I wanted a new piece of equipment, whether it was a bike or simply sunglasses, and my father couldn't afford to get it. Being sponsored by a bike shop— and Toga in particular—meant I had graduated to the next level.

But even more, Lenny became my sensei.

He was an icon, and it was devastating for the NYC cycling scene when he passed away in 1996. I remember someone pointing out a quote of his in *New York* magazine: "The real satisfaction for me is to take a young guy who has a bike and some raw speed and help him develop into a first-rate racer." Lenny was a critical evolutionary step in my development. He provided equipment as well as a coaching structure that I'd never imagined. My dad and I had gone to races every weekend and tried to win. Lenny sat us down and planned out our entire season. In 1990, we traveled to San Diego for the National Championships. Lenny welded a set of aero handlebars to my track bike and gave me a rubber skin suit to reduce drag. He was ahead of his time in his attention to the science of riding, and I benefited greatly from his knowledge.

But it was another New Yorker, Fred Mengoni, often called the Father of American Cycling, who was pivotal in helping me make it further up the pecking order. Today, the GS Mengoni team Web site proclaims they have graduated more top amateur cyclists to the professional ranks than any other amateur team in the United States.

He grew up in Italy, just south of Ancona, a center for musical instrument making, especially accordions. When he saw Marilyn Monroe in *Gentlemen Prefer Blondes,* he decided to go to New York (in March 1957) to visit some friends. Once he saw Manhattan, with all those skyscrapers, he realized that's where he wanted to be.

Mengoni turned a tourist visa into a multimillion-dollar real estate empire through hard work and shrewd investments, and though he had raced bicycles as a young man in Italy, even winning some regional races, he didn't see much of a future in a cycling career, so he let his bicycle gather dust for close to two decades.

He reconnected with his bike by riding in Central Park as a way to blow off some steam during the workday. But considering his erstwhile passion, he couldn't leave it as a hobby and decided to apply his business acumen to start his own cycling team. The initial edition of GS Mengoni lasted from 1981 to 1988, with riders like Canadian Steve Bauer leading the charge.

Mengoni immediately recognized talent when he saw it. One sixteen-year-old he spotted was Greg LeMond, who went on to become a three-time Tour de France champion. Even though they were friends, Mengoni never got Greg on his team. Greg decided to race for the U.S. national team until he turned pro, but Mengoni's eye for investment eventually centered on me.

In 1991, Mengoni introduced himself at a race in Central Park and told me he'd like me to ride for him. By this time, I had become well established not only in the New York racing scene but nationally as well. I had won on the road and the track, and the promise I had shown as a junior was beginning to be realized against the stiffest competition in the senior ranks. Mengoni had more money than Lenny Preheim, and his team opened more doors.

Mengoni made it possible for me to have the best of both worlds. Since I was paid a true salary, I only had to concentrate on riding. Since I was on the national team, I got to do all the big races in Europe and gain valuable experience, and as a member of Mengoni's team, he made it possible to contest all the best races in the United States. He fostered an accelerated learning curve that wouldn't have been possible without his support.

He lived right on Central Park, and every time I won, he'd invite me and my dad to come to his six-story brownstone, where we'd be escorted directly to his first-floor office and he would pay me a hundred dollars in cash for the win. He only showed me around once, where I couldn't help but notice how cluttered the whole place was. I suspect I was actually taking in an arrangement of priceless antiques, but to me, it looked like junk was everywhere. Mengoni's accent was so thick, I could barely understand him as he handed me the money. He finished every exchange by saying, "Keep doing what you are doing. You are going to be great one day."

RENÉ WENZEL, USA CYCLING NATIONAL JUNIOR TEAM COACH (1990-1992)

Before the first camp in Colorado Springs, there were plenty of stories about George, which people usually pronounced in Spanish as a small joke, and perhaps in homage to his Colombian roots. I kept hearing about the kid who had shaved since he was twelve. The boy who had lived as a pro, earned enough money from his racing since the same age, and was a head taller than the rest.

I went to the old Springs airport to pick him up and see for myself, even though it was protocol for a mechanic or massage therapist to do that task. Not only were the rumors true, but he was so polite, I joked I wouldn't tolerate any "brownnosers" on my team. George nervously laughed, but continued with his good manners and I could see he was genuinely eager to make a good impression. His first rides only confirmed what I had heard. He was the most talented rider I had ever worked with (and ever since). Even then, he had a gigantic physical engine (testing even better than Lance) and a rarely seen street sense.

I rode for GS Mengoni from 1991 to 1993. In 1992, I ventured to Barcelona, Spain, to my first Olympics, switching out the team's legendary green and yellow for the red, white, and blue of Team USA. It would be the first of five Olympic Games I would qualify for and attend. Even though the team got crushed in the one event we entered, the team time trial, for me, Barcelona was an important lesson. I had now been exposed to the best the rest of the world had to offer, and after being handed my proverbial hat, I vowed to train harder, longer, and faster than I ever had, to make sure I was prepared for next time.

TOM SPUHLER

George worked harder than any human being I've ever seen. I went to college with NFL players, and only one, Wayne Chrebet, rivaled George's commitment and singular focus. The only thing that ever kept George off the roads was snow, and even then, if forced inside, he and Rich would train in their basement—a low-ceilinged makeshift gym with bikes on rollers, a weight bench, and a radio.

CHAPTER 4

IF YOU COULD WRAP up and combine the Fourth of July, Christmas, New Year's, birthdays, and a first kiss, that would describe my elation upon getting the call to turn professional from Jim Ochowicz, the manager of the Motorola Cycling Team. It was late May or early June 1993, days before my twentieth birthday, when I hit the jackpot. I was upstairs in my room when my mom called up that someone wanted to speak with me.

Ochowicz was known as a no-nonsense midwestern man who cut straight to the chase. Our first exchange was short and to the point. I stood in our all-white kitchen, feeling claustrophobic among the small table, four chairs, and glistening Formica countertops. I'd been racing well that spring, having notched some notable wins, and I'd be lying if I said I didn't think I was ready to try to be a professional. Lance Armstrong, whom I had met and befriended at a USA Cycling training camp years before, had even hinted to me that Motorola was looking to sign a few guys. But "The Call" caught me off guard, making it feel as if the earth's axis had just shifted slightly.

JIM OCHOWICZ, GENERAL MANAGER, MOTOROLA CYCLING TEAM

We were primarily an American team, so I was always on the lookout for the best American kids. I'd heard about George from a variety of sources—my contacts at the national team and Lance—and his name came up in conversation with people throughout the sport, so he was on my radar. The thing I heard the most, which sealed the deal for me, was that he was a kid who could win races. I never saw George ride before I offered him a contract. I didn't need to see his résumé. That he turned himself inside out to win was enough for me.

If Fred Mengoni was the father of American cycling, Jim Ochowicz was its godfather. Ochowicz had made a name for himself as a gutsy cyclist, competing in two separate Olympic Games on the track, and had reinvented the landscape of American cycling through his management of the 7-Eleven Cycling Team (from 1981 to 1990) and its next incarnation, the Motorola team, which began in 1991.

Simply put, Ochowicz paved the way for a generation of cyclists. Not for them to dream, but for their dreams to become a reality.

As I scanned my surroundings, though my brain was busy telling me everything was the same, something deep inside was whispering, "Things just changed in a big way." I had to call my dad at work to share the news.

RICARDO

I'd actually spoken to Och earlier that day. He had called in the morning to ask what I thought about

offering George a contract. Since he was a minor, I
think it was the proper thing to do. I asked him what
his plans for George were, and told him George had
enrolled at Hofstra University for the fall. Och explained that they wanted to send George to Europe
for a couple races in October to see how he would
handle the racing. That made me nervous. I worried that if George didn't go to college and get a
degree, he'd lose out on a huge chance. But since
I had worked my whole life, I also knew I couldn't
keep him from taking this opportunity and seeing
where it led.

So, later that day when George did get the call,
even though I knew it was at the expense of his ed-
ucation, I knew there was no way he was going to
turn it down.

Then, of course, I called Rich, who was at a USA Cycling national camp on another one of those adventures I coveted so much.

RICH

It wasn't a surprise—George had been racing so
well—but it was really cool that it finally happened.
Europe was this far-off land that we only read about
in magazines like *Velo* and heard people talk about
in reverent tones. Now my brother was heading
over there.

After the phone calls had been made and we'd spread the news,
I felt like Rocky in the scene where he runs through the streets
of Philadelphia, with Bill Conti's "Gonna Fly Now" in the background. There was only one outlet for this intense energy. A bike

ride. I don't remember where I went, or if I even intended on going anywhere. In that moment, nothing mattered but that this dream of mine was becoming a reality. I'd worn grooves into the pavement ascending Long Island's Mill Hill Road and Stillwell Road, and that day, I flew faster and with less pain than ever before.

From that day, I redoubled my efforts and found ways to punish myself like never before. My thought process was simple: I knew I was going to go through more pain than I ever had when I started racing in Europe, so I had better try to equal that pain on my own before I was forced to react to others in a race.

RICH

Initially, there was some nervousness from George, the tiniest of questions as to whether he could cut it. But he took his dedication and training to a whole new level. We'd always been junk food fanatics, but once George got the call, our trips to 7-Eleven ended and he completely changed his eating habits.

RENÉ WENZEL

I was one of the first coaches he had who reminded him that even though his talent was great, when he reached the pinnacle of racing, he'd run into riders of equal or greater skill. For that reason, every little thing he did in his everyday life would matter toward the end product of being professional. For instance, take chocolate. He had to now think of the whole path, from pleasure to aftermath, of what eating it meant. What would be the benefit? What were the possible downfalls? If the downfalls outweighed the benefits, could he live without it? George was not ready for this as a junior—his talent carried him through. He did it right, he had fun during his early years, but he became extremely serious with himself and his career when he turned pro. It all clicked for him when he got the call to be professional.

If I had done ten intervals before, now I did twenty. If I'd rested five minutes between hard efforts, now I only took three minutes before hammering my body again. And again. I tried to turn off the pain, and then I tried to make the cells of my body scream so hard I couldn't see straight.

RENÉ WENZEL

I dragged the junior team out on a one-hundred-mile ride to prove to them they were not going to fall over if they did one. Near the end, as we got near the Olympic Training Center, Fred Rodriguez rode up and said to me that George had figured out if we turned into the driveway now, we'd only have ridden ninety-six miles. Freddy said George wanted to ride the extra four miles (out to the old Freddy Cappy course at the Olympic Velodrome park and back) since that was the whole point of what I had argued for so insistently. It showed me they both (and George in particular) had the capacity to want something badly enough, it didn't matter what it took to achieve it. They would do it. As for the ride, Freddy went with him. Every other member of the team rode straight into the training center.

Everything was a test, and I approached it all as if my life depended on it. The way I saw it, it did.

CHAPTER 5

THE MOTOROLA TEAM THAT year was a who's who of elite cyclists.

A sampling of the talent: American Andy Hampsten, who'd finished fourth overall at the Tour de France the year before; workhorse fellow American Frankie Andreu; England's Sean Yates, often called the toughest man in the peloton, who could make himself suffer like few before him; Norwegian Bjorn Stenersen, a time trial specialist; Australian Phil Anderson, a man who could be equally dominant in a multiday stage race or a one-day classic; Italian Maximilian Sciandri, who'd won stages of both the Tour and the Giro (Tour of Italy), and been on the podium of the World Championships; and a young Lance Armstrong, who had only turned professional the year before, but already had a multitude of wins on his résumé.

The first time we met, we both had been invited to the Olympic Training Center in Colorado Springs. He was almost seventeen and I was fifteen. Lance had already established himself as a big-time triathlete, and he was being invited for the first time to take part in a road-cycling camp. He hadn't done many road races, but the rumor was he had this really big "engine," that he was superstrong. He showed up to camp in his Camaro IROC-Z, and he just had an assured aura about himself that I liked. Sure, he was confident, if not cocky. But I didn't mind that since he had the racing results to back it up.

LANCE ARMSTRONG

Our personalities meshed from the moment we met. He was younger than me, but he was so good. I was coming from the world of triathlon, but he was already an established presence in the sport of cycling. A lot of our initial bonding was we were both just kids just having fun, being teenage boys. Stupid stuff. We were both extremely cheesy, but we hit it off at that first camp and were friends from that point on.

During the first week, we had a number of training rides where we talked and got along really well, so I drove with him to the very first race we did together. On the way there, I asked him, "What's our strategy going to be for the day?" I'd come from a background where my brother, father, and teammates had always had a plan on how to win, or at least to put someone in the best position to win. Lance just looked at me like I was from another planet and said, "What do you mean, *strategy*?"

"There are going to be some really good riders here today," I said, "even national team members. We should have a plan, so let's figure out one."

Gazing through the front windshield at the open road ahead, he paused for a moment, then matter-of-factly declared, "I'm just going to attack from the gun and get away and win. *That's* my plan."

"Dude, you can't do that. Nobody does that."

"Watch me."

And that's exactly what he did. He called his shot. And that was vintage Lance. Nothing was insurmountable and everything was attainable, in his mind.

I was never that outwardly brash, and I guess that brashness drew me in. I watched him be tough with others (for instance, he and Bobby Julich never really got along, since they were more direct competitors), but I escaped that side of his personality. I knew I could never have that exterior gruffness or toughness, and maybe he sensed that in me and was able to tell I would not confront him.

I also think Lance could see I was genuine, that I never really wanted anything from him. It helped that I never threatened him or his stature within the cycling community. But I also think he liked how different I was from him. I was a much different character and, for the most part, very happy to stay in the background.

JIM OCHOWICZ

Lance was already showing signs of the phenomenon he would later become, but I saw George simply as a sprinter, which was more than okay by me. He had an amazing turn of speed. No one yet knew his affinity for the rough roads of Belgium.

During that first call, Ochowicz made it clear the team had a use for me before the start of the 1994 season, so I traveled over to Europe in the fall of 1993. Few people gave me much of a chance to make an immediate impact on the European racing scene, even though I'd been achieving stellar results in North America.

My first race in a Motorola kit was 1993's Milano–Torino, a distance of 199 kilometers (roughly 121 miles). It is the oldest of the Italian "classics," first contested in 1876, and after its position on the racing calendar was moved from March to October, in 1987, a high percentage of top riders always had it circled as a late-season goal.

On race day in Italy, the sixth of October, Phil Anderson, Sean Yates, and Max Sciandri were the three guys from Motorola who drew the most attention. I was there simply for experience. In bike racing, the word *experience* translates to "suffering." I was there to help the team in any way they needed, as well as to begin to test my limits at this level. On the start line, I had to keep reminding myself to calm down. These were my idols, and even though I had only just turned twenty, I was now expected to assimilate my skill set with theirs.

The first ninety-five kilometers were raced in a southwesterly direction on broad, mostly flat roads. Eventually, a series of undulations gave the peloton something to react to as we approached the town of Asti. Here's where I felt more at home. These little "bumps" in the road were very similar to the hills I'd been riding on Long Island, and as the race progressed, I found myself not only feeling good, but in a break that contained, among others, the eventual winner, Rolf Sorensen of Denmark (himself a two-time stage winner of the Tour de France, wearer of the coveted yellow jersey at the Tour, as well as winner of multiple one-day classics including the Tour of Flanders).

I ended up eleventh overall, right behind my teammate Max Sciandri, and with that first result I embarked on my professional career, confident I could handle anything thrown my way. Just as important, I was happy to prove to Jim Ochowicz and the team that their trust in me was justified.

SEAN YATES

I'd really taken notice of George earlier in the year when one day during the Tour DuPont, in the locker room afterwards, I could tell he was incredibly upset because he had come very close to winning the stage, finishing second. I remember thinking, That guy's got passion. So when we lined up months later in Milan, I had a feeling he was keen. Then, when he got in the break, to be honest, my first thought was, Thank god, we don't have to work on the front! My trademark was, if it had to be done, I was never one to shy away from hard work, and that's what I saw in George, a kindred spirit who had the resolve and the will to suffer. For George to not only be in the break, but to race as well as he did in his first pro race in Europe, I was massively impressed. He was quiet and simply got down to the business of riding. There was no hullaballoo about him. It was a good start to his career.

The first team camp of 1994 took place in Italy in January. I'd been back home in New York for the holidays, but my mind was elsewhere. Toward the end of the fall of '93, I'd gotten my first real batch of training gear for the winter—all the necessary stuff you need to ride during the winter months, everything silk-screened and imprinted with the Motorola team logo and its sponsors. There's not an easier or quicker representation that you've "made it" to a cyclist than that first team kit that you're given. It's not only amazing to see piles of clothes scattered on the floor in front of you, but the most thrilling aspect to most of us is that it sends a message to the world that you now represent your team. In an overly simplistic way, it's like gang colors. I was now with the Motorola crew and the whole world knew it.

SEAN YATES

We had our training camp in Tuscany. One day, I was screaming down a descent with George and

Brian Smith (a Scot who won the British National Road Race Championships two times, as well as a British Eurosport commentator), and George tried to stay on my wheel and follow me. I thought it was funny, and it slightly pissed me off, that this young kid was thinking he could match my moves. Ultimately, he crashed. Hard. I heard the commotion behind me, but in those days, I was a bit of a tough customer, I didn't stop for anyone. I may have even chuckled that he went down. Brian ended up stopping and helping him back to camp. He got scraped up but didn't utter one complaint. He was tough as nails. He had my respect.

My two *stagiaire* (loosely translated as "apprentice") races in 1993 had exposed me to my new world. Outside of the races themselves, there'd been a bit of hand-holding to take some pressure off me so I could give my full attention to the job of being a bike racer. By 1994, I was expected to function in that world on my own and be completely self-sufficient outside of race days and camps. It was a startling and tough transition, but a necessary one that every pro goes through.

After our January training camp in Italy, I went straight to my new home near Lake Como. We chose the locale for purely logistical reasons. Max Testa, who had already worked with Jim Ochowicz beginning in 1986 with the 7-Eleven cycling team, was our coach at Motorola, and since he was based in Como, it made sense to be near him.

JIM OCHOWICZ

I'd worked with Max since we were introduced in 1985. The Italian sponsor of our 7-Eleven team, Er-

minio Dall'Oglio, who owned the Hoonved wash-
ing machine company, brought him on board as
one of two team doctors for 7-Eleven's first foray
at the Giro d'Italia (Tour of Italy). When the more
senior doctor inexplicably quit, Max, who looked all
of twelve years old, took full responsibility for our
riders' care. He instantly bonded with my guys, and
we've been together ever since. One of the reasons
a number of the 7-Eleven riders, and then the Motorola team, headed to Como was that Max was one
of the town physicians. He had tons of contacts and
helped immensely in setting them up.

He was more than a coach; we thought of him as family. He
knew everyone in the area and helped us find apartments and adapt
to the Italian lifestyle.

LANCE ARMSTRONG

Como life was anything but easy. After I won
Worlds in '93, I got my own place. This was before
the Internet was really established, and before cell
phones. We were all just scraping by. We were not
comfortable. Basically, it sucked. But we did it, and
it bonded us all.

My roommates were fellow American Frankie Andreu and Norwegian Bjorn Stenersen. It was a "marriage" of convenience—we
were all single, so it was a similar dynamic, and simpler to live together and share expenses.

It made it so much easier for me that I was with another American. Frankie became my guide—for everything. He had turned
professional in 1989, and aside from posting impressive results on

both sides of the Atlantic, Frankie, from Michigan, had that no-nonsense midwestern approach that matched Och's. He was a guy that didn't mess around and knew exactly what to do, on and off the bike.

FRANKIE ANDREU

I don't remember the very first time I met George. It was either at one of our first camps or his first races. But we all knew of him. He was a giant—in stature and in his racing résumé. It wasn't until years later, when I retired, that it hit me how talented he was. And how young, when he first came over to Europe.

Even with Frankie's help, those first few months of 1994 were rough for me. I was hit with an almost hyperhomesickness. I missed everything about the United States. The food. The language. The cars. I counted the days until I would be allowed to head back home, which was going to be in May to race the Tour DuPont. Until then, I had to suck it up and find a way to get through what was rapidly becoming a very hard time.

MARTHA

He'd call home and be so homesick. It was gut-wrenching to hear him and feel what he was going through. But this was his dream, and we told him to not give up. To do everything he could to see it through.

CLARA

Mom was so sad that George was gone. He was the first to leave the nucleus of our family. I went to

college, but I still lived at home. She used to cry, but
I knew she was so proud of him, she just missed him
so much.

Through it all, my racing was right where everyone thought it
should be, and even though I wasn't winning, I knew I was gaining
valuable experience.

Living on my own for the first time taught me self-reliance,
but also allowed for some unique bonding opportunities, like when
Frankie and I pooled our limited resources to access this thing
called the Internet.

Time would run a cover story in July 1994 entitled "The Strange
New World of the Internet: Battles on the Frontiers of Cyberspace."
Where we lived, life on the World Wide Web was not only new, it
was complicated by the myriad of AOL foreign connection numbers. As most older readers can attest, back then, you paid by the
hour to be connected, so we would have to find the different numbers to try when we were at home, see which one of those numbers
allowed us to establish a connection, and once logged on, hope the
e-mails would download quickly, so we could log off and save as
much money as possible. It was a stressful ordeal, but Frankie and I
had some funny moments working together to try to stay in touch
with our families, when by today's standards, we really were in the
dinosaur era.

My first spring campaign in Europe was highlighted by making
the front group at Omloop Het Volk (now Omloop Het Nieuws-
blad), and eventually finishing twenty-first overall. The race tra-
ditionally opens up the cycling season in Belgium, taking place
the last Saturday in February or the first in March. In 1994, it was
held on February 26, the fifteenth consecutive day of below-normal
temperatures. The race starts and ends in the East Flanders town

of Ghent, and uses a number of the same climbs and cobblestone
sections that have been popularized in the Tour of Flanders, and
therefore is considered an important preparatory event. From my
viewpoint, there couldn't have been a better race, or atmospheric
opportunity, for showcasing my ability to excel in inclement
weather.

SEAN YATES

The classics are all about having a massive consti-
tution. I could see George had the engine immediately, but what he slowly revealed to all of us was
his uncanny ability to learn through experience. His
learning curve was accentuated by his natural ability to read situations. No races test that better than
the monuments (the five oldest and most prestigious
single-day professional championships—Milan–San
Remo, Tour of Flanders, Paris–Roubaix, Liége–
Bastogne–Liége, and Tour of Lombardy) early in the
year. To excel, you need a combination of every skill
essential to bike racing.

I was immediately drawn to the early season events, and more
specifically, racing in Northern Europe, because I loved the idea of
testing *my* toughness against the toughness of my competitors.

FRANKIE ANDREU

My first races with him were the classics. I was
scared to death. The conditions, the cobbles, and the
crashes. Those races were crazy. I'd get to the finish
line and be so drained from the strain of it all, but
he'd cross the line absolutely giddy with excitement.

I just remember him smiling and saying, "Oh my
God! I loved that!" He was drawn to the scene. He
ate it all up.

Who could tolerate the most suffering was the race within the
race. Even at the age of twenty, I'd already gotten good at tuning
out any type of distraction and using focus as my fuel.

CHAPTER 6

APRIL 10, 1994

LIGHT RAIN. MY HEART raced with the excitement of getting to face my "Super Bowl" in conditions that I found appealing and in which I knew how to excel. I could barely contain myself when I saw that snow flurries filled the sky as well, each an omen that the race would be sending a message that day. I hoped I would send a message of my own.

Springtime weather in Northern Europe is never going to appeal to most people. Unless your favorite three words are *wind, wet,* and *gray.* 1994 didn't deviate drastically from that norm. February was colder than normal. March was windier than average, and early April was wetter than many remembered it usually being. Dawn forced itself on April 10 with its usual predictability, but with enough atmospheric wrinkles to turn stomachs in the peloton.

TOM SPUHLER
Before there was high-priced bicycle gear and a different piece of clothing to keep every part of your body warm, George rode in New York City in the

winters! He'd just throw on an extra jacket and another hat on his head. Northeast weather in January?
Please! That's what made him tough.

As a race, Paris–Roubaix is like a living, breathing organism.
It has a life of its own, and like a caged animal, it will fight back.
Each year, the uniqueness of the peloton breathes life into a creature
that is hell-bent on pushing men to their breaking point. The route,
while sometimes the same on paper, is constantly changing, evolving, and learning how to adapt to its creators. Its goal is to prod and
to punish, but ultimately, to provide an almost intolerable amount
of drama, so that the victor is simply the least vanquished. The cobbles create shades of gray unlike any other course, a nuanced effect
on the muscles and nerve endings that is not immediately noticeable. There's a reason it's called a race for the "strongmen" of the
sport. Riders talk of feeling as if they'd contracted the flu for days
after racing. The body is so battered and beaten down, some men
can't even sleep the night AFTER the event. It's a race where expectations rarely, and may never, intersect with reality. Where the
best-laid plans are crumpled up and tossed aside. Where the body
count is not a figurative but a literal reference to the strewn cyclists
along the reserved sliver of road not populated by the gauntlet of
people or bike-breaking stone. For most races, racers view second
place as a travesty, but finishing Paris–Roubaix at all is considered
an *achievement,* and after over 150 miles of bone bashing, finishers
feel as if they are gliding on air in the final pedal strokes.

It was into this arena in 1994 that I eagerly threw myself. It was
going to be a long, painful day, but I knew I was ready.

JIM OCHOWICZ

George's skill set came alive in the Belgian classics.
He fit into everything right away. It was amaz-

ing. He didn't fit the classics rider profile, in size
or other physiological parts, but you could tell he
loved it. And to excel in that arena you have to love
pain and battling the elements. He had speed, I'd
always known that, but there he found a place to
use it. Rather than in the mass sprints of stage races,
George's speed transferred to the pavé. He didn't
know he had it until he came to Belgium.

One hundred and ninety-one riders started. Forty-eight crossed
the finish line. I ended up thirty-first, eleven minutes and twenty-
four seconds behind the winner, Andrei Tchmil. I'd never had more
fun in my life. I'd come close to being picked up by the broom
wagon (the official vehicle that follows the riders) with around fifteen miles to go, but as I watched fans walking away from the
course, I thought, No way am I quitting! I crossed the line, completely spent, but hooked. My only thought was, This is fucking
awesome! I knew it was the race for me, and I'd spend my whole
career chasing the dream of winning it.

CHAPTER 7

BY THE LATE SPRING of 1994, I'd proven to everyone, but more importantly to myself, that I had what it took to be racing at the highest professional level. I had been entrusted with an opportunity, and I felt I had maximized my abilities up to that point. I'd been back to the United States and raced the Tour DuPont, helping Lance earn second place overall for the second consecutive year, and after doing a few other races in America, I flew back to Europe the day before the start of the Tour of Luxembourg.

The Tour of Luxembourg is an interesting race. It is a stage race that happens toward the end of May or beginning of June, and while not part of the World Tour (the hardest, most prestigious races), it is rated just below, and depending on the year, can be used by a number of cyclists who want to prepare for the Tour de France.

I didn't expect much from myself after having raced all spring and crisscrossed the Atlantic, but the stars aligned in a big way. I won two stages, wore the leader's jersey, and finished second overall against some of the best cyclists in the world—men I'd been reading about in magazines only a year before.

My results increased the exposure I received, but more importantly, they increased my bank account. Well, temporarily.

In Europe, the natural progression, or evolution, of a professional cyclist goes something like this:

Fall in love with the bike.

Dream of winning.

Train hard enough to excel in minor races.

Get noticed and sign with a team.

Place well in a few races, then buy an expensive watch.

Win a couple of races, then buy a nice car.

The particulars vary slightly, but you get the gist. The cycle hasn't changed much over the decades, but looking good was as important as racing well. The latter made it easier to accomplish the former.

I'm a speed junkie. Most pro cyclists are. I've already mentioned it was one of the reasons I got hooked on the sport, but my love of going fast trickled over into a need for speed when I wasn't racing. One of the few times I upset my parents, to the point of their getting truly mad, was in high school when I bought a motorcycle with some of my winnings from the local races. To me, it was just something I wanted, so I got it. But to my mom, my purchase of a shiny, overly loud, and in her opinion incredibly dangerous Yamaha FZR-600 was a "breach of contract." She wouldn't put up with it. Riding a pedal-powered bike made her lose enough sleep, but a teenager piloting a crotch-rocket through the streets of New York? Totally unacceptable.

RICH

I remember I was sitting at the kitchen table having lunch after just finishing a training ride, and the doorbell rings. My mom got up, answered the door, and as the door swung open, this obnoxiously loud engine started revving. George, helmet on, had ridden the bike right up to the front door and was straddling it like he was some great cavalry commander about to lead his army to victory. To say my mom was furious would be a gross understatement. Even though George never wanted to disappoint my parents or make them angry, he did have a slightly mischievous side. In his mind, he was trying to be funny while being a rebellious teenager, but he quickly found out there was no kidding around on this issue. Needless to say, he didn't keep the bike for long.

MARTHA

Oh, I didn't like that bike. I worried about them enough on the ones with pedals. I wasn't about to tolerate any with motors! But that paled in comparison to how mad I was the first time I found out he had been drinking. He was twelve years old, and he biked home after finishing a whole bottle of whiskey with a friend. I thought the parents had been there, so I got mad at the mother too. It turns out, boys being boys, they had raided the liquor cabinet while his parents had been away.

Back in high school, I may have been forced to cede my love of speed to my parents' wishes, but as a young adult, now fully living on my own, I was damn sure going to do what I wanted. I'd already bought a Rolex earlier in the season, a stainless steel Submariner that I still have to this day; now it was time to take the next step.

I wired the money I earned from the Tour of Luxembourg to my dad, and requested that he go buy me a brand-new BMW M3 and have it waiting for me upon my return to the U.S.

> **RICARDO**
> I'd reluctantly purchased the Rolex for him before the Ruta Mexico, his first stage race as a pro. I was amazed at how much that cost, and now he wanted a thirty-thousand-dollar car! I was concerned about how young pro athletes waste all their money, and I told George he needed to be smart and not blow it! He told me not to worry, that he'd be making more, and that this was his last big-ticket purchase, THEN he'd start saving. Bottom line, he was a good kid, it was his money, so I found the car he was looking for and went and got it in Nassau County.

My dad knew how hard I worked, but I'm sure he struggled on some level with going and buying his son a watch and a sports car. In fact, he probably didn't like it. But he respected my decisions. My wins in Luxembourg were absolute validation that not only was I on the proper life path, but that I was going to be successful as a professional cyclist. Rich picked me up at the airport in my new ride, and the metallic navy blue with black interior BMW M3 became my statement to the world that I had arrived.

The remainder of 1994 went well, as I continued to place in most, if not all, of my races, but it was in October that I finally had to confront, in an initial way, the use of drugs in our sport.

We were at the World Championships in Agrigento, a city on the southern coast of Italy. There was an extreme amount of pressure on the U.S. team that year with Lance the defending world champion. He had won the 1993 World Championships in Oslo, Norway, roughly twelve months prior. That day in Italy, Lance would finish in the top ten, but I was in so much pain right from the start. The pace just seemed too high. Guys were chatting, seemingly without a care in the world, and I couldn't even stay on their wheel. The World Championships are usually run as a circuit—a series of laps of the same course that eventually add up to around 250 kilometers (roughly 150 miles). That year, I was there to help Lance repeat as world champion, but I completed only five laps and got off my bike completely exhausted, drained of every ounce of energy and sapped of any will to continue pushing the pedals.

We'd always done vitamin B-12 or vitamin C shots for recovery purposes, but in recent months, rumors of something else within the peloton were beginning to grow. Before the 1994 Worlds, I had heard the whispers, but in Agrigento, I saw the speed. It's like when you see or are involved in a car crash: things just seem to slow down as your senses become hyperaware of your surroundings. I felt like I was operating in slow motion. Earlier in the year I had been on par, even at times dominant, against my rivals, winning three races, but that day I struggled to stay in last place.

I had no proof of foul play, and I certainly wasn't going to cause a stir by confirming what we all now know to be true, so all I could do was suck it up and train harder.

CHAPTER 8

I ENDED 1994 BY HEADING to Charlotte, North Carolina, where I had chosen to base myself, sharing a house with fellow racer Freddy Rodriguez. At the time, he was a great roommate to have. We were the same age, his family was likewise of Colombian descent, and with a nickname like "Fast Freddy"—well, he had a need for speed that matched mine, as evidenced by the two motorcycles in our garage.

The fun of the off-season quickly changed to the focus of getting ready to race, but 1995 was a year in which my results did not meet my expectations.

My season basically began the same as in 1994, at our training camp in Italy, but our American enclave in Como had grown. Bobby Julich, an all-rounder and GC (overall, or "general classification") contender, and Kevin Livingston, known for his climbing prowess, joined me and Frankie on Motorola, and became our roomies. As had previously been the case, it was more logistics than anything else that drove us to bunk up together. We were all Americans, so it made sense to stay together and help each other out. I recall Bobby even slept on the couch until a bed opened up.

FRANKIE ANDREU

Pizza Margherita. Every freaking meal. Pizza Margherita. He'd never waver or vary his order. It was maddening. We'd point out other things on the menu and insist he order something else. Nope. Not George. He'd simply say, "No, I like this." As frustrating and comical as it was, I admired him for that. He knew what he liked and he stuck with it. He had his comfort zone. He was very similar in his approach to cycling. He could have gone off and headlined other teams, but he knew what he was good at and stayed true to that.

Frankie had purchased a Fiat, and that became our link to the outside world. While I didn't have much success racing—not by my standards—we had a lot of fun in our apartment that year, complete with heated Sega basketball and hockey matches at all hours. It was the way we decided who would clean up after dinner every night. Bobby usually won, and I got really good at keeping a kitchen spotless.

I won only one race in 1995, the Acht Van Chaam in Holland. Instead of going to the races to compete, I went to them to finish—more specifically, to survive. I'd changed very little in my training program—in fact, the times I was doing in training were better than ever—but once I got to the races, as had happened at the Worlds in '94, not only was everyone else faster, but they seemed to be going at those higher speeds with less effort. Fat guys were beating me up climbs, never leaving their big chain ring. I'd be the last person in the bunch, hanging on for dear life.

By now, we had quite the American base camp in Italy, and after the Milan–San Remo race in March, Lance and I, along with our girlfriends, drove together back home to Como. Lance and I had long since established an impenetrable level of trust, and Lance vented a lot of frustration during the drive. He was furious because it was so obvious most of the peloton was using something. He was one year removed from being world champion, and he hadn't even been able to stay in the front group of fifty. We drove the almost two hundred miles in a time that would have made Ayrton Senna proud. If it usually took me just over three hours, that night, it took less than two. Lance made his BMW 540 caress and careen across the road as if it were his chance to show that if he had the right motor, his mind would do the rest. He'd reached his breaking point and decided enough was enough. Something had to be done so that he could prove he was the best.

Upon arriving in Como, my girlfriend at the time fled Lance's chariot quicker than a rat runs off a sinking ship, with a curt "Thanks," only too happy to have survived the experience. Long after that car ride ended, my focus never wandered from Lance's insistence that night that we needed to do something, that we were just as good as the guys beating us.

LANCE ARMSTRONG

[Some riders] had conversations starting in late 1994 about the changes going on. But that year, we held out—we assumed they'd develop a test and we wouldn't be faced with having to make the decision to use or not to use. Milan–San Remo ended up being the final straw where [a number of us] decided we'd do it.

Each time I rolled up to the start line, instead of wondering if I was going to win, I wondered at what point the pain would become too great to ignore, and then too severe to continue. That said, even though I thought about the threshold that would define too much, quitting was never an option. It wasn't in my DNA. I'm not calling anyone out for their decisions, but not finishing was never, ever a choice for me. I probably learned that from a few different sources. My father, my brother, and my early coach René Wenzel, who would tell us in very plain terms, "You aren't allowed to quit."

RENÉ WENZEL

There's a lot of quitting in sport, and the more others give up, the more the mantra of "the race is never over" rings true. George was one of the few riders who embodied this from his time as a junior to the pinnacles of international professional competition.

I wouldn't ever get off the bike and admit defeat because I didn't want to let anyone down. Not my team, my family, or myself. In the grand scheme of things, that's what I equated with quitting—causing the people I cared about and loved to be disappointed in me. My earliest memory of when that happened was enough to make me swear to myself to never let it happen again.

We'd gone to Colorado to race the Junior National Championships in 1989. I'd never raced at altitude, and up to that point, I'd rarely been beaten in any race I entered. In that race, however, I was so dead due to my lack of acclimatization, I pulled over to the side of the road and *sat down*. We didn't know what effect racing at elevation would have on me, so it was a learning process, but I couldn't understand what I was feeling. I was so used to beating everyone and winning, now I was feeling sorry for myself and asking the standard pity-party questions: "Why me?" "What did I do to deserve this?" "How can this be happening?"

JONATHAN VAUGHTERS, FORMER TEAMMATE AND CEO OF SLIPSTREAM SPORTS

George and I had met the year before. We'd see each other at all the big races, since we were the same age. That year we were both the favorites, but neither of us won. I was a climber, so I knew my best bet was to wear down the field each lap, attacking at the bottom of the climb. The field had been reduced dramatically, and before the last lap, George came up to me and said, "Hey, why don't you attack at the top of the climb, that might work better." I thought, Yeah, better for you!

I have no idea how long I sat there, or how many people saw my childish display, but I eventually got up and finished the race. I'd never seen the look on my parents' faces when I pulled up, so far behind the rest of the other kids. My dad is a very quiet individual, so he conveys a lot with a look or a stare. What I saw was a look of wonderment, mixed with a dash of despair, as if he wished he could take my pain away. But underneath it all was a wrinkle I'd never witnessed. He was trying to hide his disappointment. And that cut deeper than any knife could ever be driven.

RICH

I couldn't believe it. It was the first time I ever saw George really get beat. He came through on the last lap with the field, but when everyone finished, we didn't see him. We thought, Maybe he's crashed, or he flatted, or worse yet, he got hit by the moto. Fifteen or twenty minutes later he rolled in with a look on his face I'd never seen. He was distraught. All he said was, "I got dropped." I looked to my dad and saw a curious mix of two expressions on his face. I sensed he was worried—he felt bad for George, and wished he could take away his pain. But I also saw surprise, as in, how had this actually happened after all the training they'd done.

My dad gave his heart and soul so I could have the opportunity to follow my dream. He sacrificed so much and made my life his focus. He held a full-time job, but trying to make me into a great rider was his *other* full-time commitment. And in one race, I'd wiped away his confidence in me, and it was crushing.

RICARDO

We waited and waited, and couldn't understand what happened. Finally, I went to talk to one of the mechanics, and they told me he was "spilling his guts out" in the parking lot. George hadn't crossed the finish line; he'd gone straight to the car. It was heartbreaking to see him that way. I didn't have any answers, and I struggled to find a way to comfort him.

That moment has forever stuck with me. Every instance after that day, when I felt like throwing in the towel, I remembered that look on my dad's face and how I never wanted to see it again.

I learned how to spell *frustration* as the summer heat began to sizzle the pavement. I went to the 1995 Vuelta a España (Tour of Spain) with the knowledge of a couple things. First, since it was my first grand tour, the ultimate goal was finishing. Everyone in the media, and casual fans, always talk about the winners, but within the peloton, we give almost as much credit to the guys that finish the three weeks of racing. Like Paris–Roubaix, it requires an uncanny level of mental and physical endurance. It's an almost indescribable ordeal to haul oneself across the countryside day in and day out for twenty-three days total (grand tours often have twenty-one days of racing with two rest days built in). Whether it's Italy in May, France in June, or Spain in August/September, you earn your badges of honor in the grand tours.

Second, there was no doubt the drugs that people were talking about existed. There were too many signs to ignore, like sprinters being able to climb alongside guys who weighed twenty pounds less. There was no question the drugs were making people faster. I still didn't know what the magic elixir was, but I knew that because I wasn't one of the ones taking it, I was going to have to put myself through more pain than ever if I wanted to stay true to my mantra of never quitting.

What I didn't know, however, was that I was about to come face-to-face with what everyone was talking about and more and more of my fellow riders were relying on. The first person I ever saw using what I assume was EPO (erythropoietin) was at the Vuelta that year. It was almost halfway through the race, and up to that point, he was managing to stay with the top performers in the race. Before that year, we had been very similar in our racing résumés. He was one or two years older than me, and in 1995 was getting some attention for his racing results, whereas I was occupying the back of the bunch in every race I entered.

We were in a nondescript hotel, which is the norm for the riders during a grand tour, and after a massage, I walked back to our room. As I pushed back the door, I saw him with a needle in his arm, and his attention immediately alternated between that needle and the doorway. Surprise seized his facial features; I immediately backed out of the room, and we never spoke of it. The overriding result of that brief moment was that I felt an overwhelming sense of unfairness. I wasn't privy to what he was putting into his body, but bottom line, he was using something that was probably helping him stay within the upper echelon of riders at every stage.

I didn't know it at the time, but the effects of EPO on a cyclist, or any endurance athlete, are staggering. This drug really was a game changer.

There was another instance, involving another rider during the Vuelta, that solidified my sense that I couldn't compete on a level playing field without some assistance. This guy had been complaining about how bad he felt, how poor his results had been, and how unfair it was that he had been unable to follow his usual recovery routine. Eventually, he ended up having a friend come by with a special package (which again, I can only assume was EPO and/or other drugs), and the next day, after having struggled every single day up until that point, he was in the breakaway.

If I initially felt the situation was unfair, after the second incident, I was borderline furious. I was turning myself inside out every day to make it to the finish line, and now I'd witnessed two separate episodes that seemed to confirm the existence of the wonder drug everyone had talked about. With more than my usual fortitude, I went on a mission to finish my three weeks of hell. I may not have been on the same stuff as some of the competition, but I knew I was a better athlete and racer. It didn't matter what others did; the fuel I drew on now was derived and distilled from my take on justice and retribution.

I almost didn't fulfill my promise to myself, through what I had decided was no fault of my own. The third-to-last stage was the day before a time trial, so there was added incentive for a lot of the guys to go for the win. That's a common occurrence: since so many riders *know* they don't have a chance in the time trial, it basically becomes a day of rest, and therefore they give a little extra in the stage before. Stage 19 went from Sabiñánigo to Calatayud, and was almost 228 kilometers (139 miles) long. I can't remember how or why I felt different that day, but I did, and I took full advantage of the miraculous freshness in my legs. We'd studied the road book (the list of stages the event organizer gives each rider/team), and I knew there was a Category 2 climb about 10 kilometers (6 miles) before the finish, which then became a downhill all the way into Calatayud. I convinced myself that if I could get over the climb with the lead group, I would have a chance to win. Every second I struggled up the Category 2 got me one pedal stroke closer to the finish line. I yo-yoed off the back a couple times, but as we crested the hill, I remember bearing down with one final, desperate effort. I may have ground my teeth down a bit, and burst a couple of blood vessels, but I'd stayed in contact.

The descents were never a problem for me, and I calculated all the options as we sped toward possible glory. With less than one hundred meters to go, I shot to the front of the group, and I began to grin. I thought, *I got this.* At fifty meters to go, I sensed someone on my inside, trying to force himself between me and the barriers. In the same millisecond that my brain was relaying the words "There's not enough room," it sent a simultaneous message, "You shouldn't be flying forward like this!" German Marcel Wüst, a sprinter who'd end up winning stages in all three grand tours and twelve at the Vuelta, had decided to try to squeeze himself past me when there clearly wasn't enough room. He wasn't successful. The contact Wüst initiated catapulted me into the pavement in spectacular fashion. Graham Watson, the famous cycling photographer, took a shot of my impact that, to this day, I have trouble viewing.

The end result was that after I got blasted into the barrier, doctors thought I might have broken my neck, but eventually I was diagnosed with strained ligaments. Italian Adriano Baffi, riding for Mapei, won the stage. I finished, walking the final fifty meters, and had a whole new object for my focus the final two days of that epic adventure in Spain. As if I needed more pain to push into the recesses of my mind. After that, the time trial and the majestic ride into Madrid were a blur. But I'd done what I set out to do: I'd completed my first grand tour, and I grasped the accomplishment of, at the very least, keeping my promise to myself.

I had one more race that year, in Australia. It was a low-key affair compared to the craziness and competition in Europe. I went there to have fun, and I remember I enjoyed my time there immensely. As the sun set on 1995, I may not have had the palmarès to show for my work ethic, but I was wise enough to realize you need years like I had just had to put things into perspective and to force you to grow. I was a harder, stronger, and, most important, hungrier rider than ever before.

CHAPTER 9

FRANKIE ANDREU WAS NOT only my roommate and friend those first few years in Europe, but also my mentor in every sense. He was my guide, my sounding board, and my resource when I had questions about anything. Our dynamic was not unique; there have been countless relationships, in sports, business, and politics that have showcased how important mentors can be, and we fell into a similar pattern of teacher-student, questions and answers.

Mentoring usually takes on a positive connotation, but my relationship with Frankie that year took what some may say was a dark turn. At the time it seemed like just another small decision to become a better rider.

The year 1996 was when I took my first steps down the path of drug use. There are a myriad of ways to describe the transition that took place, or the gravity of the decision I made. The best way I know how to describe it is that I felt it was my only choice. I really did. If I wanted to be a professional bike rider, with all that that entailed, in 1996 I felt I'd reached the end of my options of racing clean. The only way to compete on a level playing field with my rivals was to do what they were doing. The memory of 1995's racing pain was all too fresh in my mind, and I knew I couldn't race another year like that, let alone if the pain and misery were worse. I didn't reach these decisions without careful consideration, and really, without one final incident that confirmed for me that *everyone* seemed to be doing it.

Others may give March 1996 a more ominous meaning, but I'll just say it was when I committed to being all-in with my bike racing. One day, I came back to our third-floor apartment in Como. Our refrigerator contained the standard bachelor-pad basics: cream cheese, sparkling water, tomato sauce, and maybe some hard cheese. In other words, it was close to empty.

So as I swung the fridge door open to the right, it made the Thermos-like container in the door that much more noticeable. I opened the cooler, and even though I had no real idea what I was staring at, I was gazing at my future. The clear, labelless vials looked harmless, albeit a little strange. I figured it was EPO, the drug I had heard about, but I was confused and a little scared to see it right in front of me. So this was what all the fuss was about? This is what I have to do to be the best I can be?

When Frankie came home, I confronted him about what I'd found, asking if the vials were his. He got irritated and defensive, and told me to mind my own business. Frankie's nickname, Cranky Frankie, was a joke, but at times he lived up to it. He had parameters and limits, and we all knew not to press an issue if he showed a certain side of his personality. And this was definitely one of those occasions.

I could tell from his tone and his protestations, that he'd already taken the infamous step, and that moment produced an epiphany for me. I had to do the same. Frankie's use of EPO was the final sign. And it was a monumental one.

FRANKIE ANDREU
At the time, I didn't have any guilt in my decision to use EPO. I felt I had two choices: not use, go home,

and not be a pro . . . or use and get to race bikes. It
was a simple decision. Now, it's a regrettable one,
but back then, those seemed like the only choices.

Cycling has always been filled with a gray area of recovery
products and mild performance enhancers—caffeine pills, aspirin,
B-12, and other vitamin recovery shots. I knew this was different,
but it was easy to justify doing EPO because that was what the
others were using.

It took me a week to work up the courage, through the course
of several conversations, to finally get Frankie to admit that the
vials were his, and to ask his assistance in getting some for myself.

At first, it hadn't been easy to get Frankie to open up. His answers to my questions were direct, and his tone implied I should
stop asking. (In fairness to Frankie, he remembers this next exchange differently.)

"It's none of your business. You shouldn't be looking at this."

"Frankie, what is that stuff? I have a feeling I know what it is.
But I need you to tell me."

"Well, if you know what it is, what is it?"

"I think it's EPO. How long have you been taking it?"

Again, he replied, "None of your business."

A light went off in my head. I'd seen people in the Vuelta, now
I was seeing my roommate with the same stuff, and for me that was
the last straw. I asked Frankie what made him decide to do it.

"I don't have a choice. We have to do it to survive. Everybody's
doing it now. I don't have a choice."

"Where'd you get it?"

"Switzerland. It's not a big deal. You don't need a prescription.
This is how much it costs."

I got the impression he was reticent in helping me—not because he was nervous about his connection to what I'd be doing, but because I wasn't yet worthy to be in the club. After that conversation, it took me a few days to summon the balls to go through with it. Frankie had no idea, at the time or to this day, of the profound effect that exchange had on me. In fact, when I spoke to him about it recently, he said that it might have taken place, but that he did not remember it or remember it 'that way'.

It hadn't been easy, but I was finally armed with the information I needed to make my own leap. And I knew there'd be no turning back. I approached my foray into Switzerland like a military operation. It took a couple days of heading to a few different ATM machines to withdraw the required money. I made sure to use different routes back to our place on Via Magenta to make sure there wasn't a pattern to my movements. Then, the day arrived. I had chosen a no-name, nondescript jersey to wear as I rode my bike. The gloomy, misty, and rainy morning only seemed to add to the suspense as I headed toward Chiasso, the Swiss town just over the Italian border. I felt a little guilty that I was embarking down this ambiguous moral path; however, I also felt proud that I'd committed to the next level. I wasn't giving up on my dream: just the opposite. I was doing what it took to be as professional as possible in my approach to attain my life's goal. The thought of cheating never crossed my mind. It was the thought of not letting myself get cheated by others that drove me.

Frankie had given me the basic info. I could go to any pharmacy and ask for a box of Epirex. He explained that in Switzerland, you didn't need a prescription, and it was not a big deal to ask for this type of medicine, because everyone did it. Once inside, I took a deep breath before approaching the mid-thirties lady with brownish-blond hair behind the counter. She stared at me for a brief moment after I nervously asked for the drug, and I wasn't sure whether I'd mispronounced the name or, perhaps worse, I'd set off some silent alarm or chain of events that would lead to my downfall. After what seemed like an eternity (but was probably only half a second), she went behind the white wall into the back, came out with the elongated box, handed it to me, took my five hundred Swiss francs, and told me to have a nice day.

I'd expected to reenact a chapter out of one of Robert Ludlum's Jason Bourne novels, and instead, it had been just as easy as buying a pack of gum. I was shocked at how simple it had been to maneuver through what I felt was such a monumental experience. I put the box, filled with those tiny clear vials, as well as the syringes I'd bought, into the back pocket of my jersey and rode home, still unsure whether I had escaped notice. When I rushed into our apartment, Frankie was there, and I didn't know what else to do but try to make light of where I'd been and what I'd just done. Pretending I was in the midst of a Cold War espionage thriller, I playfully joked that I'd been followed by the authorities and they were hot on my trail. I told Frankie to draw the blinds, lock the door, and shut the windows. He wasn't amused.

Eventually, I headed to the bathroom and prepared to do my first shot. At this point, as far as I knew, there weren't any doctors telling the peloton how to proceed. Every rider was on his own to self-prescribe and self-treat himself based on what we'd heard and been told within the circle of trust. It was a type of witchcraft wisdom, or group science. Frankie told me I needed to do two thousand IU every other day (anemic cancer patients are directed to take between forty thousand and sixty thousand units a week), and that was the best baseline to see how your performance improved. (Frankie, by the way, denies that he told me this.) I'd also heard that a box of Epirex would last six to eight weeks, and you needed to do the shots in the upper arm, near the shoulder, so that the EPO could be absorbed better. There I was, sitting on the toilet seat, tiny syringe in hand, nervous but determined. And with one final mental cheerleading note, I said, "Here we go . . ." and did my first of countless injections. I'd never done a shot there, and it didn't hurt at all. I just felt a small pinch.

I exited the bathroom a changed man. I felt completely at peace. My expectations weren't that I'd immediately feel superhuman, but I did wonder *when* I'd feel different and how that feeling would present itself. This was a new me, one without any limitations, and one without the deck stacked against him. I might have been a new pro, but a feeling of calming equality spread through me like molten steel into a metal casting. My mind raced around the room, my eyes trying to keep up. Both came to a screeching halt when I saw Frankie on the couch. I told him what I'd done, and in typical Frankie fashion, there was no fanfare, no "Welcome to the club," no pat on the back to say, "It will be all right." He just scrunched up his face with a mild look of disdain and sighed, "Whatever."

CHAPTER 10

I WAS ON THE OTHER side, but it was still an *unspoken* step in the process of preparation. I could usually guess who was "using" based on their performance and where they placed, but I wasn't omniscient. An early season race provided me with a perfect reminder that there was a large labyrinth I still had to navigate. My roommate at one of the classics injured himself and therefore knew he would be off the bike for at least two months. One evening, he opened up the dresser in our hotel room and told me to take everything—that it would be a waste if no one used all these drugs. It looked like a minibar filled with candies. I'd never seen so many drugs. I didn't know what they all did, but I took them and shoved them into my bag. It was one of the most naive things I ever did, and I paid for it.

I left from that race to head home to the United States, and after landing in Charlotte, North Carolina, was asked to head over to the side for the customs agents to search my gear. My heart sank as I remembered the myriad of medicines among my clothes. The agents' eyes got wide, and they questioned not only what it all was, but why I had it. I couldn't make eye contact as I told them it wasn't mine, I was carrying it for a friend, and I thought they were all recovery-type products. Customs confiscated most of it, and for fifteen years I didn't hear another word about it. (Until a fateful day in a meeting room with the feds, where the first question put to me was "Were you stopped with performance-enhancing drugs in Charlotte in 1996?")

At the Tour DuPont, instead of simply surviving, I felt like I could race my bike again. I finally felt my first real benefit from EPO. I was climbing with the top thirty or forty guys in the race, and it was a great reminder of how I had been able to race when I was a first-year pro, or even amateur. We knew people were abusing, but I always tried to take the bare minimum in comparison to what we heard was being injected by other riders. There were already stories circulating of guys getting sick, or worse, dying, but I never thought it would happen to me because the amounts I used were substantially less than the rumored doses done by the athletes having problems.

FRANKIE ANDREU

What people did and didn't do was very secretive. We may have all lived together, but we didn't talk about it. We all knew members of our team were dabbling with all types of drugs . . .

By the time I headed back to Europe, it was time to get ready for the Tour de France. I'd known since the spring that I was on the "long team," the group of riders being considered by Motorola, and because I'd been an alternate in 1995—the Italian Fabio Casartelli was the final rider on that roster, just ahead of me—I figured my chances were good to make the squad. Whereas in 1995 I'd been intimidated and downright scared at the prospect of starting the Tour de France, a year later I was more experienced, more confident, and nowhere near as freaked out by the pressure. I had been hit hard by Casartelli's tragic death during the descent of the Col de Portet d'Aspet on Stage 15 the year before, and by the odd co-incidence that he and I had vied for the same spot on the team, but I knew "Le Tour" was a huge opportunity for me, and I prepared properly.

SEAN YATES

George had been cut from the '95 Tour team at the last minute. It was the final Tour I rode, so I never got a chance to ride with him around France. Fabio's death hit us all really hard. As a team we were devastated. Who knows why fate takes hold the way it does, but I do think it was a good decision not to have George ride in '95. He may have been ready, but I think it helped him to have another year of experience before he got his chance in '96.

In 1995, I was terrified of the Tour, and I was fine with the decision to keep me off the squad. In retrospect, I wish I had skipped the 1996 "Grande Boucle" as well. Any pretense I had that I was prepared was quickly replaced with the pain I'd become all too familiar with and fearful of. I was buried under an avalanche of exhaustion and I dreamed of crashing out almost from the get-go. As bad as I felt, I was propelled day to day by the atmosphere, itself a natural adrenaline rush. It was a level of attention I'd never seen, or envisioned. The media and the fans were whipped into a frenzy every day. We were the chum in the water. The peloton's mere presence created traffic jams.

The Tour that year could be classified as a shocker on a number of levels. Personally, I crashed out with a week to go, soldiering on to finish the stage but missing the time cut and requiring stitches in my head. Back then, we weren't required to wear helmets. I thought nothing of zipping down a mountain pass on wet pavement at sixty miles an hour. It didn't matter that if I miscalculated a turn I could catapult myself into an abyss, or that a mistimed fall could hurtle me into a rock wall. We did not think about disaster; youth and adrenaline only fueled desire.

Even after my injury, I refused to get in the broom wagon, not wanting to send any sort of a message that I was willing to give up or quit. The team had already decided I would not start the next day, but I wanted to make it to the finish line on my final stage.

The explosive news for the *team* had happened earlier when Lance had simply gotten off his bike and gone home. History would later reveal a much more detailed account of the war being waged inside Lance's body, and his long road to recovery and back to bike racing. But before that day in July 1996, there had been no indications, and zero questions, about Lance's health. It hit our team hard. It was very demoralizing to lose Lance, but the Tour is a fickle mistress, she feels pity for no one, and we were forced to forge ahead.

The only good thing I can say about that year's Tour, other than that I got my first taste of cycling's greatest race, is that in the midst of my misery, my prayers were answered: they actually shortened Stage 9, which was supposed to start in Val d'Isère and run close to 175 kilometers, to only 46 kilometers (28 miles). A horrible blizzard had blown into the Alps, and on a day when we were supposed to suffer over multiple mountain passes, the organizers decided we'd just race up the valley to Sestriere, Italy, the original finishing town. Mercifully, I missed having to climb the Galibier and Télégraphe passes that day, although I'd be back to pay my tab in later years.

CHAPTER 11

It's HARD TO EMPHASIZE how much 1999 changed the way America, and the world, looked at the Tour de France. The new perspective was made possible by a change of attitude in how we, as a team, approached the race. A lot had happened since my first Tour. For one, in 1997, I'd managed to survive my hardest day ever on the bike. It was Stage 10, from Luchon to Andorra Arcalis, a whopping 252.5 kilometers (156.9 miles) over six mountain passes. It was a level of suffering I'd never experienced before and, thankfully, haven't since. I was in the gruppetto (the last big group on the road that tries to stay together to make the time cut) after the first climb, on the brink of exhaustion almost from the start. It was over 100 degrees, and with the time cut hanging over us, our group of fifty-plus willed ourselves onward. My back, neck, and arms hurt just from maintaining my body position for such an extended period of time. By the end of the day, I had spent eight hours and forty-five minutes on the bike. It's not natural to be seated in the saddle that long. You can't train for it. I wouldn't *want* to train for it. I was driven by the aura of the Tour. I wasn't going to miss out on that experience because of something so basic as pain.

I've often wondered, how do you compare levels of suffering between sports? How do you decide which is the most demanding? ESPN once did a study where they identified ten skills of athleticism and asked eight panelists to give a number, 1 to 10, to each of the skills as they were needed within a specific sport. They ranked sixty different sports, and cycling came out as tied for twentieth. Twentieth?! Please! After looking at endurance, speed, power, and agility, to name a few, boxing was named as the most demanding sport. Cycling tied with distance running for the top score in endurance, but other than that, the illustrious panel didn't think riding a bike was very noteworthy. I'd like to take each of those eight and bring them along for a ride in the Pyrenees. I've ridden myself into such a mental black hole, I've been unable to remember my phone number. I've drained myself of every ounce of energy, to the degree that after a race I've sometimes been unable to stand for more than an hour. Multiple times during the Tour, as well as in training, I lost more than *eight pounds* during a ride.

So in 1997, after torturing myself for almost a month, riding onto the Champs-Élysées for the first time was spectacular. Few people ever get the peloton's view of Paris, and as I whizzed by the landmarks that had defined the City of Light for centuries, I had no idea I would end up seeing the Seine on so many of those sultry July afternoons.

1998 was a turning point in our sport, encapsulated in two words: *Festina affair.* The drug investigation, raids, confessions, and subsequent arrests that were all part of the 1998 Tour de France forever changed the landscape of how doping was perceived. Only a few days into the race (which started in Ireland that year, for the first time), our soigneurs told us all the teams had heard what was going to happen, and dumped all their stash into the English Channel after leaving Ireland and before landing in France, at the port of

Roscoff, in Brittany. The big joke was that in a few years the fish in the area would be gargantuan and able to outswim their cousins from other parts of the Atlantic! We all knew there were teams that still used PEDs during that Tour even after arriving in France; we could tell based on their level of racing and results. After Stage 7, no one on our team took anything, not even recovery vitamins, we were so paranoid about a possible similar outcome to the teams already embroiled in the scandal. Ironically, I was close to yellow that year, but it was the time trial that removed any hope I had of donning the leader's jersey.

Jim Ochowicz had disbanded the Motorola team in 1996, after the company decided they no longer wanted to sponsor cycling, but for the 1997 season, I was fortunate to seamlessly transfer over to another mainly American squad, the United States Postal Service team. It was the brainchild of businessman Thomas Weisel and managed by Eddie Borysewicz—Eddie B., the man who coached the 1984 U.S. Olympic cycling team to nine medals. It was from humble beginnings, and high expectations, that our new U.S. squad set out to conquer the competition. Lance would end up joining the team in 1998 after his recovery from cancer. The unbreakable will he had used to defeat cancer, he now refocused on anything that stood in his way of winning the world's biggest bike race.

The 1999 Tour was labeled the Tour of Renewal. What it meant for all of us on the U.S. Postal team was a renewal of our commitment to be the best, and in particular, to make one man rise above the rest. I mentioned earlier that there had been a definitive change in how we approached the race. Lance was back, and with him came a new directeur sportif, former pro racer Johan Bruyneel. As a duo, they brought a level of planning never seen before. What Lance and Johan envisioned was a strategy that combined reconnaissance, nutrition, team structure, and, yes, conservative doping, whose *only* objective was to see Lance wearing yellow on the Champs-Élysées in Paris.

LANCE ARMSTRONG

Before cancer, George had been there from the start to help me win bike races. Early on in my career, I'd never dreamed of winning the Tour. It was Johan who convinced me that I could do that. And George bought into the idea as well, wholeheartedly.

Where other teams in the past might have had one or two components of this formula, we were a squad built on the premise of leaving no stone unturned and nothing to chance in order to achieve our desired result. Previously, where other teams had been good at simply cheating, we strived to be better at being professional in *all* aspects required to win the Tour. A lot's been written about how Lance was the first rider to "recon" specific Tour stages, and while that undoubtedly helped, it was only one piece of the puzzle in our attempt to be prepared.

I'd had an amazing spring campaign that year. I'd finished second in numerous sprints, but my proudest result was my fourth place in Paris–Roubaix. I finished the ninety-seventh running of the "Hell of the North" just one spot off the podium, which was occupied by all Mapei–Quick Step riders. Lance had helped me win the U.S. title in 1998, and I repaid his work by assisting him that same year at the Tour of Luxembourg. That was the race when I knew he was back, and it made it that much easier to buy into the overall plan for 1999. Our first race together in 1999 was the Tour de France, which marked his return to our Super Bowl, his first time among the two-hundred-strong peloton since he had stepped off his bike in the rain during Stage 5 in 1996. I knew my fitness was good, if not at an all-time high, and everyone else on our team (Frankie Andreu, Kevin Livingston, Jonathan Vaughters, and Christian Vande Velde among them) was primed to fulfill his role and, hopefully, our destiny.

CHRISTIAN VANDE VELDE, TEAMMATE
1998-2003

I'd met George in 1996 when I was on the U.S. track cycling team. I was starstruck when he came into our hotel in Atlanta at a pre-Olympic event, but it was at our first U.S. Postal training camp in 1998 that it hit me. I was on a team with one of my idols. I'd had his posters on my wall growing up! So at the Tour in 1999, even though every day felt like I was biting off more than I could chew, I looked to him, and his humble, calm nature, as a guide. I aspired to be like him.

When Lance blitzed the field in the prologue in Le Puy du Fou, we could barely contain the excitement that night at the hotel. However, there was also a level of nervousness as we all realized, "Oh shit, now we've got to defend yellow!" The festive atmosphere was a tad tempered by the mountain of questions created by his victory, not to mention the increased stress level. We all knew based on Lance's result from the Vuelta a España the year before that he had the ability to do well, but we honestly never imagined we'd start the Tour with a win! We ended up losing the jersey to Jaan Kirsipuu after the second stage, but when Lance crushed everyone in the Stage 8 time trial in Metz, the *maillot jaune* was ours for good.

Lance and Johan made quite the pair and a formidable team. Some have called it a "dictatorship." I'm just not sure who was the dictator, Lance or Johan. I'd known Johan only superficially while we raced together in the peloton. My first impression of him was that he was a smart guy with high expectations. Johan was keenly aware Lance was his chance to prove he could manage and be a directeur sportif. Lance liked someone with a clear plan, and Johan was a master tactician and organizer. On top of that, Johan would only accept 100 percent devotion to the ultimate goal. Lance wearing yellow on the podium the last day in Paris was all that mattered. He didn't like input from anyone except Lance. And as I evolved, we butted heads over that aspect.

Every team, especially at the Tour de France, comes with its own ambitions. Some bring sprinters, and the team works together to win on the flat stages. Others are made up of opportunists, so that on any given day, anyone has a chance to go for the win. The 1999 Tour was the first time I had ever heard *both* a directeur sportif and top rider, Johan and Lance, tell the other members of the team that we were not there for personal ambition, so if we had designs on individual glory, we'd better pack our bags. Because of Lance's story, we knew media attention surrounding the team was going to be high, and that played into the pressure we felt. It wasn't just the usual cycling-centric fans that would be watching our every move; it would be a large percentage of the country. Johan was still allowing me to go for sprints that year, but there was definitely a sense of two teams within our squad.

I didn't take any EPO that Tour because I started with a high hematocrit, or red blood cell count (my mother suffers from polycythemia vera, a condition where the body produces too many red blood cells). Plus, Johan drilled home a conservative approach, which had already been tested a month earlier when Jonathan

Vaughters, one of the new additions to the team, scorched the time trial up Mont Ventoux in the Dauphiné Libéré and set a new record in the process. Wins meant mandatory testing at the finish line. That was not the kind of attention Johan wanted any of us to bring. He wanted us under the radar.

Jonathan, now the manager of Garmin-Sharp, at the time was known as the Professor. As has been written in other books, he questioned everything—the doctors, the timing of when we took the drugs, the measurements and dosages. He was as knowledgeable about what we were taking as the team doctor giving us advice. That was uncommon. Most of us just took what we were told, when we were told to take it. What also made Jonathan different, however, was that he was actively searching for new and better ways to dope. We'd all heard about the blood transfusions that had taken place on the U.S. cycling team at the 1984 Olympic Games, but the first time I ever heard about one of my teammates looking into blood doping (taking out blood to then reinfuse it at a later date) was when a mutual friend told me Jonathan Vaughters was researching how to do it himself. He was trying to figure out how to do it on his own because he had heard, even though it was an older method, it was a great way to improve performance, and most important, had a low risk of being detected.

JONATHAN VAUGHTERS

I was always curious, and I wanted to know what I was doing to my body. I didn't want the team doctor just giving me something. From a self-preservation standpoint, I felt it was important to know if there were any side effects and what the costs versus the benefits were. I never blood-doped, but from everything I learned, it seemed like a logical step in the evolution of what guys were doing.

Everyone had a role to play in our cycling soap opera. We were a ragtag group that first year:

LANCE: Determined as ever, but different from when we'd first met. He was on a new mission in life. He'd stared death in the face and hadn't blinked.

FRANKIE ANDREU: Cranky Frankie. His wife, Betsy, would call almost every day and wonder why he wasn't getting in the breakaways. One of the field generals, he'd already raced in seven Tours. Totally dedicated to the mission.

TYLER HAMILTON: My roommate in Spain at the time. Excited to be taking part in his first Tour with such a strong team. Expected to be Lance's right-hand man in the mountains.

KEVIN LIVINGSTON: The comedian and joker. All-American kid from St. Louis, Missouri.

PETER MEINERT NIELSEN: A hardworking Danish rider. One of our veterans. Old-school in his approach and training techniques. Could ride all day, every day.

CHRISTIAN VANDE VELDE: Youngest of the team. Totally green, but adapted quickly to the pro peloton.

JONATHAN VAUGHTERS: The Professor. Very good climber, but terrible spatially in the peloton. Was out of the 1999 Tour after Stage 2.

PASCAL DERAME: Workhorse Frenchman who liked to have fun at the right time. Incredibly nice guy who didn't speak much English, but let his riding do the talking.

People questioned our ability, but we had a lot of fun. Others have said and written it, but it was true: we were like the Bad News Bears. This little three-week excursion was a learning experience, but with everything on the line. The experts had us so far removed from serious contender status, we weren't even in the Underdog zip code. We all felt like we were in way over our heads, but nobody was going to give in. Every morning, we woke up to the unknown.

FRANKIE ANDREU

We had one goal—to win. And we had nothing to lose. Our team got along great. Me, George, Lance, Tyler, Christian, and Kevin were all good friends. We would have done anything for each other, and sacrificed everything.

JONATHAN VAUGHTERS

When Lance told me his power numbers from training, I was very scientific in my assessment and said to him, "Well, you're going to win the Tour." It was that simple to me. I thought, We'd better be ready to have a guy win the Tour de France. His riding, and eventual result, didn't shock me at all.

An early sign of how things would go for us that year was Stage 2, the jaunt over the Passage du Gois, a narrow strip between the Île de Noirmoutier and Beauvoir-sur-Mer. Because it's underwater most of the day due to the tides, the Passage du Gois is exposed and passable for only four hours a day, and it is always slippery. It was going to be critical to have Lance at the front of the group as we headed into the wet and tricky cobblestones. For me, it had the feel of a classics race. I don't ever need extra motivation when conditions are at their worst, but I had a feeling I was going to be relied on that day. I could sense I had to be "on."

The Tour is an endless stream of tiny skirmishes that, added together, often make the difference. Everyone knew they needed to be at the front. Everyone fought for positioning as we entered. But I got Lance where he needed to be and through the carnage. Who knows what might have happened had Lance been caught behind? But it is one of the things I'm most proud of, not just that year, but in all the years we raced together. Nobody shepherded people through the craziness better than me. Nobody. That's what I did. If it makes sense to phrase it this way, I *humbly* took immense pride in my ability to analyze, calculate, and execute in a millisecond. Doing my job, helping out my leader, and putting Lance in a position to win the Tour was a thrill. Swiss rider Alex Zülle, twice a winner of the Vuelta a España and two-time runner-up at the Tour de France, lost six minutes that day and would never come close, eventually losing the Tour to Lance by just over seven minutes. On a day when no one expected the overall contenders to have to worry about their rivals, we'd shown that destiny demands constant attention.

LANCE ARMSTRONG

Looking back, it was just a no-brainer that anyone who wanted to be safe needed to be in the front. I had 100 percent confidence in George, and the team, to get me in position. At the time, I didn't even give it any thought. We knew we needed to be there, and I knew George would do his job and get us properly placed.

Lance's position in the lead dictated extra work, but as the weeks went on, what we lacked in energy, we more than made up for in motivation. But the work still had to get done. I don't care what anyone says, we were not doing anything different than any of the other teams that year.

Overnight, Lance became a celebrity. Even our profiles, as his support riders, skyrocketed. We were all more respected. I was young, and enjoyed the extra attention. Eventually, it would get old, and I'd want to spend less and less time outside the nucleus of my family and teammates, but that first year, I wanted to gulp it all down. Absorb all the accolades and hope it never ended.

The biggest result of the 1999 Tour was that we started the gradual process of teaching a new generation of Americans about the sport, what it entailed, and what it took as a team to make Lance the best. Greg LeMond's years in yellow had helped break the ice and make people notice. Others had tickled the surface of success and shown the public what was out there. Now it was our turn to help the United States earn its Ph.D. in professional cycling. The Tour was our canvas, and none of us wanted to miss our opportunity to show what we knew and what we had learned.

CHAPTER 12

No TWO TOURS ARE ever alike. Each Tour de France is unique for a variety of reasons: The route. The circumstances dictated by the riders. One's teammates. We won in 1999, but no one was ready to rest on his laurels. If we felt pressure during our first win, it was exponentially greater the following year. For Johan and Lance, doing the back-to-back double was their chance to prove Lance's (and Johan's) talent wasn't a fluke, which made the stakes even greater. Throw in the fact that Italian Marco Pantani, the 1998 winner, and German Jan Ullrich, victor in 1997, both returned having missed the '99 Tour, and there was plenty of motivation to go around.

If 1999 was our year for having fun, 2000 was the year we turned winning into a science. Johan upgraded everything about the team and its approach to winning the Tour. Still around to help Lance were me, Frankie, Tyler Hamilton, and Kevin Livingston. But Johan brought back Russian strongman Viatcheslav Ekimov to the team, and added Benoît Joachim and Cédric Vasseur. "Postal Tour 2.0" tried to leave nothing to chance.

Due to the fact that I was naturally already close to the cutoff, numerous times Dr. Luis García del Moral needed to give me saline transfusions in order to keep my hematocrit level below the threshold. Both Dr. del Moral and Jose "Pepe" Martí were brought onto the team in 1999, del Moral as the team doctor, Marti as the trainer.

Stage 10 was the first day in the mountains, with five categorized climbs. Lance woke up that morning with a huge grin on his face, excited by the possibilities, since it was already raining outside and the forecast was for the weather to get worse. He was at the breakfast table clapping his hands, riling us up like a college football coach at halftime.

"With the weather like this, half my competition is already beaten!" he roared.

It was a brutal run-up to Hautacam in the mist, rain, and fog, the moist air of the Pyrenees almost too thick to breathe. Lance had told us that morning to just do everything we could to have him at the front over the Col d'Aubisque, which was the ultimate *hors catégorie* (HC) climb: steeper than even a Category 1 hill. We had done our jobs, had turned ourselves inside out to keep Lance in the proper position. To quote Phil Liggett's call on worldwide television that day, "Armstrong moves on now, relentlessly cutting his way through the Tour de France . . . letting them all run like a great fisherman, and then reeling them in, one after another."

Lance's dominance on the day against his main rivals was set in motion by Marco Pantani, the man known as the King of the Mountains. At the time (or perhaps even since), no one was considered better at flying uphill. When he launched, Alex Zülle followed, and Lance rounded out the trio who attacked. Back in the gruppetto, we got news from the team car that Lance didn't just ride up the road, he tore into his pedals with such purpose and force, I knew he was on a mission to send a message. He started the final climb more than ten minutes down on eventual stage winner Javier Otxoa, but by the finish, he would end up only forty-two seconds

Family vacation. I was the most high-maintenance of the kids. I hated to leave my mom's side.

With sister Clara and brother Rich.

Even at an early age, I preferred to be outside rather than in a classroom.

All dressed up. I had big plans.

That's me, third from left. Tour of Somerville. Even though it doesn't look like it, I was really excited to race.

1986, Long Island, New York. Left to right: Rich, my dad (Ricardo), and me in our backyard. Getting ready for one of our weekend rides with our matching Atala jerseys.

My dad was a good rider in his own right, and is still passionate about the sport today.

Rich and I were not the coolest-looking at the time, but riding our bikes made us feel cool.

At the Velodrome in Trexlertown, Pennsylvania. Not just my dad, but my pal and my biggest supporter. Never missed a race in those days.

Every kid's dream: cash for riding a bike.

Mengoni team in Brooklyn— our jerseys tried to show off the NYC skyline.

Jeff Evanshine, me, and coach Renee Wenzel. Jeff went on to win the Junior World Championships that year.

1992 TTT Olympic Trials: me, Dave Nicholson, Scott Mercier, and Nate Shafer. The team time trial is one of the hardest events in cycling. All-out for more than two hours, with no room for error. (*John Pierce, PhotoSport International*)

U.S. National Team with Freddy Rodriguez, May 1993. Good friend of mine, and roommate at the time. We grew up racing our bikes together.

1994 Tour of Mexico, my first pro stage race. Most of the riders didn't have their parents there.

1994 Paris–Roubaix. My first time on the course that would consume me the rest of my racing career. I was determined to get to the finish line. I did the last thirty miles by myself. (*John Pierce, PhotoSport International*)

1994 Tour du Pont. Me and Lance (in the world champion's jersey). I never would have imagined all the ups and downs our relationship would bring. *(John Pierce, PhotoSport International)*

Lance and me. Overwhelming to think how much we've shared over the years.

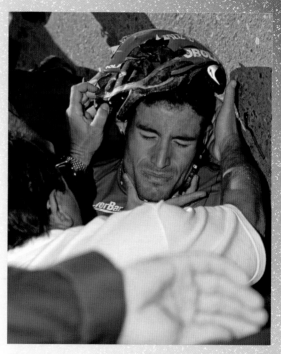

Even though my mom was never a huge fan of the sport, she was always there to support me.

1995 Vuelta, two days before the finish. Thank god for helmets. Things would have been a lot more serious without one. (*Graham Watson*)

With Sean Yates, 1996. One of the legends of the sport and one of the hardest men I know. I really looked up to him.

The infamous showers of Paris–Roubaix (with Frankie Andreu). Toward the end of my career, thankfully, we didn't have to use these anymore. We'd use the ones on our team bus. *(Graham Watson)*

Moments like this defined most of my career. Even though I hated these conditions, I excelled in them. *(Graham Watson)*

2002 Paris–Roubaix: me and Tom Boonen. The worst bonk of my life. Ended up in a ditch two kilometers after this picture was taken. *(John Pierce, PhotoSport International)*

2004 Paris–Roubaix. Me in front, leading a man who would come to own the cobbles, Fabian Cancellara (in third position). *(John Pierce, PhotoSport International)*

in arrears. Most important, anyone who had designs on winning that year's Tour *before* that climb now clung to very little hope as they watched Lance pull on the yellow jersey that evening. In the bus and that night at dinner, we were on cloud nine. Our team had been criticized and Lance's leadership questioned, but Hautacam silenced the doubters.

Lance loved making the first mountain stage miserable for his rivals. We were always an integral part of that plan. Anytime the plan was executed to perfection, the satisfaction shared between Johan, Lance, and the rest of the team was tangible. He needed us, and we delivered.

We put Lance in position not just on Hautacam, but two stages later on Mont Ventoux. Lance relished his role as a finisher. If his ride up Hautacam was intended to send a message, Ventoux was a chance to destroy the will of his rivals. To suck any last ounce of hope out of their souls. We were his two-wheeled version of meat tenderizer. He lived to take the final swing of the sword and cut the head off the snake. Everyone knew the "Giant of Provence" would be a battlefield, fought not just on the pavement but against the elements and within the mind. As had happened on Hautacam, a few of the expected players dropped off earlier than anticipated, but by the time the lower forests abdicated to the lunar landscape of the upper altitudes, only the Titans of the day remained. Pantani, Ullrich, Lance, and a handful of others.

I wasn't around to witness the historic and heroic struggle. Having already done my work, along with Viatcheslav Ekimov and Frankie, on the flats leading up to Ventoux and into Bédoin, I went through my own nightmare to the top. As we ticked off the miles toward Ventoux, Johan had been screaming at us over the radio for what seemed like an eternity. He and Lance kept demanding that we go faster. The struggle to maintain my cadence and velocity was all-encompassing. My vision was blurry, but I found a focal point in my mind. A slice of sanity the size of a pinprick that tauntingly kept repeating, "The pain is almost over." It was the carrot at the end of the stick. And it worked.

Johan wanted us to give everything, blow up, and crawl to the finish. That's what we were paid to do. So we did what we were told. But my Ventoux experience that year was the antithesis of Lance's. At one point, I had to pull off to the side of the road to try to recover before resuming and honoring the deal with myself, to never give up or give in. While the cameras followed Lance upward in his quest for immortality, I suffered silently. Even though I was amid the gruppetto, I suffered alone, as every cyclist learns to do.

Up ahead of me and most of my fellow professionals, we all know what happened. Pantani, after struggling through a bad patch, managed to claw his way back to the lead group as they left the shelter of the tree line. Il Pirata (the Pirate) always loved to live up to his nickname. In typical swashbuckling style, seconds after connecting to the rear of the group, he swept past them all, so clearly throwing all his energy into every turn of the pedals that each revolution seemed as if it could be his last. No doubt fueled by his futility on Stage 10, Pantani wouldn't accept anyone on his wheel. Each time the group regained contact, Pantani would burst forward again, seemingly shot from an invisible cannon. It took three or four Herculean efforts, but eventually it looked as if he was free to soar to one of the most celebrated summits of the sport.

Lance had designs on a different outcome. We'd rehearsed the scenarios in meetings, pre-Tour training, and in the bus the morning of the stage. Now, it was up to Lance to prove yet again why he had no equal. With Pantani well up the road, Lance launched an assault on the leader and on the Ventoux. The finish of Stage 12 has been debated and discussed since the millisecond both men crossed the line. Depending on who you believe, either Lance "gifted" the stage to Pantani, or Pantani was able to eke out one last surge at the line, swoop in, and steal the victory.

I'm here to verify, as have others, that Lance absolutely gave that stage away. Earlier, we had decided as a team that if an opportunity arose to build an alliance between Pantani and his Mercatone Uno squad, we should take it. A magnanimous gesture would hopefully provide us with an ally later in the race against some of Lance's other, tougher, rivals. Instead, the gesture only infuriated Pantani's already overly enlarged ego and set in motion his mission to single-handedly destroy us for the rest of the Tour.

Pantani's kamikaze approach has been written about extensively in other books. His panache caused us plenty of headaches, but ultimately cost him more. He abandoned the Tour after Stage 16, citing the fact that he was "completely empty" after the mountain stages were completed. The Tour doesn't blink when any one cyclist gets off his bike. We still had several stages to go and another Tour title to achieve.

CHAPTER 13

AT THE TOUR, WE'D conquered our own demons and proved to ourselves, and to the world, that our team was now the standard for the sport. Even though the turnaround was short, I was very excited to head to the Olympic Games in Sydney.

There are more prestigious races for a cyclist than the Olympic Games. It may sound harsh, but within our circles, that's the truth. World Championships, the Tour de France, Paris–Roubaix: all of these are considered a bigger win than a gold medal in the Olympics.

But even though it might not be the ultimate achievement for a rider, it still is the *Olympics*. It is the most universally recognized sporting event in the world. To win it *does* mean something, no matter how jaded, or successful, you are heading into it.

I found myself traveling down under for my third Games, and they would end up being my favorite of the eventual five I attended. I loved Australia. I loved the culture. I loved the weather. I loved the food. It seemed like the perfect country to host the Olympics. Welcoming, warm, and without question, ready to celebrate.

The United States went there with a stellar team—me, Lance

Armstrong, Tyler Hamilton, Tony Cruz, and Freddy Rodriguez. As at past Olympiads, our multipronged approach involved trying to get a rider in an early breakaway, and then watch how the complexion of the race developed. For me, this Olympics was notable because my expertise in one-day races was now well known, and I went into the Games as a "co-leader" for the team. I was there as a weapon, not just as a worker.

My experience at my first Olympics, the 1992 Games in Barcelona, Spain, was quite a bit different. I went into the Games of the XXV Olympiad as wide-eyed and eager as any first-time Olympian. I was nineteen years old, and having been one of the youngest riders ever named to the U.S. Olympic team, I was determined to prove my worth. Not just to the officials of USA Cycling, who had selected me along with Scott Mercier, Nathan Sheafor, and John Stenner to take part in the team time trial event, but also to my friends, family, and fans who had seen me progress up to this point. This was my first real exposure to the world's best. A chance to gauge my talent against names I'd only read about in results columns and articles detailing remote races in exotic locales.

The team time trial had been on the Olympic program since 1960, but this was the last time the event would be contested at the Olympics. This was also the last Olympic Games where only amateurs were allowed to compete. Starting in 1996, the Olympics became open to professional cyclists, and with that decision, in rushed the modern era of racing.

In 1992, the race I took part in was listed as 100 kilometers but was actually 102.8 kilometers (63.9 miles), and even though bigger names took part in the individual road race, including a certain twenty-year-old American by the name of Lance Armstrong (who was also competing in his first Games), the team time trial was a perfect representation of why I wanted to be a cyclist—teamwork and pushing myself more for a group than for myself. The race itself took place on the highways surrounding the city of Barcelona, and years later, when I lived in Spain, I felt comfortable getting around because I knew the roadways thanks to that one day of racing.

I already mentioned how eager I was to test my skills against the world. Well, that eagerness died early on July 26, 1992. We finished sixteenth out of twenty-nine teams. The gold medal was awarded to Germany, silver to Italy, and bronze to France. We were almost twelve minutes behind the winners, and I remember thinking afterward, We just got our asses handed to us. I've got a lot of work to do if I ever want to compete against the world's best. It was a wake-up call, but I had already established a pattern in my life: whenever I was faced with a challenge, I figured out a way to conquer it.

Since my racing wasn't a highlight, my greatest memory of my time in Barcelona was getting to go see the four-hundred-meter semifinal at the Olympic Stadium. Great Britain's Derek Redmond had won his quarterfinal and started well in the semi, but with about 250 meters to go, his hamstring snapped, and he fell to the ground in intense pain. As medical staff rushed onto the track to treat him, Derek somehow stood and began to gingerly walk forward. In one of the most inspiring, and touching, moments ever in an Olympic Games, Derek's father, Jim, burst past security to help hold up his son, and both men forged ahead toward the finish. By the time the duo crossed the line, I was cheering along with sixty-five thousand other fans, and crying. I thought of how if I ever fell, that's what my dad would do, and it reinforced the knowledge that I was not and had never been alone in my quest for sporting excellence. If I needed him, my dad, or anyone else in my support network, would be there for me, just as Derek's dad had been.

Most people associated Barcelona with Michael Jordan, Larry

Bird, and USA basketball's Dream Team, but for me, I ended up filing my trip under "learning experience" and using it as fuel for later on.

By 1996, I had a whole different approach to the Olympics in Atlanta, Georgia. It was a home game for the U.S. team, and even though we were riding for Lance, between Frankie Andreu (who would ultimately end up finishing one spot out of the medals in fourth), Greg Randolph (seventy-fourth), myself (seventy-sixth), and Steve Hegg (ninety-third), we felt we had a team that could contend. As it was the first Olympics in which they allowed professionals to participate, the biggest names of the sport were there: five-time Tour de France winner Miguel Indurain from Spain, Italy's Mario Cipollini, Denmark's Bjarne Riis (who had just won the Tour days before), and Germany's Erik Zabel.

Lance ended up finishing twelfth overall, last in a group of six, one minute and twenty-eight seconds behind the winner. Earlier in the race, he had launched off the front in an attempt to stun the field by making his move much sooner than anyone anticipated. He was just over two months away from being diagnosed with cancer, so his body had to already be ravaged by the disease. It was a bold move. Nothing Lance did was ever with less than 100 percent conviction, but it cost him. Road races, especially one-day races like the Olympics, are a calculated chess game. Usually, a team has a general strategy going in, but within that game plan, there are numerous scenarios that everyone is aware of and able to act upon if things fall into place. At the start of the day, 184 cyclists left the line. By the end of those 221.85 kilometers (137.85 miles), 116 would finish. I was one of the players, one of the pieces on the board that tried to move my king into the right position. Even though we'd failed as a team to get someone on the medal stand, I didn't feel I had failed as a teammate. It just wasn't our day.

Looking back on those Games, two things stand out. First, there were barely any spectators on the roads during the race. In Europe, the whole route would have been lined with people. Cycling still had a few years to go before it would become more mainstream in the United States, and that was evident as we sped by. As racers, we don't *need* the fans to push us, but we can tell when the excitement spills over the barriers and elevates the energy level around us.

The other, more chilling memory is the time I spent with my family in Centennial Olympic Park. Thankfully, I wasn't there on July 27, when the bombing took place, which was four days before my team raced through the streets of Atlanta, but of course, I was as stunned as the rest of the world at the senseless destruction and loss of life.

In 2000, I'd been promised one of the coveted protected spots on the team, where if all went well, I could have a realistic shot at a medal. On September 27, 2000, forty nations—156 cyclists—were at the start for the 239.4-kilometer (148.75-mile) romp.

Australians love sports. It doesn't have to be a sport they know a lot about, let alone follow religiously. As a culture, they seem to crave competition. The Aussies were out en masse for our road race. Afterward, the global TV audience would be estimated at 600 million, and over every inch of the course, I felt the eyes of the world upon me. To boot, Lance stated that he would work to help me win gold.

The Aussies had high hopes for Robbie McEwen and Stuart O'Grady. The only medal their country had ever won was Clyde Sefton's silver in Munich in 1972. In Sydney, the organizers felt their course, fourteen laps centered around Queen's and Centennial Parks, gave their sprinters a good chance for victory. McEwen, in particular, packed a powerful punch, having won his first stage (of an eventual twelve) of the Tour de France the year before.

A number of riders, and journalists, thought that the climb

up from Bronte Beach would prove decisive and provide a perfect launch pad for any opportunistic soul. What made this ascent especially hard was that it came immediately after an incredibly fast downhill with a sharp left-hand bend, where we reached speeds in excess of fifty miles per hour. At only 1.2 kilometers long (seven-tenths of a mile) and an average gradient of 6.6 percent, the pre-climb tactical maneuvering made this rise seem steeper and longer than it was. It had rained the day before for the women's race, and even though the ground was wet for our first few laps, eventually sunshine ruled the day and put the focus squarely on our skills, rather than on the elements.

I felt great through the first half of the race. Attentive. In control. Responsive. With two laps to go, I was well placed. I had put myself in a large lead group with plenty of powerful pros—among them, Jan Ullrich and Andreas Klöden from Germany, Kazakh-stan's Alexander Vinokourov, Belgian Axel Merckx (son of legend-ary cyclist Eddy Merckx, who had traveled to Australia for the first time to watch Axel compete), Italian Paolo Bettini, and France's Laurent Jalabert. A one-day race like this always comes down to a simple criterion—how good do you feel? From a planning stand-point, I'd accomplished everything I set out to do, and I was where I needed to be. Now it was up to my body to respond.

Paolo Bettini, who had already won Liège–Bastogne–Liège, one of cycling's "monuments," earlier in the year, as well as a stage of the Tour de France that summer, took a flyer and tried to break away almost immediately once we were into the last two laps. I had to put in a huge amount of effort to claw my way back to the group that followed his surge. I managed to do it, and I was now the fifth in a group of five guys, but I had expended a lot of energy in the process. The Olympic road race never has as many guys as a Tour stage, but you know all the guys there are the best.

In cycling, we use the phrase "burning a match," or "burning matches," to denote when you put in a big effort (any rider will tell you it's important to save your matches for as late in the race as possible). I'd just burned a couple. More than I wanted to, but at least I was still in the mix.

On the descent toward Bronte Beach, I surged to the front, not because I felt fantastic, but because I did not want to take any chances with my positioning. The safest place is always at the lead, but it's also where you get drained of the most energy. The peloton was quickly closing, and I felt if I could just get past the speediest section safely, I could catch on with whoever surged up the hill.

And here's where my memory goes blank for a time, which illustrates a unique perspective of cycling. Where did the chunk of time go in my head? I've referenced how "into the red" we all go in this sport, and perhaps that played a part. Even though I felt as if I was in control, perhaps I had exhausted too many subtle energy stores to coherently recall my surroundings. Our team radios had stopped working midway through the race, so instead of being able to ask an easy question, I had no way of gauging where my rivals were.

That late in the race, I not only needed the ability to *surge,* I needed a gear for turbo acceleration. I asked my body for more, and when it didn't answer back, I begged it for anything. When the response I got was another echo, I knew I was cooked. Mentally and physically I was so spent that I didn't realize I wasn't still in medal contention. When Lance rode up on me among the group, he asked me what was going on, and I told him excitedly, "This is it, this is the sprint for the podium!" To which he replied, "No, there are three guys up the road!" He pointed at one of the huge Jumbotron screens lining the course, and I looked up to see three oversized, pixilated figures fighting for their own glorious finish.

One I wouldn't be a part of. Everyone on the U.S. team had done all that was asked of him and played his role to perfection. I just didn't have what it took that day to stay with the leaders. By the end, I would finish a respectable eighth (my best placing ever at the Olympics).

That was a blow—to think that I was going for a medal, but actually be out of contention. I just didn't have anything left in me. Crossing the line, I was devastated, but oddly satisfied. I'd given 100 percent. Effort, more than results, was always my yardstick.

Some people questioned how I could so quickly move on after the outcome of the 2000 Olympics, but I'd been racing since I was eight years old, and I knew how hard and unforgiving this sport could be. It's brutal, but addicting at the same time.

People who fall in love with the sport at the level I was know that it's your everything—it's your wife, your dad, your mom, your kids. It's totally encompassing. So when you fail, you don't throw in the towel; you keep trying to win. And that's why it was easy to flip the switch and move on, because I was immediately concentrating on what I wanted to win coming up. In many ways, my success from such an early age allowed me to take a more mature outlook on my losses later in life. I won so much as a kid that I never had to deal with defeat when perhaps I wouldn't have been able to handle it. By the time I got into the pro ranks, my mind-set was so cast in stone that nothing shook me from that foundation.

MICHAEL BARRY, TEAMMATE, 2002-2006

Sure, George would get frustrated after a loss, but he could move on to the next target better than anyone I ever trained or raced with. It was just easier for him, which in turn minimized the angst associated with the offending result.

In Sydney, Germany ended up winning the gold and the bronze—Jan Ullrich triumphed, while his teammate Andreas Klöden won the bronze. Kazakhstan's Alexander Vinokourov slipped in between them to win silver. All three riders competed professionally for the Deutsche Telekom team, and since Ullrich was the designated leader of the squad, his status secured him the gold once the three worked together to establish the winning move. All three men would factor greatly into my future on the bike, as rivals who would help define a generation.

CHAPTER 14

Even the most seasoned veterans can, at times, get claustrophobic in the middle of the peloton. But I never did. I'm convinced it's because I grew up weaving my way through traffic on the streets of New York City. Anyone who's ever visited the Big Apple knows that cars, taxis in particular, rule the roads. It's gotten better over the past decades, but when I was first learning to navigate the myriad of manhole covers, potholes, and pedestrians, I quite literally took my life into my own hands every time I was on two wheels. But as a kid, that just made the intensity of the game that much greater, and it made the simple reward of living through it that much more fun. For that one reason, my comfort level was always high when I was in the midst of other professionals, and it became one of the cornerstones of my career that I could pilot my leader through the peloton as easily as some people thread a needle or walk through an open door.

In the midst of two hundred other riders, there's no time to *think* if someone falls—it's pure reaction, a reflexive motion honed over hundreds of thousands of miles in the saddle, each an opportunity, a processing moment, to store for later reference and instantaneous recall. A cyclist's bank of biking scenarios is never-ending, and he develops instincts that let him exit a critical juncture the right way.

CHRISTIAN VANDE VELDE

Positioning in a bike race is like a dance with close to two hundred other partners. You can't force it. You have to flow and be graceful. George was the best at finding the right spot. He was a bigger guy, but he never fought for his place, he was just seamlessly there. It's an art form that some people have, and most do not. Over his billions of bike races, he built a bank of knowledge unparalleled. His eyesight, co-ordination, clarity, and reaction time all developed into an amazing ability to be "in the moment." He seemed to always be the first to see, and the first to react. He had poise in impossible situations.

Our über-focused family, a kaleidoscope of Lycra and neon, usually travels at mind-blurring speeds. Even though our top speed on a descent can be between sixty and seventy miles an hour, *within* the peloton, everything slows down and seems accentuated. You hear conversations in multiple languages, laughter, or the labored breathing of a hard effort, and all seem to be amplified in the close quarters. Crammed together like we are, a hungry thief would have a field day, a cornucopia of nutritional items at his fingertips—gels, energy bars, and drinks.

I always felt I was comfortable enough riding so close to another pro that I could pickpocket his thoughts. If I was on a good day, I could peer inside his mind, and instead of having to use my energies to assess the safety of a situation, I could read a rider's face and body language to my tactical advantage.

The Tour de France is particularly tricky when it comes to staying safe. It's the race that has the most riders on the road, but also the most at stake each and every day. That day in 1999 on the Passage du Gois had provided an all-too-memorable example of just how fine the line is between being in the *right* and the *wrong* place. Four years later, I had to tap into my situational sixth sense again.

In Stage 3, the Tour organizer, Amaury Sports Organization (ASO), decided to bring back the cobblestones for the first time in over a decade. Even though the two sections totaled only a little over two miles (3.5 kilometers) and were considered mild by pavé standards, they required plenty of planning and caused substantial stress.

The first section was the longest, about 1.75 miles (2.9 kilometers), and came with just under 42 miles (70 kilometers) left in the race. Like a real-life Peter Parker, I could feel my "spider sense" tingling as we got close to the Erre cobbles, and a quick scan of the surrounding suffering confirmed it was time to take charge. With the subtlety of a violin virtuoso, I began to calculate my path to the pole position. In that situation, a seemingly infinite number of small, deft, almost undetectable maneuvers eventually add up to "the" move—the one that finally telegraphs your intentions to your competitors and thus fully commits you to the chosen course of action.

I could feel the wheels all around me. Through my years of racing, I'd developed a way to gauge where not only my bike, but my passenger's bike (the man I was in charge of protecting), could fit while slicing through the peloton. Part eyes-in-the-back-of-my-head, part peripheral spatial awareness, once I saw, or sensed, an inch opening up, I could predict how that space would widen, or could widen, through my efforts.

July 6, 2004, was one of those days where all my skills were needed. The parts of the infamous Paris–Roubaix course we were doing couldn't be taken lightly. We knew we had to protect Lance, and in those final milliseconds before the first section of cobbles, marshaling him to the front was my only purpose. Every calculation, reflex, and intuitive thought centered on that goal. At the opportune time, Viatcheslav Ekimov (Eki) and I became a two-man battering ram as we badgered our way forward and got Lance into the lead. It was a quintessential moment, as one of Lance's main rivals, Iban Mayo, crashed, never recovered or reconnected with our group, and eventually lost almost four minutes on the day. It illustrated perfectly a Tour axiom mentioned often in the first week, or on flat stages. "You can't win the Tour on a day like today, but you can certainly lose it."

LANCE ARMSTRONG

The greatest job of "guidance" George ever performed was getting me to, and through, the cobbles in '04. There would inevitably be times, in every Tour, when I'd be fearful of what might occur. Everybody gets scared. But in this case, I was scared for my life. I did not want to be anywhere near an accident. And the only way to make sure we avoided a catastrophic scenario was to be in the front. Once George and Eki started getting us in position, I got completely calm and knew we'd get there first. George gave me that look that said, "Stay right here. We got this."

While wearing the yellow jersey (*maillot jaune*) and winning the overall classification at the Tour de France is the pinnacle of pedaling performance, it's unrealistic for every rider to have "yellow" as a goal, which is why the organizers, ASO, provide different awards each day, and throughout the three-week-long race. I was no different than almost every racer, having dreamed of the yellow jersey since I was a kid. The dream grows, like a pulsating, fluttering entity inside of you, constantly propelling you forward. Once I made it to the Tour, I saw what it was like to wear it. Witnessed the other riders in awe of whomever's shoulders it sat on. That was when it became a yearning to feel what it would be like to wear it myself—to be the one everyone would stare at. It was a craving, where if given a chance, any chance, I'd snatch for it, the way a junkyard dog that hasn't eaten in days goes after a scrap of food. That's how I felt about the *maillot jaune,* but other riders had their own prize.

The best climber wears a red polka-dot jersey to denote himself as the leader in the King of the Mountains classification. The points leader wears a green jersey as a badge of incredible consistency in his finishing places, as well as in intermediate sprints along the way. Historically, the green jersey is worn, and ultimately won, by a sprinter, but there have been years when that is not the case. Most notable were in 1969, when Eddy Merckx won the *maillot vert,* and 1979, when Bernard Hinault took home the prize, also winning yellow in the process. In fact, Merckx is the only cyclist in history to win the yellow, green, and polka-dot jerseys in the same year (1969).

A white jersey was introduced in 1975, and while its requirements have morphed a few times, it now denotes the best young rider (age twenty-five or younger) of the Tour. Six men who have won the white jersey have gone on to win the yellow jersey— Laurent Fignon, Greg LeMond, Marco Pantani, Jan Ullrich, Alberto Contador, and Andy Schleck. On four occasions, a cyclist has won the young rider classification and the general classification (yellow) in the same year—Fignon in 1983, Ullrich in 1997, Contador in 2007, and Schleck (retroactively, due to Contador's disqualification) in 2010. The only cyclists to win the young rider classification in multiple Tours are Marco Pantani (two wins), Ullrich (three wins—also finishing first or second for the general classification on all three of these occasions), and Andy Schleck (three wins).

There are also intermediate sprints held within every stage, and a "most combative" award given to the rider who usually rides at the front of the race the longest each day. If a rider wears one of these jerseys for just one day, he is hailed as a hero and set financially for a career. All this adds up to the most intense collection of cyclists all year racing for the most coveted prizes offered.

To try to put it into perspective: Imagine getting in your car every day for three weeks straight and driving on a highway filled with vehicles. Each day, you know where you need to go, and you know that you'll have to drive between four to six hours, but at no time can you take your eyes off the road or let your concentration lapse from the cars darting around you. The highway, while wide and clear at times, might unexpectedly go from four to two lanes. There could be an island in the middle of the road that appears out of nowhere. Or worse, a pedestrian could run out from the side and cause everything to come to a screeching halt. The thinking involved to keep the necessary focus becomes not only all-encompassing, but also mind-numbingly fatiguing. It's one of the reasons why you see a lot of crashes toward the end of the Tour. Everyone's response time has increased due to how tired they are. The crashes at the beginning of the Tour have more to do with everyone being fresh and over-confident in their expectations of what they can accomplish. Not to mention in the first week of the Tour, the stages are usually set up to favor the sprinters, which means each team wants to marshal their man into the best position possible leading up to the finish, in the hope of the sprinter sealing the win with an explosive effort for the line.

In my later years, that's what I got paid to do: escort the likes of Mark Cavendish through the critical moments of a sprint stage, where the difference between being on the right wheel versus following a fatiguing rider was a decision made in a millisecond, but always produced a result that was explosive—either the exultation of victory or the anger of defeat. Looking back on it, it would have been easy to attach a ton of pressure to those moments or to those decisions. Without sounding nonchalant, I guess maybe *others* would have. But for me, it was fun. It made me feel alive.

MARK CAVENDISH

George lived for the bike. He was just a natural cyclist, and enjoyed it. He was born to do it. It was never training to him, it was just bike riding. All that experience ended up giving him an ability to just know when things were going to happen. No one could ride up the side of the peloton like him.

CHAPTER 15

THE YEAR 2003 REALLY tested us as a team. I keep using the word *pressure* to describe not only our motivation, but what we felt before and during those days of racing in July. It's overly simplistic but true: we felt pressure year-round. And going for a fifth consecutive Tour title brought whole new levels of angst. Lance wanted to grasp cycling's Holy Grail. He was looking to etch his name alongside the legends. Jacques Anquetil. Eddy Merckx. Bernard Hinault. Miguel Indurain. They had all won five Tour de France titles. Indurain was the only one to win five consecutively, so Lance was looking to become the second man on an even more exclusive list.

Because 2003 marked the centennial of the race, all the stages took place in France, and they created a special prize, the Centenaire Classement, to be given to the rider who cumulatively placed the best in the six stages finishing in the original towns of the 1903 Tour: Lyon, Marseille, Toulouse, Bordeaux, Nantes, and Paris.

By Lance's own admission, and supported by various statistics, it was his weakest Tour. And the hardest title to win. Even though he would end up wearing the yellow jersey for thirteen days, it felt like we aged as a group in dog years. Each race always had its defining moments, but in 2003, two stood out. Both illustrated Lance's sheer will to win, but also the fact that Lady Luck has to be smiling on you at times.

Stage 9, which ended in Gap, will forever be known as the day Lance went cross-country, saving the yellow jersey and his Tour hopes in the process. Lance was following Joseba Beloki, who rode for ONCE-Eroski, into a right-hand turn on the descent of the Côte de la Rochette when, due to the intense heat of the pavement, Beloki's brakes locked up and he went crashing to the concrete, breaking his right femur, elbow, and wrist and ending his Tour instantaneously. Lance's only option was to go left into a recently harvested field (the corner was too tight to make it to the right, and straight would have run over Beloki), where he showed off his mountain bike and cyclo-cross skills by plunging through the rutted terrain, eventually using a cross-dismount (getting off, then on the bike) to climb over a huge ditch to get back on the road. It was an audacious display of adept bike handling, but also of Lance's ability to think in the moment.

We knew he was filled with adrenaline after the stage, having averted disaster, his reaction time never better. We rarely saw Lance right after a stage, because instead of heading to the team bus he usually had different transportation arranged. That night, there was more than a little nervous laughter and jocularity shared at the dinner table, and we all remarked how easily it could have been the end of our dream to help him get number five.

Every experience was amplified during the Tour. Any energy expenditure seemed to take a greater toll as well. I was unique in my dichotomous dedication to my yearly double duty. Spring meant one-day races, usually devoted to myself, the war of attrition usually lasting between five and six hours. Teaching my body to parcel out my reserves over that month in summer was very different than allowing myself to be completely spent after a day. The Tour forces you to respect yourself and listen to your body on a whole new level. Management of my resources always made the difference. Most of the time I got it right, but there were plenty of other times I paid for my mistakes and/or hubris.

My worst "bonking" (completely depleting myself of energy reserves) had occurred the year before, in my favorite event, Paris–Roubaix. It happened to be the one hundredth anniversary of the race, and for most of the day, I felt invincible, as if my body was not only energized but protected by an invisible force field. It was the best I ever felt during my career. The weather was cold and rainy. I eschewed any extra layers of clothing early in the race in a foolish display of machismo, and I paid tenfold later. Around fifty kilometers (thirty miles) from the finish, I started feeling a bit weird, a little fuzzy in my mind, with a slight tingle in my stomach. Forty kilometers out, I knew I was starting to bonk, but I was in the thick of the hunt and used a substantial amount of willpower to convince myself that I could ride my way out of the bad patch I was in physically. While in the midst of my mind games, Johan Museeuw, in search of his third Paris–Roubaix title, took off with a leg-ripping acceleration that eventually only Tom Boonen (in his first pro season) and I could follow. If I'd been at the limit before Museeuw muscled his way clear, I then waded into very deep water, with no clear plan to stay afloat. Twenty kilometers from the velodrome, at what should have been the time for me to put in a signature push to the finish, the proverbial wheels came off, and I was done. Cooked. My legs were rubber, my mind unfocused. My body had run through its power sources.

The spring classics, and Paris–Roubaix in particular, are a study in physics and math. Over a thousand times throughout the race, you have to make minute calculations to keep you in position, each one a reaction to a situation that is unique, never to be duplicated.

At my best, reaction time was my strong suit. But on Pavé Sector #4, only eighteen kilometers (less than twelve miles) from the finish, my bad luck, or perhaps bad judgment from earlier, caught up with me. I miscalculated a simple maneuver, and lacking basic energy in my brain and body, I fell into a ditch on the left side of the road and watched Tom Boonen ride away from me. Contrary to some of the insinuations people made after the race, it was neither that my competitors were on better drugs nor that I wasn't prepared. It was something simpler. The elements, and my ego, had gotten the better of me.

There would be no such mistake many months later. In stark contrast to my bonking because of the cold, it seemed the daily headline in 2003 was the heat. The newspapers and commentators invented new ways to describe the thermometer's grip on our collective fate. Triple-digit mercury was the norm. Lance had lost twelve pounds during the first time trial alone. But while the temperature was a topic of immense and intense conversation for others, as riders, we didn't even talk about it. It was just something you dealt with. At the time, the standard practice was to drink more and add a pinch of sea salt to your water bottles. Also, back then, you could do a saline drip at the end of the stage for recovery purposes. (Now, with the "no needle" policy, this is not allowed.) We'd also tried some new ways to stay cooler during warm-up (lining the bikes up in the shade, fans blowing on us before the time trial, ice strategically placed within our jerseys, and ice vests), anything to alleviate feeling as if we were melting.

We were all on edge after Lance's cross-country adventure in Stage 9, but one of the great things about the Tour is that something new is always happening. It's easy to forget past problems, since survival depends on being in the moment, existing in the now.

Stage 15 was from Bagnères-de-Bigorre to Luz Ardiden in the Pyrenees. It was the last, crucial mountain stage, and the final uphill finish of 2003. Lance had yet to win a stage, so he was highly motivated to honor the jersey and finally send a message that he deserved a record-tying title. Plus, the proverbial stage was set for a general classification battle that had not been seen in years.

Three days prior, Jan Ullrich had crushed Lance in the time trial, and the German only trailed him by thirty-four seconds afterward. But by the morning of Stage 15, Ullrich had trimmed his deficit to a minuscule fifteen seconds, with Telecom's Alexander Vinokourov another three seconds back. We knew this was the last chance for Lance to gain time before the final time trial, and since he had been so soundly beaten in the previous race against the clock, we were all extremely nervous and focused on coming through for him that day.

I knew Lance was a bit lost that year. On paper, T-Mobile had a much stronger team, and I'd tried to instill in Lance a return to our underdog mentality. I knew we'd need him in the right frame of mind up the final climb, and the best way to assure that was to always make his day as stress-free as possible until the very end. Johan had instructed us to not let any breakaway get too much distance, and since the first hour of racing is always a cornucopia of attacks, we were tired straight from the start. It also didn't help that the following day was a rest day, which meant a lot of riders were willing to give a little extra to try their luck. Their roll of the dice cost us countless calories as we rode down each attempt. Johan was like a casino boss, ordering us to get back the money (or in this case, time) that had been lost to the house.

I had ridden my body and mind to their limit to help get Lance to the base of the Tourmalet, and once my job was complete, my body imploded. Every cell seemed to cave in on its neighbor, the eye-blurring pain the main reminder I was alive. Through my earpiece I was still close enough to hear Johan exclaim, "Vino [Alexander Vinokourov] is dropped," then later, when Ullrich dropped Lance, Johan repeated sternly, "Keep your pace, keep your pace." (Lance later remarked that he didn't feel he needed to answer Ullrich's acceleration due to the distance still to come.) Once we crested the penultimate climb of the day, the Tourmalet, there were still thirty-five kilometers to the finish, including the climb up Luz Ardiden.

Heading to the final summit, all the protagonists were at the front, eyeing each other and calculating their options. The uphill amphitheater was alive, and the expected explosions commenced with just over ten kilometers (six miles) to go. Euskaltel's Iban Mayo shot ahead, with Lance pouncing to answer the move. Ullrich wasn't able to respond, his diesel style of riding never suited to fast accelerations. In typical Lance fashion, matching Mayo wasn't enough: he had to show who was in charge. After taking Mayo's wheel for only a moment, Lance fired his turbo rockets and catapulted ahead.

Lance's dominance was on display, but in an instant, he was on the ground. Milliseconds later, Mayo followed him to the pavement. Ullrich, who had somehow managed to keep relatively close, had just enough time to swerve to the left and avoid them both. It has now become one of the most analyzed crashes in Tour history. Lance had hooked a spectator's souvenir *musette* (food bag) with his handlebars, causing his bike to be swept out from under him like the legs of a roped calf. Jan Ullrich looked almost confused upon seeing his two rivals mixed with the mass of their machines. He slowed down, and in a great show of sportsmanship, waited for both Lance and Mayo to return to the lead group. Interestingly, Tyler Hamilton, who had since moved on to Team CSC, also went to the front to instruct everyone that the proper code of conduct was to wait for the yellow jersey.

Even though Ullrich was only fifteen seconds behind overall, and many believe he could have gone on to lead the Tour after that fateful day, he said afterward that leaving Lance behind was not the right thing to do, that he had to honor the leader in a situation like that.

Lance's trials and tribulations weren't finished quite yet. Another mishap, this time with his right pedal, sent his crotch careening into the top tube, which should have toppled him over again. Miraculously, he stayed upright, and with the help of our teammate Chechu Rubiera, Lance not only returned to the front pack, but went on to win the stage and fire a salvo, not over the bow of his rivals, but directly into their hearts. If 2001 was epitomized by "The Look" (when Lance looked back to size up Jan Ullrich while climbing l'Alpe d'Huez, almost daring him to try to match his acceleration), then 2003 was ultimately tied to what Lance did after "The Crash" (while descending, navigating around a fallen Joseba Beloki, through a field, and remounting his bike). It was typical Lance, snatching victory from what seemed to be inevitable defeat. He made a career out of moments like those, and as much as the world showered *him* with praise, he made sure that we all knew the accolades he received were shared with us. No one understood better than Lance the extent to which cycling is a team sport. No one appreciated the work we did more than him. It's why I was so devoted to him year after year, and to the goal of winning the Tour.

There's a picture Lance gave me of him on the Stage 15 podium. In it, he's got a look of focused exhilaration, his right index finger emphatically pointing at something out of the frame. I'm the subject of that stare, smile, and gesture. It's me as I crossed the line, nineteen minutes and forty-nine seconds after he had won the stage. It was his way of acknowledging all the work we had done together, not only that day but throughout the Tour. It's signed "For George, Much Love. LA."

As I mentioned, we all knew it was going to be a day when, if you held the aces, you'd have to throw them on the table. We didn't win the Tour atop Luz Ardiden, but it was huge for Lance's confidence. And as the whole peloton knew, in his fight for supremacy, confidence usually counted a lot more than seconds for Lance. He'd gotten both that day in the Pyrenees.

LANCE ARMSTRONG

The year 2003 was a disaster for me. Fans always remark that they loved that Tour the most. It sucked! No question T-Mobile had a great team, and it was probably Jan's best year. But I was just off. And I had never needed George more. We had our routine every day on the bus. We'd both sit in the same place so we could see each other's faces. I'm sure that year he didn't like what he saw, a lot. But before the start of Stage 15, we made eye contact, and all he said was, "This is your day." And for the first time that Tour, I believed him. Afterward, that photo I signed for him really summed up my myriad of emotions. The excitement of the day, the relief that I'd finally won a stage, and the renewed possibility of winning in Paris. George was the guy who, once again, made it all possible.

Lance always left in his own vehicle, nicknamed Air Force One, a Subaru with dark-tinted windows so you couldn't see inside. About forty-five minutes into our crawling descent off the mountain that evening, his unmistakable vehicle pulled alongside, then in front of, our bus. There was no ignoring the grin of the man who leapt out of the backseat and in an instant was inside the bus, high-fiving every hand in sight. In all the years I've known him, Lance has had an expression he lives by: "Keep your highs low and your lows high." While he was racing, it was his way to deal with the multitude of race situations and to help keep himself focused.

That night, he broke his own rule. It's the one time I saw him get really excited. He stayed with us on the bus all the way down the mountain to the hotel. In all my years of racing with him, I can count on one hand the times he rode with us after a stage. We spent the whole ride reliving the day, feeling his enthusiasm and approval wash over us, reinvigorating our battered bodies and getting us ready for the last few days ahead.

The 2003 Tour was my favorite because I felt needed more than on any other Tour. Lance relied on me enormously that year, on and off the bike. His demeanor was always the key, and a large part of the time those three weeks, he lacked his killer instinct and his unique confidence. He needed me to prop him up, and even though I knew I was telling him what he wanted to hear, I wasn't sure we would eventually win. That year had begun with a lot of question marks, but by the end, it became a fifth exclamation point.

The end of the year might not have yielded great results, but it produced a valuable lesson. I raced the Vuelta that year as a tune-up for the World Championships, which were held in the beginning of October in Hamilton, Ontario, Canada. I had missed the classics earlier in the season due to what eventually would be diagnosed as the Epstein-Barr virus, which causes mononucleosis and is linked to various forms of cancer and autoimmune diseases. Early in the season I had tried to race, but my fatigue kept getting worse, and even though I could ride, I lacked top-end speed, as well as any ability to push past my usual pain thresholds. So, by the fall, I felt I needed race days in my legs to be better prepared. It was the only time I raced the Vuelta a España, and I withdrew about halfway through, satisfied that my form was where it needed to be in order to peak a few weeks later in North America.

I got to Ontario and physically had never felt better. Before traveling, I'd allowed myself to envision a podium placing, but I started to dream a little bigger as I realized the form I had. The day before the race, I broke one of the cardinal rules of sports, "Thou shalt not deviate from your routine!" Instead of eating with the team and sticking to the bland buffet, I chose to have lunch with my parents and Melanie. It was a dumb decision.

I came to Canada ready. I knew it. My team knew it. All I needed to do was follow through with my preparation for one more day, and then I'd unleash the form I'd timed to perfection.

One lunch, and a plate of pasta arrabbiata, changed everything. I never got to test myself against the world's best. At least, not in the state I should have raced in. Any athlete will tell you, you never want to admit that you're sick, let alone at an event with so much on the line. I tried to fight the feeling building inside of me. The gurgling turned to grumbling, and finally to a gut-bursting pain too hard to ignore. Within an hour of finishing my spicy Italian dish, I was sprinting to the toilet. If only relief had come with one trip. I spent all day, that night, and the next day, race day, more concerned with how far away I was from a restroom and how much toilet paper was left on the roll than with how I was going to beat the best cyclists in the world. I'd come to Canada hoping for a medal. I left happy to have my health and knowing where way too many of the city's toilets were located.

CHAPTER 16

WITHOUT TRIVIALIZING IT, THE 2001 and 2002 Tours left little impression in my mind. As all-encompassing as the Tour can be, both campaigns were approached much in the same way our second win had been—always looking to silence the critics, always finding a way to exploit our opponents' weaknesses, and never relaxing until we got Lance onto the Champs-Élysées for the final few laps. But after years of building an aura and brazenly backing up all the rhetoric, it was 2003 that held the most significance, for a multitude of reasons. The racing was electrifying. Lance wasn't at his best, and Jan Ullrich was on fire, so it was the year I felt Lance needed me the most. I had a lot more of a role.

But it's a memory of a vision *off* the bike that brings an immediate smile to my face. The day I met my angel.

We had just won the 2003 Tour de France Prologue Team Classification (awarded after the prologue stage to the team whose top three riders have the best cumulative time), and because we won, we were invited onto the podium the next morning so that the organizers could present us with the customary Crédit Lyonnais Lion, a cute stuffed animal symbolic of excellence.

At the end of each day of racing or on the next morning, it's tradition for the women who present the awards, more commonly referred to as podium girls, to place a well-timed photogenic smooch on each celebrated cyclist's cheek. Before Stage 1, for me, a mere kiss on the cheek connected like none other. It was more than a kiss; it was a kick in the head. The shock wave went from my cheek, through my spine, and out my toes.

MELANIE HINCAPIE, GEORGE'S WIFE

I had done the Tour (and Paris–Nice, too) in 2002, and the custom was you got one year as a sponsor liaison and then moved on. (The casting process was quite intense, starting with over eighty girls who were eventually whittled down to only four.) But two weeks before the 2003 Tour, the head of Crédit Lyonnais called and said that a couple of the main sponsors had asked if I could come back and take part in another year. It was just fate that I was on that stage. I remember laughing when I had to place the medal around George's neck because he was so tall. We made eye contact and giggled at the glaring discrepancy between our heights, even with me in heels.

I rushed back to the team bus and began exclaiming to Lance and the other team members within earshot that I had just met an angel—that I had just met The One, and I was in love. At the time, I'd had a bunch of girlfriends, and I tended to attach substantial significance to each one, so for my teammates to hear me now extolling the virtues of yet another girl—well, they thought it was comical and that this infatuation would only end the same way all the other ones had. But this wasn't just somebody-tapping-me-on-the-shoulder different, this was scream-it-from-the-top-of-the-tallest-mountain revelatory.

The next morning, I went to the "Village Départ" (Start Village) to try to find Melanie and eventually work up enough courage to give her a note. I didn't speak French very well, so I figured if I wrote something down, then it would be easier for her to have a friend or colleague translate, figuring her English was on par with my French.

> MELANIE
> I got this note from him that read: "Hello, I am not sure if you speak English. I hope you do. If not, I will do my best to learn French. Call me sometime if you want to speak. I would love to get to know you. George."
> I didn't speak English at all. And I really didn't want to get involved with anyone, especially a cyclist.

The note got returned to me on the podium the next day with a simple "Not Interested" scrawled on it. But then I noticed that there was a phone number, in a different color of ink, written as well. I was a tad confused, but decided that perhaps she didn't understand English that well, and even though "Not Interested" seemed pretty clear, I took a chance and texted her anyway.

It turned out her boss was a big cycling fan, and a fan of mine, so he had read the note, and after seeing her response, had written her cell number on it before handing it back to me.

We began a slow, simple dialogue via text, with both of us cobbling together a unique gibberish of French, Spanish, Italian, and English in order to get our thoughts across. We agreed to meet on the second rest day, in Pau, and sat together by the pool. Between my friends and hers, it was like a mini–United Nations summit. So many languages were being used, and all of us strained to understand or to help communicate to the group. I couldn't take my eyes off of her.

MELANIE

After visiting George in Pau, and having an amazing afternoon, the next morning my boss was very accusatory and wanted to know what I had been doing with George. It was always frowned upon for us, as girls working the Tour, to interact with anyone outside of our sponsorship duties. But I didn't feel I'd done anything wrong, and made sure to stand up for myself. Even though I still had a myriad of things to work out with George, I knew I was beginning to like him, and I didn't see a problem with that, as long as it didn't interfere with doing my job.

With about a week to go in the Tour, she got fired. Someone had seen us together, and she was issued an ultimatum.

MELANIE

We just happened to be staying in the same hotel as George's team, and needless to say, I was excited to see him. I had stolen a kiss from him the day before and was thrilled that we were going to have a few moments together. My boss was not happy to see us together in the lobby, and eventually told me I had to choose—my job or George. I didn't like my boss's attitude or tone, especially after I had done my job to perfection, and as well as anyone that year. It was an easy decision. I didn't even hesitate before saying, "George."

As I watched her bags get loaded into the car, I felt bad for her, and guilty, yet secretly relieved that now we might have one less hurdle between us. After she left, I texted her and asked if she would be my date for the final night's festivities in Paris. Thankfully, she agreed. It turned out to be the perfect ending to my month of racing, and the perfect beginning to my life with her.

MELANIE

Why was he so special? I have no idea! I was cold and very protective. In our first encounters, he was so pushy, so sure of what he wanted, and so nice. He made me feel happy and secure. At the end of the Tour, I was starting to be in love with him. Throughout the Tour I had called my mom, and she remarked that I had never sounded so happy. And the feeling just kept getting better.

A budding romance in the City of Lights is one thing, but I was determined to see this through all the way. I invited Melanie to visit me in Girona, Spain, the week after the Tour ended, and after dizzying days and nights, there was no doubt in my mind that she was the woman I wanted to spend the rest of my life with. Eventually, I asked her to come back to Greenville with me that fall.

MELANIE

By the fall, I felt like it would be an impossible relationship due to the physical distance between us and our differing cultures. The day I had hit "rock bottom" just happened to be the day George texted me and asked me to come visit him in the U.S. I took a chance. He asked me to come to Greenville for two weeks. I ended up staying for three months.

I'd gone to the Tour in 2003 completely focused on notching number five for Lance and my teammates. I left Paris at the end of July not just a better biker, but a more complete man. I had long since learned to control the pain and manage the fear of bike racing's pressure cooker, but letting my restraint go and giving in to the uncontrolled waves of emotion scared me more than a sixty-mile-per-hour descent.

CHAPTER 17

IN 2004, OUR TEAM hoped to set ourselves apart in a way barely dreamed of, and only talked about in hushed tones, for fear that vocalizing the goal would jinx its completion. Six consecutive Tour de France titles. My most notable results, personally, were the overall win in the Belgian stage race, Three Days of De Panne, and a fifth overall in Paris–Nice, the early-season stage race done by a number of top riders and Tour de France contenders. My classics season went well, with a fourth-place finish at Gent–Wevelgem, tenth at the Tour of Flanders, and eighth the next week at Paris–Roubaix. What my results showed me was that my training had paid off.

I always put pressure on myself to do well in the spring, and as we continued to help Lance win Tour de France titles, I put even more pressure on myself to be there for him and to never be the weak link. So I worked harder. I rode more. I concentrated on my nutrition. I'd look at cookies, ice cream, or any other indulgence, salivate, and tell myself, "No: after the season is over, not before." In the beginning, I'd experimented on my own to see what effect certain doses of drugs had; then, eventually, my drug use took on the significance of simply taking vitamins. You didn't forget to do it because it was part of a defined schedule. About two weeks before a major classics competition or the start of the Tour de France, I'd begin taking EPO every other day. That pattern would continue until roughly two days before the event, when I'd leave home and travel. Sometimes I would mix in testosterone or growth hormone twice a week. There was no guilt; it was a part of the training. I knew my competition was riding for six hours a day, then taking their recovery routine, and I had to do the same if I wanted to have a chance to beat them. It was a monastic existence, but one I constructed of my own accord. My religion was cycling improvement and success.

As spring transitioned to summer, Lance became increasingly concerned with the drug techniques of his competitors. He was constantly talking about what other guys were using, or doing, to enhance their performances. He'd heard rumors of synthetic hemoglobin and use of multiple blood bags. He constantly scoured the Internet trying to find out what the other pros were taking, what new methods existed, and whether the benefits outweighed the cost. At the same time, he had begun to express a distaste for this pharmaceutical arms race. I'd even heard that he'd written letters to the UCI (Union Cycliste Internationale), the governing body of the sport, telling them to test for certain substances based on what he had learned through his own research. Nerves were frayed. Money, reputations, and history were on the line.

April 11, 2004. Paris–Roubaix. Another shot at the Hell of the North, and another instance where I was close, but not good enough. To be honest, I really didn't care. I'd had a lot coursing through my mind the few weeks before. I planned on asking Melanie to be my wife, and the only other people who knew were my parents and my brother, Rich. Being in Belgium, I'd used a couple of connections to get in touch with one of the premier diamond distributors in the region. Antwerp is one of the diamond capitals of the world, and to top it off, my contact knew I was racing Three Days of De Panne, so he brought the diamonds to me at my hotel in Kortrijk, in West Flanders. He showed up at my hotel room with a bag full of uncut stones as well as rings that were already set. I couldn't believe this guy was just walking around the street with what seemed like a bag worth millions of dollars. I spent a long time studying his merchandise, and then, the moment I saw Melanie's engagement ring, I knew. I'd been staring at sparkling things for what seemed like an eternity, but the ring I chose had a special quality. I just knew. I kept the ring in my suitcase as we traveled around Europe, but I knew our gear was in good hands with the soigneurs.

After I finished Paris–Roubaix, my dad, Melanie, and I checked into our hotel near the Gare de Lyon. We went out for a nice Italian dinner, during which my dad, knowing my plan, kept saying we should see the sights and just drop him back off at the hotel. Melanie felt guilty not including him, and alternated between insisting he join us and questioning why I even wanted to go out. Wasn't I tired from the race? And shouldn't I be smart about getting to bed and my recovery? My dad kept saying, "You should go," I kept insisting that we enjoy the evening, and finally, we were in a cab to Notre-Dame. My mind had been on very little else since the end of the race, and during dinner, as anyone who has proposed will tell you, everything that was said to me came through a haze. I knew I was being spoken to, but the words didn't make as much sense, or were never as loud, as I thought they should be. For hours, all I heard inside my head were the litany of questions surrounding how I was going to pull off proposing and not looking stupid, and if she would say yes.

As the cab pulled up to Notre-Dame, Melanie said, "Okay, we've seen it, now let's get back so you can rest." Once again, I broke character and deviated from what had always been my normal postrace pattern. I said, "No, I think we should walk around."

I had held on to this romantic idea of our engagement. We'd met in Paris, under the Eiffel Tower, the most recognizable landmark of France. I wanted to bookend our Parisian experience by sealing the deal at another one of Paris's iconic structures.

Once we were in front of the cathedral, I dropped to one knee to prepare to propose. Melanie thought I was tired, and in a concerned tone asked, "What are you doing?" I had to tell her, "No, let me finish." Upon which I asked for her hand in marriage. Thankfully, she said yes.

Adding to the excitement about having a new fiancée was the fact that Rich and I had started our own company, Hincapie Sportswear. It was a bit awkward because Nike was our team's sponsor, and yet here I was, the face of our family-owned and -named sportswear enterprise. Rich had been working on it for years on a smaller scale, but in 2004, we decided to make the leap into an already crowded market. We thought our selling points were our family story, the dedication to quality, and our connection to the clothing industry in Colombia, which would keep our costs down. The boutique size and aspect of our brand helped me justify my involvement. We stood, and stand, for family and handcrafting, not mass production. Nike was a world apart, a whole different galaxy, in terms of their vision and goals.

The first time Rich, and a couple of our crew, showed up with hats and jackets at the classics in 2004, I thought, Oh, man, we are actually doing this. I was nervous, but so happy for Rich, since he had put so much work into getting the company up and running.

The plan for me was to focus on product development. At home, since contractually I couldn't be seen riding out of my team colors, when I wore Hincapie, I'd train out of the public eye. Stealth mode included only wearing black, or blacked-out logos, as I tested our product line for comfort and fit up and around the hills of Greenville. It's hard to reinvent the wheel in terms of cycling clothing, but it's easy to screw it up. We were, and still are, always looking at cutting-edge fabrics and making our brand one that people want to be the first to try, then be the first to have.

Before I went to Europe for my final Tour prep race, on May 13, Mel and I made it official. Due to the timing of my season, we knew we couldn't plan a big wedding, so we headed to Greenville's City Hall. It wasn't the ceremony I wanted to give her, or that she deserved, but I promised I'd make it up to her at some point.

Feeling more than a little guilty, I was back on the road soon after. My lead-up to the Tour in 2004 included another trip to the Dauphiné Libéré. This stage race, the annual Tour testing ground, would be a who's who of contenders again, but that year there was a twist to the tale. Tyler Hamilton had left our team a couple years earlier and was now riding for Phonak. The Swiss entrepreneur Andy Rihs owned their squad, and they had assembled a formidable collection of talent. Beating us—well, beating *Lance*—had become a personal quest for Tyler. The Dauphiné was Tyler's chance to make a statement and send a message. Both were delivered loud and clear. Lance lost a large chunk of time to Tyler on the critical time trial up Mont Ventoux, and what that meant for us was a problematic few weeks of preparation. Worst-case scenario—this was an indicator that Lance was vulnerable. After the Dauphiné, we were told by both Johan and Lance that we were all on notice—that we needed to dial it up to be prepared for the Tour.

I had headed back to my European base in Girona, and had planned on going to Belgium right before the start of our annual foray around France, when out of the blue I got a frantic call from Lance stating we had to leave two days early for our training camp in the Pyrenees. Unhappy with his form and how he was feeling, he was panicking and wanted to squeeze in as much training as possible.

Our destination was a remote Spanish town, Puigcerdà, near the border with France. At over three thousand feet in elevation, it was a perfect area to do our final Tour training, and secluded enough that we were almost 100 percent positive Lance's "positive" wouldn't be detected by any testers. Our Americanized posse was made up of Floyd Landis, Lance, Sheryl Crow, me, and Melanie. We were an hour east of Andorra, and what I remember most about those days were the weather and the riding time. It was miserably cold. Since we were at altitude, the temperature hovered in the forties. And it rained nonstop, making our six-to-seven-hour sojourns in the saddle a literal and figurative pain in the ass.

Melanie wasn't too happy herself. She was pregnant, had been rushed off to an obscure village in Spain, and spent her days huddled in a cold and dank apartment. This was not the Spanish vacation she had read about in brochures. This was business. For years, business had been good, but I couldn't help thinking that here was another instance where I was affecting the people I loved with what I had always done—thinking of myself first, and justifying it because I called it *my job*.

MELANIE

Puigcerdà? What a nightmare! I was about six months pregnant, and in the middle of nowhere. George was riding his bike all day! No TV, no music! Depressing. Weather was cold, rainy, gray. Really, it was that bad. So I had to find something to do. I would just get in the car in the morning and go buy groceries. Then I'd cook all day for everybody that

was there. I was glad I had Tina, our Westie, there
with me for company. They would come back shiv-
ering around 4 p.m. I would have to help George
take off his gloves, socks, etc., and he would have to
start the shower with cold water, which felt warm
for him, and little by little go warmer. It was just
crazy for me to see him suffer like this.

Throughout our time near the border, we trained, and we were
also tested. The drugs, the spinning centrifuges once a week, all to
make sure we were "good." By the time we got to Liège, Belgium,
for the start of the Tour, all was in order. Lance was nervous, edgy,
but satisfied with the work we'd done in the previous weeks, and
the doping plan had been refined to perfection and to his liking.

Another wrinkle arose right before the Tour. Lance wanted
to get everyone together in Europe early. For me, there was one
big problem. Melanie had planned a surprise birthday party for me
(which she only told me about when I said we needed to leave early).
Melanie had put a lot of work into the party, and she was none too
pleased to have to call people and tell them it was canceled, but I
wasn't in a position to say no to Lance, so off I went to Liège.

Others have written about what transpired on the road, and
it's been talked about in great detail, but I remember 2004 as the
year of no gifts. Lance wasn't going to *let* anyone win a stage as a
sign of respect, or to garner favors. It is ironic that when Lance and
Johan partnered and set their goal for our first Tour de France title
in 1999, the only thing that mattered was Lance wearing yellow on
the last day in Paris. Fast-forward to 2004, and what mattered most
to Lance was crushing his competition. Winning the Tour was no
longer enough of a reward. Proving beyond a shadow of a doubt
that he was the best biker was all that mattered.

More days in yellow meant more work for us. As a team, we were perfectly happy with riding onto the Champs-Élysées with the leader. But now, our leader wanted it all. U.S. Postal won the team trial that year, held from Cambrai to Arras. (That was Stage 4, and Lance would also have five individual stage wins, though all were later disqualified.) It was a show of dominance rarely seen, and as much as he, and we, celebrated, his critics and doubters only got more vocal. Ultimately, the history books would erase the work we did that summer in France, but a month later in Greece, my work was as defined as ever.

The years in between the Games of the XXVII Olympiad and the Games of the XXVIII Olympiad were the halcyon days of American cycling. With the worldwide attention our team got each July in France, the sport of cycling continued its meteoric and historic growth in the United States.

By the time the U.S. Olympic team went to Athens, Greece, in August of 2004, cycling was riding a wave of media exposure never seen before. Lance had just won his record-breaking sixth Tour de France, and at the time, all of us benefited from the limelight his win brought to our team and our sport.

In the Olympic Village, all the teams hung their country's flags outside their windows, but we, the United States, weren't allowed to do that because of security concerns. No one wanted our positions within the compound to be given away. We were the only country that was not allowed to put a big flag on our roof.

Every Olympic Games is somewhat the same. It's a bit like Groundhog Day, just every four years. We may compete in a different locale each quadrennial, but the IOC and organizers purposefully try to make the athletes as comfortable and stress-free as possible. The Olympic Village itself is awe-inspiring. There's food from all over the world representing ten to twenty countries. Everyone is served buffet-style, and you have the whole world dining twenty-four hours a day. Some athletes might have just gotten up to train, others have just finished their events and are coming back from celebrating. So many athletes are around, connected in so many ways. It's perfect for people watching.

Aside from the dining hall, in Greece there was an Internet room, video game area, a place you could call home, and of course, the visitors center, where families could come and see the athletes. Visits had to be set up in advance—a competitor would apply for a day pass if they wanted someone to come, and then there would be a thorough prescreening process that took place before anyone could come to that part of the Olympic Village.

The room that was used the most was the massage and therapy area. It may sound like a pampered lifestyle, but one of the best things about being an elite athlete was the constant massage and body work that was required to keep my frame ready to perform at its peak. I miss those days. Getting daily work done is the equivalent of fine-tuning a guitar, car, or piano. Whether it was massage, chiropractic care, or any number of therapies, as athletes we were always searching for a better and more efficient way to recover.

Tyler Hamilton won the gold medal in the time trial, and I wasn't surprised when weeks later he tested positive. I'd seen him doing dodgy shit, occasionally clandestine and noncommittal in his actions. There were times when the whole team would be together in the Village except for Tyler, who would later appear and tell us he "had a meeting." At the time I thought, He's got some balls to go to those lengths. We all knew that if you only did enough drugs to be *even* with the rest of the peloton (small amounts of EPO, or using a blood bag [transfusing one's own blood] only one time a year), you would probably be able to stay under the radar, but if you were taking massive risks then you were definitely on your own and the peloton wasn't going to raise a finger to try to protect you.

These days, 5 percent of the peloton is probably using. It's the guys on the small teams trying to make a name for themselves. Look at the grand tours: if a guy on a small team defeats the best in the world and makes it look easy, it should throw up a red flag. But for some, it's still worth rolling the dice.

In Athens, our team went into the race with no clear leader. Who had the best legs would be decided during the race between me, Bobby Julich, Tyler, Levi Leipheimer, and Jason McCartney. Some of my teammates wondered why we were starting the race at 1 p.m., the hottest part of the day. I didn't mind. Sure, it was hot, but Greenville on a summer's afternoon can be brutal too. It wasn't the heat that sapped my will, it was the Italians' race plan and their perfect execution. Paolo Bettini won gold ahead of Portugal's Sérgio Paulinho (who later became my teammate for one year on the Discovery Channel team). I finished in the bunch, twelve seconds back, a respectable twenty-fourth. In the same group, Tyler was the highest placed rider on our team, in eighteenth. The Italians had done what few countries had ever been able to do: control the race with only five team members. The rest of us seemed to be at their mercy all day long.

I'd put in a huge effort with just under thirty kilometers to go in the race, right before a tricky section of pavé, but it was covered, and I began to realistically think I didn't have much left. On the penultimate climb up Lycabettus Hill, Bettini took off and only Paulinho could follow his wheel. Once those two were away, the natural letdown was undeniable. Later, Axel Merckx made a move on the last lap right before we climbed by the Acropolis, and that was the last straw. I wasn't going to risk my life in a sprint for fourth place. Mentally, I was done. My legs locked into autopilot until the finish. As callous as it may seem, my focus immediately transitioned to my family, and before I was even off the bike, I was thinking about being home.

Earlier in the summer, I'd gone back to Girona with Melanie. It was very low key, and once I got to Greece, I couldn't wait to leave. I really just wanted to get home to Girona to be with Mel, who was near the end of her pregnancy, so after I raced in Athens I left Greece immediately.

CHAPTER 18

NOVEMBER 3, 2004. MOST fathers will admit, if the change hadn't happened already, it happens the moment you see your child for the first time. I was no different than the fathers before me, but my metamorphosis was no less stunning to me.

We'd decided to induce, so we knew we were headed to the hospital the evening of November 2. On the bike, I'd made a career out of perfecting the art of detachment—my outward demeanor almost always masking my intentions to my competitors—so I was happy we didn't have to worry about the timing. It melted away a lot of the stress. I didn't have to hide that I was anxious, nervous, and a little unsure. Like any expectant father, my excitement was tempered by my worry for Melanie and my list of questions.

I wanted to document and remember it all, so I decided to video-tape as much as possible. As new parents, we didn't know what to expect, but the doctors told us everything was normal and there were no complications. At 5:04 a.m., I laid eyes on my daughter.

Everything I had done up to that point faded into the background. Julia was the biggest, and greatest, thing I had accomplished in my life.

The euphoria of the moment melted away quickly as the weight of responsibility began to squeeze the air out of my lungs. How was I going to care for her, provide for her? It was as if someone handed me a parenting version of 3-D glasses. The world looked completely different.

Mel wanted me to cut the umbilical cord. I was hesitant, fearful I'd screw it up and do something to hurt Julia. Sure enough, the second I made the incision and severed the former lifeline, Julia started screaming, and I jumped out of my skin, convinced I'd caused the pain and irreparable damage to my daughter. Mel was the first to hold her, and as I looked at my wife and saw how happy she was, I realized everything I had ever dreamed of had come true. It was a contentment I'd never experienced.

MELANIE

I thought it was just amazing to be pregnant, to give life. The first time I felt Julia move I cried, and I couldn't wait to feel that sensation again. Delivery was very easy. But the first day back at home was a bit overwhelming! We weren't two anymore but three! And Julia seemed just so fragile, so little, and I was so young. I wish my mom had been there to show me things. She said to me on the phone that giving life and becoming a mom were the most beautiful things she had experienced, now it was my turn and I shouldn't be scared. She also said that as soon as I became a mom, I'd know what my baby wanted and needed—it's just inside you. And she was right. Julia and I just learned from each other, and every day I did my best to be a better mom.

DAVID ZABRISKIE, FRIEND AND FORMER
U.S. POSTAL TEAMMATE

Ever since I'd met George back in 2001, he'd impressed me with how nice and personable he was. My respect for him only grew when I saw how he developed and worked at his relationship with Melanie. Then when Julia was born, I saw how happy he became, and it made me want to have kids. I could see how fulfilled he was, and I wanted to feel the same thing.

CHAPTER 19

AT THE END OF 2004, I'd begun to believe I could compete without the help of drugs or other doping practices. Not only had Julia's birth kindled a spark in me, a natural transition from my centric way of thinking to one that extrapolated further down life's road, but testing was getting better, so the peloton was shifting its ways out of necessity. Tyler Hamilton had tested positive at the Olympics for a blood transfusion after winning the gold medal in the individual time trial, as well as at the Vuelta a España a month later, which was an all-too-obvious reminder that the times, they were a-changin'. There were more drug busts at the Athens Olympics than there had ever been. Once again, I reevaluated and tweaked my training habits, committing myself with even more purpose. I'd been minimal in my doping approach in '04, and I was determined to do even less in 2005. The logistical nightmare of purchasing, scheduling, and transporting weighed heavily on me, and accelerated my experiments with not only minimizing but eliminating my use of drugs.

The new methods I used to try to naturally increase my red blood cell count were altitude tents and masks that regulated the

amount of oxygen I would breathe. I'd felt good in training before
the 2005 season's racing began. Whether or not it was a placebo
effect, my results were great during the early season. I flew from
Greenville right before the start of the Ruta del Sol, planning to
base myself in Girona for the remainder of the spring. I had a better-
than-average race, and it was an omen of things to come.

I became the first and only American to win Kuurne–Brussels–
Kuurne, the one-day Belgian race held at the end of February. It was
a miserably cold day, snowing at times, and as always, the pace and
the attacks were relentless. From the start, it was a war of attrition.
The win was nice, but it was the confidence I gained from it that
mattered most. At that point in my career, I was no longer worried
about garnering respect from the peloton—my time among them
and my results had already done that—but the win elevated my stature even more. I'd always excelled in Belgium, and like a banner
across the road, the victory was a signal to me I was on the right path
with my decision to minimize my doping. This win meant more to
me than my 2001 victory in Gent–Wevelgem, even though that race
had shown that Americans could mix it up with Belgium's best.

TONY CRUZ, U.S. POSTAL TEAMMATE, 2001-2005

When we won Gent–Wevelgem, we thought we
were on our way to killing it in the classics with
George as our cornerstone. We set out to show the
other teams we weren't filler, and George helped
me achieve a level I never thought possible. I'd have
given everything to help him win. It was hard for
me to see him never win Paris–Roubaix or the Tour
of Flanders. I wished with all my might I could have
helped him do that.

After standing on the top step of the podium in February, I entered into the standard month of training and racing I'd always embraced. When I was back in Greenville, I'd begun to work with a "performance mind coach" by the name of Christina Maddox. She was my neighbor in the condo complex we lived in at the time, and our work together unlocked a level of focus I didn't know I had. It amounted to a stripping away of the noise so that I could concentrate only on what would enable me to train, then race, well. Her work with the Pacific Institute had given her experience with a wide range of athletes and professionals, and her advice gave me a new weapon in my arsenal.

March continued my trend of solid stats. A sixth overall in the Italian Race to the Sea, Tirreno–Adriatico, had me primed to take a shot at La Classica di Primavera, the Spring Classic, Milan–San Remo—the longest professional one-day race on the calendar, at 298 kilometers. I'd felt superfit at the end of Adriatico, buoyed by a surprise visit from Mel and Julia. The Thursday before the race, we were set to drive down to Milan when I got the first indications I wasn't feeling well. It's an athlete's first instinct to question why they are feeling a certain way and then almost immediately to go into hyperdenial. I tried to convince myself that nothing was wrong and that I'd be able to race in two days. By Friday, the tickle in my throat had turned into a full-blown fever. My confidence that I would beat the bug working its way through my body was replaced with prayers that I'd be miraculously healed and revitalized. Those prayers went unanswered. Saturday's sunrise didn't bring a miracle, or a trip to the start line in Milan.

Hello flu, good-bye bike. I didn't ride for over a week. Each day, each minute, I was stuck in a claustrophobic state where my fitness fell away and my confidence eroded.

Even though I was slipping further off the back of my peak

fitness level while my competitors were logging mile after mile, I hadn't broken my deal with myself in terms of using EPO or blood bags for the spring races. I won't lie. I thought about how easy it would be to prepare the old way, but now I was emboldened not just by results but also by my own commitment. My transformation, admittedly, was in baby steps. Even though I was willing to bear the burden of not using what I termed the "heavy stuff," I was still using testosterone patches, but I classified and justified them as minor compared with the Big Two.

One of my biggest goals, the Tour of Flanders, started only three days into April. I didn't know what to expect from my form after having lost so much training time. I secretly hoped for an out-of-body experience, where I'd finish and not really remember anything except a good result. That's almost what happened. I ended up missing a late race move, and finished seventh. The week between Flanders and Roubaix was an anxious one. The best indicator of my form was always how I felt in the Flanders race, and in 2005, I'd felt good enough that a small glimmer of hope began to grow inside of me. Maybe, just maybe, I'd be able to match the best when I rolled to the start of the Hell of the North.

The 103rd edition of my favorite race, the one that more than any other defined me, began with 190 brothers-in-arms. Mild temperatures and moderate winds brought a smile to my face. I was happy to be feeling as good as I did on the start line. A few weeks prior I'd been unable to get out of bed, and now I was as energized as ever. The first part of the day was dominated by mind-numbing, myriad maneuvers. Everyone fights for his turf, every inch is constantly earned and agonized over. You can't rest. Ever. The second you take pride in your positioning, you've lost concentration and fallen back fifteen spots.

At around eighty kilometers to go, the critical move was made.

Filippo Pozzato launched, and his teammate Tom Boonen attached himself to his wheel. I reacted, as did Marcus Bäckstedt (Liquigas), Lars Michaelsen (CSC), Juan Antonio Flecha, and Fabian Cancellara (both Fasso Bortolo). We broke clear of the peloton and set off to hunt down the break.

With fifty kilometers to go, we caught the riders who had slaved at the front most of the day. We now totaled eleven. But not for long. Whether due to punctures or the pain associated with all the effort, we began to lose guys from the group. True to the course, Paris–Roubaix weeded out the weak. Fabian Cancellara, not yet wearing the crown of greatest classics rider ever, punctured not once, but twice. There are twenty-seven sections of cobblestones: the first, numbered 27, comes a little before the one-hundred-kilometer point; the last is right before the entrance to the finishing velodrome. I tried my luck in Secteur 6 (with 25.5 kilometers left), hitting the front and throwing in a large effort, but it wasn't anywhere near enough to get a gap or work anyone off my wheel. I had a huge group of friends and family waiting for me at the finish line, but the adrenaline of seeing them quickly wore off, and I realized riding smart would have to be the plan for the rest of the day.

As we entered the pivotal Secteur 4, the Carrefour de l'Arbre, even though Juan Antonio Flecha led us onto the cobbles, I could tell Tom Boonen was strongest, and although I felt worthy of being among this group, I reconfirmed with myself that I should mark Boonen, no matter what. We ended up losing a couple guys shortly thereafter, Michaelsen due to a puncture and Bäckstedt based on our pace. He simply blew, and he watched us ride off. There's no more frustrating, or sickening, feeling for a cyclist than to have to watch guys pull away. But that wasn't my fate this day.

We had been reduced to a band of three. A trio of suffering. Flecha, whose name means "arrow," had made a career, like me, out of the classics. Also like me, winning Paris–Roubaix was his dream. He alternated turns on the front, and I began to question my initial assessment that Boonen was the strongest among us. Tom Boonen and I had been teammates for one year on U.S. Postal, but being Belgian, he made the right call transferring to Quick Step after his first year. It was a team made for nurturing classic specialists, and Tom was cut from that mold. And then, I think they broke it. As youthful as he was, he had shown his mastery a week earlier in winning the Tour of Flanders, outsmarting the competition by attacking earlier than anyone suspected. Now he was in a three-way dogfight for a slice of immortality. The Flanders–Roubaix double is rarely accomplished—before that day, the last man to do it had been Peter van Petegem in 2003, but it had been twenty-six years since the previous occurrence, when Roger De Vlaeminck pulled off the feat in 1977.

In cycling, any sign of weakness, any indication of vulnerability, can be used to advantage by your competitors. In a race like Roubaix, those implications are magnified. I searched for any "tell" that the two men I was with were reaching their breaking point, or had exceeded their system's limits. Nothing. No extra sweat. No uneven pedal strokes. No overly labored breathing. No change in body position. All mentally noted and processed in an instant. The outcome? This race was going down to the wire. I made sure I was sending the same message, the same poker face, I was reading from them.

Over the final kilometers, as we rode closer to Roubaix, none of us was willing to wholeheartedly make a move, convinced it wouldn't amount to the winning one and serve only to destroy our chances for victory at the end. Even though I tried to look like I was riding comfortably, I was at my limit. Just concentrating took energy I didn't have. After almost six and a half hours, we took the

right turn into the velodrome, and I was in front. It wasn't ideal to
have both powerhouse riders behind me, but my impulse to always
be in the safest position through the turns was too hard to ignore.

It's surreal to go from the jarring, bone-breaking feeling of the
cobbles to the silky-smooth sensation of riding the last laps. Even
with the crowd, everything seems to become quiet, and the silence
bleeds up through the tires and frame of your bike. Having been
shaken for six hours like an overprepared martini, my body wanted
to keep vibrating on a molecular level, but it was time to ignore
the cellular "hum" and transfer what remained of my energy to
cognitive function and colossal pedal power. I kept looking behind
me, slowed my pacing, and stayed high on the boards to try to force
either of my foes to make a move. It was time to try to remember
all my track training. Flecha dropped down first and took the lead,
allowing me to fall in behind him.

As the bell signified the last lap, our order was Flecha, me,
Boonen. Boonen was in the best spot, but I felt I could react if
Tom launched, then make my own move off his wheel and squeak
by him at the line. I needed to make sure I was in the right gear
to surge when Boonen went. I kept looking down at the cassette,
making sure it was where I needed it to be.

Our critical cat-and-mouse game continued, each of us un-
willing to change position, until finally, coming into the final
bank, Boonen bolted down and to the inside. His acceleration,
even though I knew it was coming, was so intense, so immediate,
I thought, How can he be so strong? My body reacted while my
mind played catch-up, and I too used my weight and strength to
steer my bike down the incline and vault toward Tom's back wheel.
I made contact, finding his slipstream, but out of the saddle, at full
throttle, I didn't have enough to come around. I had given absolutely everything I could, and second place was the result as Boonen

became only the fifth man to win Flanders and Roubaix in the same year.

It was small consolation to know I was a part of a historic ride, but I did draw strength from the fact that I'd bounced back from the flu so well. I didn't win, but I was emboldened with a renewed commitment and attitude.

I took a week off after Paris–Roubaix. My spring had gone almost as well as I could have hoped, and I began to phase into summer mode. It didn't seem possible, but I trained harder. I rode more, with longer climbs. I became obsessed with the idea of losing weight, as being skinnier equaled faster. I started skipping lunches and only had a protein shake during the day. I dropped down to 162 pounds and 4 percent body fat. It was brutally hard not to eat, a constant struggle. On one shoulder sat the angelic voice of my racing results, telling me I could be on the top step of the podium, every race, with just a little more dedication. On the other shoulder squatted the louder, never-ending nagging of his counterpart, extolling the virtues of every type of junk food, not to mention questioning why any sane person would deny themselves the pleasure of food and the contentment of a full belly. I always went to bed hungry, and one of the few indulgences I would allow myself, mostly to trick my belly into thinking I was full, was a sip of a protein shake before bed. *Never* allowing myself to finish it, for that would be too many calories.

My plan, all along, was to race drug-free through the spring, then for the Tour, use a small amount of EPO, as well as reinfuse a blood bag that I'd drawn out earlier in the year. I considered this consistent with my tapering off, or phasing down, my dependence. Even though I wasn't totally clean, I'd already begun to try to influence younger riders I knew not to go down the same path I'd taken. My results were proof—success was there for the taking, especially

in the shorter races, without enhancement. I'd had a training partner who came to me in 2005 and told me he had started taking
EPO; he had actually gone to my supplier and gotten it. I lost it.
I got so pissed at this young kid, who had so much talent. I told
him I wasn't going to let him do it, and that the sport had changed
since I'd gotten involved. I *had* to do it, I told him, but it was up
to him to be part of the change as well, to think long term. In that
instance, I'd like to think I helped, or at least made a difference. My
die was cast, but I could still help shape others. The more I raced in
'05, the more steadfast I became in my resolve to ride clean.

The 2005 Dauphiné Libéré started in southeastern France with
a 7.9 km time trial, and I was ready. All indications were that I was
going to have a great week. I didn't disappoint myself, or the team.
I won the prologue in Aix-les-Bains by two seconds, and ended
up winning the final stage as well. I'd gotten in a breakaway with
teammate Yaroslav Popovych, and on that final day of racing, eventually Discovery Channel (U.S. Postal had stopped sponsorship of
the team at the end of 2004, but the team infrastructure and the
riders basically stayed the same, with Discovery Channel becoming
the main sponsor) commandeered the podium, with Lance finishing in third. I left the Dauphiné convinced I was ready for the Tour
and one last heroic ride around France with Lance.

CHAPTER 20

I LEFT THE DAUPHINÉ AND went to Belgium. That had been the plan all along. There, we drew out blood to be used during the Tour. I then went down to the Côte d'Azur, between Nice and Monaco, and stayed in a small seaside town called Beaulieu-sur-Mer. Lance was close by in Cap Ferrat, and as I stated in my affidavit to USADA, it was here that I borrowed a vial of EPO from him, and over the course of six days of training, injected EPO a couple of times. I didn't think anything of it. There was no guilt or remorse as baggage. It was the agreement I had made with the team, the coaches, and myself. I was tired from a full spring of racing, and I saw it as a necessary recovery tool. I justified it completely.

Others have written about how they were torn apart by the weight of the secret they kept concerning their drug use. I was never like that. In the later years of my usage, I was honest with my close friends and family about it. I didn't telegraph to the press, or to the general public, what was happening within the sport, but anyone who was in my inner circle had an idea of what was necessary at the time.

The days leading up to the start of the ninety-second edition of the Tour de France combined the usual craziness and last-minute training I'd always experienced. We knew this was going to be Lance's last hurrah, and there was an unspoken bond between us all. He knew we'd give everything for him, but he also knew that this year we'd find a way to give a little more. In the first stage, an individual time trial to the island of Noirmoutier via the slippery Passage du Gois, I placed fourth, two spots behind Lance, who was two seconds behind our former teammate CSC's David Zabriskie. It was a fortuitous start to my month. After our Stage 4 team time trial win, Lance moved into yellow, although he didn't want to take the jersey after David Zabriskie crashed close to the finish line. Only when the organizers threatened Lance with expulsion did he relent and wear yellow for Stage 5. We fell into the same pattern and workload we had come to experience every year. Lance was in yellow, so we rode the front, dictating the day's pace and protecting our "patron."

There were times, however, when we disagreed on the best course of action. With only three days left in the Tour, Lance was leading the overall classification by around five minutes when we got to the base of a climb. Lance told us all to crank it up so that we could make the rest of the peloton suffer. Johan was on board to crush the collective will of the group too. I told Lance, "No, that's bullshit. You're already winning the Tour, we don't need to send any more of a message!"

Feeling it was in poor taste and showed a lack of sportsman-ship to follow their course of action, I sat up. Got dropped by the whole group. A couple of days later, Lance made a speech at dinner, during which he mentioned that moment of defiance, saying that's why he liked me so much—because I was so different from him, that my voice was the calming and more rational, always opposite to his. I balanced out his charge-ahead-at-all-costs style. His mentality was always to win, not only to show that he was the best, but that nobody was even close to him. There were times I tried to temper that resolve with a little realism, that perhaps simply winning *was* enough.

LANCE ARMSTRONG

He's the greatest, bar none, teammate the world of sport has ever seen, the one guy who made my success possible. My wins do not happen without George Hincapie. Anyone who thinks differently is kidding themselves.

As the days ticked off and we rode closer to Paris, I started to think more of myself. Lance was comfortably in front; he was going to win his seventh consecutive title and make history, again, as the greatest Tour rider ever. I was feeling good, having followed the prerace plan, reinserting my blood on the first rest day. I began to look for opportunities for myself and actively search out breakaways. Everything aligned perfectly on Stage 15 in the Pyrenees. It was called the Queen Stage, so named because it was considered the hardest of the race. Five categorized climbs, ending in the *hors catégorie* (beyond category) ascent to Pla d'Adet. With little more than a tenth of the stage completed, I responded to an attack by Rabobank's Michael Boogerd. Atop the first climb, the Portet d'Aspet, we had almost eighteen minutes on the peloton, and as we descended, we passed the monument to my former teammate, Fabio Casartelli, who had died almost ten years prior to the day. It was a grim reminder, but also an uplifting testament to how much I loved cycling and how much it had given me in the time since Fabio lost his life. An almost imperceptible tingle crept up my spine. An omen? Perhaps something special was in store.

The imposing heat and Lance's grip on the leader's jersey only helped drain the peloton of its urgency, and our lead group continued to push the pace and build our advantage. Aside from my personal ambitions, my position in the break was a smart tactical move for the team. If Lance and the other General Classification leaders did claw us back, I'd be in a perfect place to help Lance up the final climb. But once Johan saw that we had more than an eighteen-minute lead, he got on the radio, said there was little chance the peloton would catch us, and told me to race for myself. Once I was given the green light to go for the stage, I began to conserve as much energy as I could. The unwritten rules of the road dictated that since Lance was in yellow, I did not have to take turns at the front of our group, pulling our pack and pushing our pace. The other riders knew it, and like it or not, it's just an element of cycling. One of the codes of conduct followed by the peloton. In a weird way, after all I'd given Lance, he was now giving a gift to me. As the race leader, he had relieved me of any responsibility. I was able to save so much by sitting behind the rest of my pack.

The sweltering, shimmering, sunflower-laden countryside came and went. With each climb, our baker's-dozen-plus-one band of stage-success dreamers began to whittle down. By the base of Pla d'Adet, we numbered only four—Spain's Óscar Pereiro (who would win the 2006 Tour), Dutchman Michael Boogerd, Italian Pietro Caucchioli, and myself. It was here I hatched my plan to take a page out of Lance's playbook. The final climb to the finish was over ten kilometers long, and I decided to play possum with the remaining riders. I began to feign fatigue, and made it look like I was suffering a lot more than I was. Our Belgian directeur, Dirk Demol (the winner of Paris–Roubaix in 1988), was in the car following me, along with Sheryl Crow, and Dirk kept telling me, "You can do it, you can do it, just hang on!" About a quarter of the way up, I dropped back to the car, telegraphing that perhaps I had had enough and wasn't able to keep up any longer. I leaned into the driver's-side window, Dirk's face a mixture of excitement and fear. I could tell he wanted this win for me almost as much as I did. Before I could say anything, he launched into a litany of positive reinforcement: "Don't give up. You can do this. Just hang on. It's not that much farther. The other guys are tired and they're about to crack. You could win the hardest stage of the Tour."

I smiled and told him not to worry.

He saw in an instant that it had all been a ruse. I'd even faked out my directeur. Barely above a whisper, I leaned in and said, "I'm not even feeling the chain." The car erupted in screams and excitement, and I rode up to finish the job.

The attacks began in earnest, and I just did my best to cover every move that was made. With about five kilometers to go, Phonak's Pereiro played his hand, intensely accelerating ahead. I got on his wheel, and it was down to two. The sea of spectators was deafening. Just when it seemed we'd run into a crazed wall of fans, the mass of humanity would part and make room for us to pass. Tactically, I knew I'd have to wait until the very end, but I was more than confident that I could outkick Óscar, especially since he had done the lion's share of the work throughout the stage.

I watched, planned, and prepared. He was struggling. He'd given everything. He was completely drained, and had to have been praying I was either going to give him the stage, as a token of all the work he'd done, or somehow a miracle would happen, and he'd find one more gear to hold me off. At altitude, each meter ascended feels like an eternity. With less than half a kilometer to go, I ran through the checklist. *Stay on his wheel. When you do go, make your move decisively. Be prepared for him to have a final surge. Shut out the pain.*

We were both out of the saddle at three hundred meters from

the line, when Pereiro put his final card on the table. Call it a queen, in honor of the stage. But I was holding an ace. I'm sure it didn't seem like an explosion, but to me, my surge felt like one, as I moved up and past him on the right side with around 250 meters to go.

It was a crushing blow to Óscar's confidence, as I looked back, his body seemed to shrink into itself atop his handlebars. But I needed to press my good fortune. I still wasn't convinced I'd done enough to win. Every pedal stroke was painful, but each was also blissful ecstasy. In the final two hundred meters, I looked back half a dozen times because I couldn't believe I was about to win a stage of the Tour de France. The last of the six anxious glances was after I had started to celebrate, ever so slightly, but then I caught myself, still unsure it was real.

I held my hands up to my face, more out of disbelief than to hide any sort of reaction. I'd dreamed of this moment since I was a little kid. I'd worked an almost infinite number of hours to make the dream a reality. I'd ridden the Tour for a decade, always devoted to my teams. Now personal success had arrived, and it was overwhelming.

History recorded a record seventh win for Lance, and the last night in Paris was one to remember, but many who were there have probably forgotten. King Louis XV commissioned the Hôtel de Crillon in 1758, and from 1999 to 2005, it became ground zero for our afterparties—and 2005 was one for the history books. Hollywood had hit the Place de la Concorde. Lenny Kravitz and Sheryl Crow were in attendance. Jan Ullrich came to the party to show his support for Lance and what he meant to the sport. It was the hottest ticket in town; riders from other teams had begged to be let in the door. Sunrise didn't make a dent in anyone's celebration. Even though we'd just ridden almost thirty-six hundred kilometers, what we'd accomplished over the past years was all the fuel we needed.

SEAN YATES

Lance always said that George was too nice to be
a bike rider. And he meant it as a compliment. It
was always so clear George was happiest working for
others. He was okay skipping the extra pressure of
being a team leader. He could have definitely gone to
other teams and been "the man," but George found
his niche. He didn't like, or want, to have a selfish
side, and every leader has to have that. George had
an ability to work harder than anyone, day in and
day out. And one of the reasons he had such longev-
ity was he was totally at peace with himself and his
decisions.

CHRISTIAN VANDE VELDE

One of the few frustrating things about George was
he didn't seem to believe in himself at times. His
personality was such that when he needed to, he
didn't see himself as "the guy," with everything that
that entails. He was always a fair and honest captain.
You wanted to help him succeed. When I saw him
doing everything he could, it made me want to give
everything for him. In the end, I'm not sure George
was 100 percent comfortable putting himself out
there. It's a huge leap to be okay with failing. Michael Jordan used to say, "You miss every shot you
don't take," but, at times, George was fine with not
being the guy to take the shot at the end.

The races I excelled at were held earlier in the year, and required a completely different style of racing than Lance's focus on
winning grand tours—more specifically, the most important grand

tour. I was fine with putting all of my energy early in the year into the spring classics, and once spring slid into summer, that emphasis switched. I chose to focus on what I was really good at, and that was getting somebody (more often than not, Lance) into the proper position within the peloton. It's one of the few things I am not afraid, or hesitant, to brag about. There was nobody better at getting Lance into position than me.

I looked at it as an art form. Sure, I needed to get him strategically placed—whether that was at the front before a tricky section of cobblestones, or behind the right person before the start of a climb—but it wasn't just about placement. It was about economy of effort and seamlessly maneuvering through that large mass of humanity. I had a moving 3-D canvas on which to mold my performance art. Every day was a chance to create a masterpiece. I focused on being great at that, and even though I might not have gotten a lot of credit for it from the outside world or the casual fan, I garnered a ton of respect within the peloton and my inner circle of friends. That's what mattered to me most.

If my brother watched on TV, then told me I had done an amazing job marshaling my man into place, *that* was all the validation I wanted and needed.

RICH

Stage 17, 2009. George crashes and breaks his collarbone. He didn't tell anyone for fear he'd be forced to leave the Tour. He was so instrumental in Mark Cavendish's six stage wins that year, and they'd developed such a close bond in their time together. He didn't want to let Mark down, and when 99.999 percent of the peloton (who are considered some of the toughest men on the planet) would have quit the race, he kept going. Then, on the Champs-Élysées, with those nasty, bone-jarring cobblestones, when anyone else would have just gone to the back of the pack and hoped to finish the stage, George was in the front setting Mark up for one final win. With one kilometer to go, he even jumped out of the saddle (putting all his weight on his broken collarbone) to give his last ounce of energy. It was pure guts. And pure George. I sat in my living room, thousands of miles away, in utter amazement. I couldn't wait to talk to him and tell him how proud I was to be his brother.

Whenever a teammate (whether it was Lance, Mark Cavendish, or Cadel Evans) came up to me after a stage and thanked me for helping him stay out of trouble, I couldn't have been more thrilled.

CADEL EVANS

It was an early stage in the 2010 Tour. I wanted to be near the front to stay out of harm's way, but George told me to stay back in order to avoid the inevitable melee at the finish. Robbie McEwen ended up crashing, which in turn caused a chain reaction, and George had the foresight and expertise to know there was a possibility of it happening, and he kept me safe. I thanked him for looking out for my best interests.

Those were my victories. The behind-the-scenes scenarios and sentiment were what drove me to succeed and fueled me for the future. On the surface, many might argue that my goals were minuscule in comparison to standing on the winner's stage in front of millions of viewers, but I never craved the limelight or the attention. So those minimoments were massive in what mattered to me most—the respect of my peers.

In the early years of our success, America didn't know much about my role, or how someone in my role actually helped a guy like Lance. Explaining to a noncyclist something as simple as "sitting in the wind" versus "being tucked in behind a rider" became part of my daily routine. It was a fun side effect of the team's growing notoriety. Once the race in France was over, for a large part of the year, we became cycling minstrels, singing the praises of teamwork and what it took to win the toughest race on the planet.

Lance, like Michael Jordan, Tiger Woods, Roger Federer, or Wayne Gretzky, was a once-in-a-generation athlete. He happened to come along at a time when the rules of the game were different than they are now. Lance and Johan never asked us to take drugs. They never forced us to dope. I, along with all my teammates, knew what was at stake and what was expected of us to perform at the highest level. And in order to win the Tour de France, in the years that we raced, against the other teams who were doing exactly what we were, we did what it took to be 100 percent committed to the cause. We all wanted to win the Tour. I believed then and believe now that we were lucky to have a man like Lance as our closer.

I had one more stellar result in me that year. After heading back to Girona for a couple of weeks, and not touching my bike much, at the last minute I entered the GP de Plouay, in northwestern France. It was a World Cup event, so there were plenty of top-tier guys in attendance. Before the start, I made a deal with myself. The race itself didn't matter, I was merely riding in order to get kilometers in my legs, in a hope to be ready for the GP San Francisco. I didn't care if I finished: my mental odometer was set to the goal of completing two hundred kilometers.

I knew it was going to hurt, due to my lack of training and the field's pace, but as we got deeper into the race, I realized I was suffering on a level I hadn't experienced in years. Each lap made my legs feel progressively worse, as if the muscles were melting from the inside out. The pain got so severe that I contemplated quitting, which of course triggered my innate "never give up" response. However, in my head this time, instead of an army of reasons rushing to my aid, the pain, aided by reason, dispatched my willpower with a flick of its mighty dominance. In a last-ditch effort to avoid stopping, I made a new deal. Just complete the lap, then reevaluate my status. The trick worked. I survived the initial takeover attempt, and while the pain still tried to overrun my defenses, I kept pedaling.

We hit the halfway mark. Each of the six laps so far had increased their toll, so I didn't hold any illusions as to what was in store for the next half dozen. I tried to hide as deep within the group as I could, conserving precious calories, not just for my legs but for my brain. It hurt to think. Autopilot kicked in, and the next real memory came with one lap to go. I looked around. As far as I could tell, I was in the main group, we were all together, and we totaled around one hundred. I let out an audible, incredulous gasp: "I'm still here?!"

A flutter of hope hit my adrenal gland and my racing sensations switched back on. I took stock of everyone around me, what the course conditions offered in the way of opportunity. The pain was still there, but it had taken a backseat to my calculations. Even though I'd suffered every single time over the one five-hundred-meter climb in the route, I knew I needed to be at the front of the field at the top if I had any hope of challenging for a high finish. From there, it was a downhill two-kilometer run to the line.

I've said before, I was good at positioning, even in a fatigued state. At times, trying to remember a race, how I moved into position is an unknown—a bit like sleepwalking. I wasn't sure how I got there, I'd just all of a sudden be aware I was in a different place in the peloton. My honed sense served me well as I crested the hill with the front fifty and did a quick recalculation. If I went full gas for one kilometer, I'd be set up for a left-hand corner with only five hundred meters remaining. I played that card, accelerated, then dove into the corner at an almost reckless angle and came out in tenth.

Top ten, baby!

Now, not only did I have adrenaline on my side, I had an unquenchable desire to fight until the end.

I'd done the high-speed chess in my head and outmaneuvered my competition again. Almost immediately, taking the inside of the next right bend brought me from tenth to fifth. Holy shit. For the first time in over four hours, I didn't feel any pain, only the anxious joy of possibility. A final brief, rolling downhill was all that stood before the last 150 meters. The dash to the line was up, and I exploded past the remaining guys as we bottomed out and began our slight ascent. I caught them all off guard. No one was able to jump on my wheel or cling to my slipstream. I'd gone from feeling as bad as any day on the bike, top three worst ever, to winning against an incredibly tough field.

Afterward, Jan Ullrich came up to me with a huge, wry smile on his face. I'd been honest with him before the race, saying that I felt horrible and just wanted to survive. He reminded me of my words, then, in a joking manner, said he hoped he felt as bad in his next race as I just had. He was completely convinced my honesty had been the usual gamesmanship that goes on prerace, a white lie to hide my true intentions. Nothing could have been further from the truth.

CHAPTER 21

AN OFF-SEASON FILLED WITH appearances, charity rides, corporate events, and dinners finally faded into the background, and I concentrated on getting my soft frame back into a recognizable shape. I'd done the celebratory Crits (circuit races) in Europe and in America after our seventh Tour de France title, but now, in 2006, I'd be starting LAL (Life After Lance). I was committed to two things: shattering everyone's expectations of me and exceeding my own. I'd always been categorized as the Loyal Lieutenant, but my success in 2005 got me, the team, and cycling aficionados thinking that perhaps I could ride a grand tour for myself. After consulting with a few key people, we arranged my season plan around trying to podium at the Tour de France. It was a lofty goal, especially considering I was not going to deviate from my 2005 minimal doping structure. No use during the spring, and then an EPO hit before, and a blood bag during, the race in July.

My early-season success only fanned the flames of possibility. In a slight twist from prior years, 2006 marked the first time the Amgen Tour of California was held, so instead of heading to Girona for the first few weeks of the season, I left Greenville and came out to Southern California to train. It paid off. Racing clean, I notched two stage wins—Stage 2, which finished in San Jose (and included the Category 1 climb up Sierra Road), and Stage 5, where we ended in Santa Barbara—and fourth in the General Classification in the inaugural race. Floyd Landis won the overall, but I was more than happy with my form after being tested amid the famous cities of the Golden State. It felt good to race in America on roads lined with crazed fans—almost one and a half million people in attendance throughout the week.

I headed to Europe immediately after racing in Cali, and even though the time zone displacement was brutal, by all indications my form was lining up perfectly. I was sprinting and time trialing where I needed to be if I wanted to contend in the Tour. My next big test was the Tour of Flanders. It had been a little over a month since I'd raced in the United States, and I'd acclimated well. The Tour of California had been great training, but it had taken me a little out of my comfort zone, since I'd broken from my usual routine. As one of the favorites, I was a little nervous, but cautiously optimistic about what I could accomplish.

It was raining slightly in Bruges's Grote Markt when 199 of us clipped into our pedals on April 2. The weather didn't end up being much of a factor; we had the usual winds and light drizzle for the first half of the race, but then brilliant sunshine brought us through the critical sections and to the finish line.

Physically, I felt great, but mentally I struggled mightily the first half of the race. One of my best friends and teammates, Michael Barry, crashed less than fifty kilometers in. The first few hours are always insanely nerve-racking. Just as in the traditional first week of the Tour, winning doesn't happen early on, but plenty can happen to take you out of contention.

We were going through the city of Roeselare, in the midst of a wide four-lane road, when the peloton swung to the left and I passed a guy, covered in blood, lying motionless in the middle of the pavement. It was Michael. I thought he was dead. An overwhelming feeling of nausea enveloped me. It was early in the race, so I dropped back to the team car to ask my directeur, Dirk Demol, what I should do. I wanted to quit the race and be with my friend. He told me Michael was going to be okay, that he had spoken with him, and that I should get back to the task at hand. I reiterated I didn't think Michael was all right, that I hadn't seen any part of his body moving. Dirk placated my anxiety, repeating his first statement and adding, "He'll be fine."

MICHAEL BARRY

I hit a barrier that was in the middle of the road as I came through a corner in the town of Roeselare. I don't remember the crash at all, but Eki (Viatcheslav Ekimov), who was on my wheel or close to me near the front, said we went from a four-lane road into the town. I came from the larger road to the smaller, the barrier was misplaced in the road, and I hit it straight on. I was either the first or second rider into the turn and couldn't avoid it.

Usually, an accident gets washed from my mind almost immediately, but for the first one hundred kilometers, nothing took my thoughts off Michael, what I'd seen, and how upset I was. It was incredibly hard to concentrate on the minutiae of the moment, given the bigger-picture questions that started to creep in. Besides what medical state Michael was in, I thought of my daughter, Julia, and whether or not my racing, and risking my life, was worth it.

I must have asked Dirk about Michael's status more than ten times, and each time he told me the white lie he knew I needed to hear. Michael was fine. He'd be okay. Everything would work out. Dirk knew all too well, from his own successes and time in the peloton, that in a race situation, even on the best of days, a rider's confidence is tenuous and needs to be protected.

MICHAEL BARRY

At the time, the team actually thought I might have died. The Discovery Channel team car turned the cameras off when they saw me on the ground.

Meanwhile, my teammate Matt White shepherded me back to the front, reiterated Dirk's mantra, and hoped I'd recommit to the cause of conquering the cobblestones underneath us. The key moment came on the Valkenburg climb with just over thirty kilometers left. My teammate Leif Hoste attacked up the climb, and only Quick Step's Tom Boonen could react. On the descent, Boonen's teammate, Paolo Bettini, acted the perfect foil, slowing down just enough to block our path and not allowing us to chase back on. By the finish, I had come close, winning the sprint for a place on the podium in third.

But it was a placing that perhaps could have been augmented. Deals are made in cycling all the time. Whenever you see two guys chatting in a breakaway, usually it has to do with brokering an outcome. Often the deal benefits both riders—one gets the win, the other gets some form of payment for helping, in a very subtle way, the desired result.

But immediately following the race, I wasn't concerned about my placing or prizes. I showered in the bus and headed straight to the hospital to check on my friend. It was a heavy situation.

MICHAEL BARRY

He came to the hospital to see me as soon as he was
finished, which meant a whole lot more to me than
he likely knew, as nobody else from the team had
come yet.

His wife, Dede, also a bike racer, was there by his side. Unbelievably, Michael started to apologize for not being there to help
me. He had watched the race, saw what had happened, and, battered from head to toe, focused more on his regret that he hadn't
been there for me than on the fact that he was almost roadkill.
There's a pro cyclist for you.

A week later, I was back at my main yearly objective, Paris–
Roubaix, looking to avenge my misfortune from Flanders. As was
the case the previous week, I went in as one of the favorites, based
on my form and my affinity for the conditions. Simply put, I was
ready. So was our Discovery Channel team. I'd done a massive
amount of visualization work leading up to the race, and all signs
pointed to me having a successful day.

Fifty kilometers in, however, a stupid crash wasted needless
energy. My teammate Benjamin Noval looked to the right at an in-
opportune time, and his bike drifted into mine, accidentally sending
me to the ground. I hurt my wrist, but I was so consumed and focused, I felt no pain, and eventually caught back up to the leaders.
As we passed sector after sector of pavé, my teammates turned themselves inside out in order to keep me in proper position near the front,
and it was the always intense race for positioning before the entrance
to the Arenberg Forest that caused the major split in the race.

The Arenberg has held its notable place in the Queen of the
Classics since 1968. It's not just the jarring element the cobbles
bring, but due to the path's narrowness, if anything happens to a

rider during the one-and-a-half-mile stretch—puncture or crash—
it's much harder for the team cars to reach and service them. The
cobblestones have been improved over the years, but the elements
add such an unknown factor that more often than not, I'd just hope
to guide my bike in a general path, rather than concentrate on
steering it to an exact place. No matter how much planning I devoted to the Arenberg, I never felt I was prepared enough for all
contingencies. It often gave me the impression I was riding into the
eye of a hurricane, hoping a mere umbrella and rain boots were
enough protection. In 1984, the legendary French manager Cyrille
Guimard, who at the time was running the Renault-Elf squad,
best described the respect this stretch of land deserved when he
commented, "By the end of Arenberg half of my riders were flat on
their backs, and the other half were flat on their faces."

Charging out of the Forest, there were only seventeen of us with
a legitimate shot, and I couldn't believe my luck. Not only had I
made it through unscathed, but I had two teammates with me—
Leif Hoste and Vladimir Gusev. Nine teams were represented, but
none had more riders than us, and surprisingly Tom Boonen, the
defending champion, had no one from Quick Step to aid his chances.
Numbers in a race like Roubaix are everything, and it was nothing
short of a miracle that the Discovery Channel's colors were the most
abundant in a lead group of that magnitude that late in the race.

As we rode through Sector 10, the three-kilometer stretch of
Mons-en-Pévèle, I was about two-thirds of the way back following
the wheels in front of me, focused on staying out of the worst part
of the path. All of a sudden, I felt like I was floating or skating on
a patch of ice. Incredibly, my handlebars had cracked completely
through. Instantly, my body awareness popped up my torso so I
was sitting with my arms in the air, trying to keep my balance as
if I were in the midst of a high-wire act. I drifted to the left of the

road, already running the scenarios through my head. To minimize the severity of the crash, I knew I needed to try to land in the dirt on the berm, but I had no way to direct my bike, so I leaned to the left and subtly shifted my hips as well. It might have worked had the handlebars not gone into my front wheel. I might as well have been launched from a cannon. I was thrown forward and down, as my bike stopped and my body kept going. Due to the angle of the edge and the way my body landed, my right shoulder took the brunt of the blow, and I knew instantly something was broken.

Shock took over. Even though my body hurt, and I knew something wasn't right, the tiniest of voices kept trying to be heard, saying, "Get up! Get back in the race!" I'd always been able to get up and soldier on, but this felt different. I sat in the dirt and dust and tried to cope with the disbelief. I'm not sure if it was more from the pain or the bad luck, which seemed to have robbed me of my best chance ever to achieve my dream.

I was soon surrounded by fans, cameramen, Johan, and the team mechanics. With the world watching live, everyone tried to assess me and my bike and make sense of the damage. With my right arm hanging limp by my side, all I could do was hide my head and wonder why. It had all seemed within my grasp. Anger welled up inside me.

Recovery should be a four-letter word, at least in terms of coming back from injury. It's as much of a struggle mentally as it is physically. I was carted off to a French hospital, my despondency at having missed my best opportunity to win Paris–Roubaix as painful as my shoulder. Even though I was treated on French soil, I immediately flew back to the United States and went to see my doctor at the Steadman Hawkins Clinic in Greenville.

The shoulder was set, and the slow process of healing began.
I spent only a few days off the bike. My depression, compliments
of the Hell of the North, was quickly replaced by the white-light,
mind-splitting pain of my shoulder, and I was further fueled by my
eternally optimistic forward focus. I couldn't ride outside; there was
no way the doctors would allow me to risk reinjuring the bone. Not
that I wanted to. I embraced the notion I would be on the indoor
training bike for the foreseeable future. Besides the monotony, the
hardest part of the recovery was regaining mobility. My shoulder
wanted to protect itself and freeze in the least painful position, both
on the bike and off.

I spent two weeks inside, moving my legs and passing scen-
ery that only existed in my mind. The rehab went smoothly and
uneventfully, and finally, I was able to ride outside. A short time
later, I headed off to our home in Girona with my family to begin
the European phase of my season. I dropped Mel and Julia off and
traveled south, straight to Valencia, to draw out blood to be saved
for the Tour. My early-season success confirmed that there was no
reason to diverge from the road map I had followed in 2005. Aside
from my injury, I'd raced extremely well in the first part of the year;
now it was time to follow the plan for the summer.

CHAPTER 22

IMMEDIATELY AFTER HAVING MY blood taken, I headed back to Girona and prepared to settle back into my routine. I couldn't have been more unprepared for the shock I received forty-eight hours after returning home.

I was getting a massage when Mel texted and said the testers were at our apartment. They had been sent by the United States Anti-Doping Agency (USADA), but were a contracted company out of Barcelona. I told her that I'd be back in an hour, then texted our team doctor to tell him I'd injected myself with one thousand units of EPO the night before, and to ask what I should do. His texted response was that I should definitely avoid taking the test. After another text exchange, I needed to be absolutely sure, so I took the risk and called Pedro (Dr. Pedro Celaya) to make sure I was correct in my interpretation of his messages.

In as veiled and coded a way as we could, he put any questions I had to rest.

"The process is a lot more refined."

"I did it last night."

"Way too risky. There's a chance maybe you are okay, but maybe not. And then that outcome could be very severe."

Comparatively, our team doctor was one of the good guys. He cared about our health and what happened to us. For him to be this direct made me sweat and my hair stand on end.

My massage continued to go on while I listened; then I started feverishly texting on my BlackBerry again. I told Mel to tell the testers I'd be back in an hour, and then told her to wait until they left, then get out of the house. I typed, "Bring Julia, rent a car, and I'll meet you at the train station as soon as I can." She replied that she was worried, but that she'd do it. With the masseuse's every touch, I became more agitated and less relaxed. Every minute, the knots might have been reduced in my legs, but the knot in my stomach multiplied exponentially. It was the worst massage ever. I was trying to keep my life from being ruined. Plus, to minimize any red flags, I figured I needed to stay on the table and finish the massage. It would be harder to explain abruptly leaving than to deal with the torturous thirty minutes I had left lying prone.

After what seemed like an eternity, the massage ended and I made my way the one kilometer to the train station, furtively glancing at each person I passed, wondering if they were one of the Barcelona testers. I found Mel at the train station, waiting in the car. Julia was in her baby seat in the back. Mel, to put it mildly, was not happy, but I was affected more. She had been aware of my drug use—I had confided in her early in our relationship—but not what I had done the previous evening. Even though she'd been peripherally aware, this was the first time my drug taking had had a direct effect on her. Aside from her incredulousness, I had to deal with the immediacy of getting out of town. We just drove toward the Costa Brava, but with no real destination in mind, just to get away. Away from Girona. Away from the testers. Away from what I'd just put my family through. Away from my past life.

I'd already been leaning toward not using drugs, but I'd finally had my epiphany. It wasn't worth it. None of it. Risking my career, abruptly uprooting my family, the nervousness, the planning, the attempts to fool the governing bodies. Out-of-competition testing wasn't as refined as it is today. We knew testers wouldn't show up after 10 or 11 p.m., and our injections were at night. Due to our conservative approach, usually anything we took would be out of our systems, or could be flushed out to undetectable levels by drinking copious amounts of water, by the morning. That said, missing a test was still preferable to testing positive, so our core group of American riders in Girona always had a system. If one of us was being tested, we'd send an alert to everyone in town. Our early-warning system had worked like a charm for years, but it was a form of Russian roulette, and now I wanted out. I was sick of it all. I made the decision, driving a rented Peugeot on the backcountry roads of Spain, staring over at my wife, that I was never going to use drugs again. Aside from deciding to marry Melanie, it was the firmest, most concrete decision I've ever made.

TEJAY VAN GARDEREN, FRIEND AND FORMER TEAMMATE

He took a leap of faith. He was used to a certain standard, and without knowing whether he'd be able to stay there, he decided it was important to TRY. That's worth a lot of respect. I can't imagine having to do that.

If I'd been seeing life through rose-tinted glasses, now those lenses were crystal clear. And it was such a relief. The floodgates had opened and the drive to change my sport took hold. I texted Michael Barry from the car to tell him what had happened and that Mel and I would be out of town for the night. He suggested we spend the night at his place, which I eventually did, deciding, however, that Mel should return home with Julia in case the testers came back again the next morning. We didn't want to make it seem too obvious that we had avoided my test by fleeing town.

At Michael's, even though he knew, in general, the methods I'd been using, I finally shared in detail everything I'd done. I followed up by saying I had reached my breaking point, and was now going to do everything I could to steer the sport in a better direction. Michael had never been on a Tour de France squad, so he never went to the lengths that many of the rest of us did to assure ourselves the best chance of winning. But he had had his own doping regime, and upon hearing my story, he agreed to stop as well.

MICHAEL BARRY

For me, it was a clear moment. I decided it was not how I wanted to live my life. It was not why I started biking. Even though we protected our past, we wanted a better future for the riders coming up. George stopped when he felt a form of guilt. You know you're doing something wrong when you put the people you love at risk.

The blood bag I took out in Valencia never got put back into my body, but I never felt healthier. I knew it would be a big challenge to stay at the same racing level, but I liked that aspect of it. The integrity of my new goal gave me the drive to give everything. I told Johan that I was done with it all. I explained that I had hit my fork in the road, and the reasons behind it, and he understood, agreeing that I didn't have to do anything. From that moment on, he never forced me to go back on my word.

With my decision and fresh outlook weighing heavily on my mind, I headed to the 2006 Dauphiné Libéré. I was nervous, even though my training showed I shouldn't be. My deal with myself also included reaching out to others to try to convince them that clean racing was the change the sport needed. I talked to my Discovery Channel squad, and convinced those who were thinking of doing blood bags at the Tour to forgo them. It was a small victory with a profound effect on me and the team. I'd taken a chance reaching out to them, and they'd reacted the way I had hoped. They were making a small step in the right direction, knowing full well it was going to affect our results. Fans and press would question why we weren't contending in stages as well as other teams, and as well as we had in the past. We were all willing to take that risk, and we did so together.

Aside from my teammates, I spoke with most of the Americans who lived near me. Christian Vande Velde, David Zabriskie, and Michael Barry didn't need any convincing. I was like an overeager, newly converted Hare Krishna you'd see at an airport. If I sensed an opening, I'd talk to anyone. I spoke with Óscar Pereiro and Alejandro Valverde, whom I could converse with in Spanish, and implored them to help me change this fucked-up sport. The doping had been going on way too long and it needed to stop. If we could start change from within, it would be a lot more effective than any new tests that might be in the pipeline. If we could convince enough people, we wouldn't have to worry about the majority having an unfair advantage.

Once I made my decision in Girona, I never wavered. My elation after meeting with my teammates continued through the prologue, where I finished second, just two seconds behind my friend David Zabriskie, who was racing for Team CSC. If I felt I was batting a thousand as an agent of change, I got brought down to earth pretty quickly when my next attempt to convert one of the sport's stars was an epic strikeout. After Stage 2 or 3, I can't remember, I sat down with Floyd Landis and tried to convince him we had a chance, and a responsibility, to help our sport. With more passion than I'd outwardly shown in a very long time, I laid out my points: We're the top American riders. Why risk getting caught anymore? We can *lead* the change in cycling.

Floyd, racing for Phonak at the time, squared his jaw, looked me right in the eye, and said, "Fuck you, George. I want to win the Tour de France."

CHAPTER 23

I ENDED UP TENTH OVERALL at the Dauphiné, almost seven minutes behind the winner, American Levi Leipheimer. Floyd finished sixtieth, almost an hour behind. He didn't care; his focus was only on July. Everything we did, we did for the Tour. Even after Lance, after we all split as teammates, our old mentality was what we knew. It's what made my breaking away from that way of thinking so rewarding.

The Tour de France began in Strasbourg, and with Lance's retirement, it was billed as the most wide-open race in years. But what blew the race apart, before it even began, was the Spanish investigation into the practices of Dr. Eufemiano Fuentes, dubbed Operación Puerto.

The first news broke on May 23, when the Spanish police arrested the directeur sportif of Liberty Seguros-Würth, Manolo Saiz. But the biggest bombshell exploded just two days before the start of the Tour, when details compiled by the Spanish paper *El País* were finally made public, and fifty-six riders, including Jan Ullrich and Ivan Basso, were listed as being clients of Fuentes and were subsequently pressured by the Tour organizers, ASO, to not take part. As a result, none of the riders who placed in the top five of the 2005 race were on the start line for the 2006 edition. The podium possibilities grew exponentially due to the withdrawal of so many riders. It was a scandal on par with the Festina affair in 1998, and it was a public relations body blow to the sport. I hated to see the negative publicity surrounding what should have been our biggest celebration of the year, but selfishly, I was happy I didn't have to worry about looking over my shoulder. I felt absolved, and relieved, because I was out of the doping game and didn't have to worry about my results coming back to haunt me.

I completely redefined my tactics for the three weeks. I knew I no longer had a chance to contend for the overall win at a grand tour, even though I'd been close to Floyd and the others during the early part of the year. I approached the Tour as a series of one-day races, each giving me a chance for greatness, but collectively, I'd have to concentrate on survival and being highly selective in my energy expenditures. As my approach broadened, my focus narrowed. My mantra became "My family loves me no matter my results."

Day after day during the 2006 Tour, I knew who was using. I could read the "tea leaves" in the results. At times, it was hard to accept the successes of others, knowing it came at the expense of honesty and that for all intents and purposes, it could have been me standing onstage. The world expected and assumed one thing, while I was able to tell that certain riders blatantly flaunted their disregard for the boundaries. I'd been a member of the pro peloton for a long time and thought I'd seen it all, but nothing before or since topped Stage 17 of the 2006 Tour, the final mountain stage and the last day in the Alps.

Floyd had lost the yellow jersey the day before, having one of his worst days on the bike, at the absolute worst possible time. He lost close to nine minutes to a number of his rivals and had to hand back the *maillot jaune* to Caisse d'Epargne's Óscar Pereiro. Everyone counted Floyd out after his miserable performance. He was now eight minutes and eight seconds out of first with only one mountain stage and one time trial left. Floyd had already shown, via his response to me at the Dauphiné, that he was willing to risk everything to be the champion. Desperate times called for desperate measures. Floyd Landis needed a miracle. The one the world thought he got was really a nightmare he created on his own.

Stage 17 was two hundred kilometers (122 miles) long, with five climbs and incredible heat that was already eighty-six degrees at the start. At the base of the first climb, the breakaway had over eleven minutes on the peloton. Before we got there, Floyd had ridden around the whole bunch, taunting us all by pointing and proclaiming, "You'd better take your caffeine pills, you'd better take whatever you have, even if it's just aspirin. I'm going to destroy you all today!" He seemed to relish riding by me, David Zabriskie, and Christian Vande Velde in particular. He gave us a focused stare: "Guys, get ready. I'm going to shred." He mocked us, and showed a level of arrogance I'd never seen.

CHRISTIAN VANDE VELDE

That was one of the fastest days on the bike I've ever seen, or been a part of. I was very happy I'd made the decision "enough is enough" before that Tour. I didn't have any animosity toward Floyd. He'd made his own bed. Our directeur at CSC, Bjarne Riis, had made a point before the race: "Worry about yourselves." So it didn't matter to me what Floyd or others did; I was just doing my job. But I rode my guts out that day, and we didn't even make a dent into his time.

Like a cycling version of Babe Ruth's famous called shot in the 1932 World Series, Floyd proceeded to make the world's best professionals look amateur. On the Col des Saisies, Floyd's team, Phonak, gave it their all and whittled down the peloton. Floyd grew impatient, passed his whole squad, and took off on his own, pulling, at least momentarily, the other GC contenders with him. Mick Rogers, riding for T-Mobile that year, told me afterward that Floyd was going so fast and holding more than five hundred watts for so long on the climb that there was no way Mick could even stay in his draft after a few seconds. Along with Rogers, Andreas Klöden (T-Mobile), Cadel Evans (Davitamon-Lotto), and Carlos Sastre (CSC) all dropped back to the yellow jersey group in an attempt to regroup and hit back. Floyd Landis had just ridden the best in the world off his wheel. And he wasn't done.

At the top of the Saisies, Floyd was three minutes behind the leaders and three minutes ahead of his other rivals for the title. He'd made up eight minutes on the lead group in one climb, and gapped some of the best climbers in the world by 180 seconds. The rest of the climbs followed the same script. Floyd flew up and over them all, making mountains seem like mere hills. Everyone else suffered. By the end, Floyd had won, with Carlos Sastre in second, a colossal five minutes and forty seconds back. Óscar Pereiro kept yellow, but only barely: twelve seconds ahead of Sastre and thirty ahead of Floyd. In one fell swoop, Landis was back in control.

The world was amazed. Astounded. Effusive. Anthony Tan of cyclingnews.com used the subtitle "Raging Phonak Freak Turns *Groupe Maillot Jaune* Upside Down" and wrote, "Without a shadow of a doubt, today will go down as one of the finest stages in modern Tour de France history. Today, a twenty-eight-year-old American by the name of Floyd Landis, written off by most after his collapse of yesterday, staged a comeback that defied logic. And in one fell swoop, he finds himself back in contention to win the 2006 Tour de France."

Tan had recounted something he thought was amazing, but it was based on a lie. I knew it. Everyone in the peloton knew it. The switch had been flipped on the ticking time bomb.

DAVE ZABRISKIE
At the time, a part of me thought it was impressive,
but I knew he was doping.

We all said the right things afterward, attempting to draw attention away from what we felt was the obvious fact that Floyd was doped to the gills for the stage. Four days after the Tour finished and Floyd had fulfilled his dream of winning the Tour de France, his downward spiral began. Phonak announced he had tested positive. And his saga was only beginning. When I heard the news, I thought, Oh fuck. Not for Floyd, but for our sport. I would have preferred not to see him get caught, only because of what it meant to cycling. I didn't care that he lost his win, but I did care how much it was going to cost us all. Still, a part of me acknowledged that it served him right for being so stupid. It had been hard watching him get all the attention as he became an instant rock star, and I'd be lying if I didn't admit to being a little envious—for those few days. My envy was quickly replaced by relief as I watched him struggle through press conferences and interviews, his half-truths designed to give himself possible legal loopholes in his defense.

Floyd's bust overshadowed what, for me, was a Tour filled with mixed emotions. I finished second in the prologue, only one one-hundredth of a second behind Thor Hushovd (Crédit Agricole). I was devastated to lose out on wearing yellow by such a close margin, but the margin gave me a goal for the next day. To take that yellow jersey right off his shoulders.

Stage 1 had three intermediate sprint bonuses and on the last

one of the day, I figured out that if I won the bunch sprint, I'd
get two bonus seconds and place third. Luckily, my lunge for the
intermediate line paid dividends, and when coupled with Thor
Hushovd's accident near the finish, I found myself in the lead of
the world's biggest race.

It was the first, and only, yellow jersey of my career. That night,
at our team meeting, Johan used my result to try to rally the rest of
the team. He noted that even though we didn't have an overall guy
for the race, what I'd done earlier in the day showed what all of us
could do this Tour. See a move. Act on our instincts. Employ split-
second tactics. Get results.

My day in yellow was almost like an out-of-body experience. It
was weird: the eyes of the world were upon me, and even my fellow
riders acted differently. I never won Paris–Roubaix or the Tour of
Flanders, the two races that meant the most to me. But I wore the
leader's jersey at the Tour de France. And it mattered. That morning, I got goose bumps putting it on and riding to the line to start
the stage. I knew I would probably lose it by day's end, so maybe
that made my time a little sweeter. I didn't want Stage 2 to end.
The last half of the day I spent with an almost overbearing feeling
of longing weighing me down.

Ironically, I was almost able to feed my addiction a second time,
when in Stage 3, near the end, the climb up the Cauberg gave me
a surprise chance. My teammate Yaroslav Popovych and I found
ourselves right next to each other in the closing kilometer, and I
screamed, "Go, Popo, go!" He led me out, and we were passing
people like they were standing still—our speed was a full four to
five kilometers per hour faster. About one hundred meters before
the line, Italian Alessandro Ballan (Lampre) moved to the left, cut
in front of us, and killed all the momentum we'd built up. The precious bonus seconds I was after were gone in an instant.

As good as I had felt as the leader of the Tour, by the time we entered the Pyrenees, in the race's second week, I was close to cracking. Stage 11, from Tarbes to Pla de Beret, brought me face-to-face with my new reality, and even though I tried to project bravery outwardly, my wife, Mel, was able to see right through me.

On the penultimate climb, the Col du Portillon, I blew up, the pace and heat too much to handle, and lost contact with the main group of contenders. By the time I had made it to the climb of Pla de Beret, I was barely able to keep my legs moving or hold on to the handlebars. Mel had positioned herself at the bottom, on the side of the road with Julia in her arms, about eight miles from the finish. I was more than twenty minutes behind the leaders, and all I wanted to do was get off my bike. I had been down on myself for a large part of the stage, believing I'd never be competitive again. I wanted to quit more than at any other time in my life. I looked at her as I passed, and I could see she knew how much I was suffering. She started to cry. I became almost crippled with devastation. It was one thing to be in pain, but I felt that to make her share in that was totally unfair.

It seemed to take forever, but I finally made it to the finish. Crossing under the banner, any hope I had of somehow being a grand tour rider was extinguished, and any dream I had of quickly influencing my competition to race *pane e acqua* (Italian slang for racing clean, literally meaning "bread and water") was gone as well. I knew Floyd was going to use during the Tour, but Levi Leipheimer had told me he was on board the "clean train," so when he finished second to Denis Menchov, and ahead of Floyd, on the stage, I guessed he'd gone back on his word to me (he later confirmed his usage in his affidavit). It was like a kick in the gut. But it was also a stark reminder that I had made my decision for *me,* and I couldn't expect anyone else to be on the same timetable. I was confident that eventually other people would change too.

The only time I lost my cool throughout the three weeks was

when Lance came to visit us in the Alps. At that point, we'd been racing almost three weeks, and even on the best of days I had little patience for stupidity. He was enjoying his time as a VIP and riding in the car on stages, but one night he spoke to the team and told us that we were all sucking and needed to pick it up. It really pissed me off to hear him call us out, when part of the reason why we all felt the way we did and were not getting the desired results was that we had decided to not use doping products. And that directly related to him. We were being cautious, in a small way, to protect his legacy. Lance being Lance, he just wanted results, and in the heat of the moment, he didn't think through the idea that if we got busted for anything, it could ultimately come back on him. At the time, I thought, What the fuck, dude, really?! You're saying *this* to *us*?!

By the end in Paris, the Tour had been a complete disappointment for the team, but I left satisfied. Even though I'd come close to throwing in the towel in the mountains, by the time I rode onto the Champs-Élysées, I was able to embrace the broader significance of the past three weeks. Winning a stage and wearing the jersey "clean" were major stepping-stones in reaffirming my choices. During that month, I'd confirmed two things to myself. One, I'd made the right decision weeks prior when I chose to forgo doping, and two, I knew I could still be successful in the sport.

Next, I headed to the Tour of Benelux in Holland, and almost won the eight-day race, crashing on the final stage and finishing second by one second. In September, as I got ready to race the U.S. National Road Race Championships, held in my hometown for the first time, my confidence was at an all-time high. I knew I was in shape, I knew the course like the back of my hand, and I knew it was my last race of the season.

I'd lived in Greenville for six years, and this was the first chance a lot of my friends had to see me race. The climb up Paris Mountain (a little over two miles long with a gradient of almost 7 percent) was hard enough to make us all suffer, and as it was the highest local point of the Blue Ridge Mountains, the race organizers made good use of it. Since each of us lacked teammates, David Zabriskie, Levi Leipheimer, and myself all agreed to form an alliance and help one another throughout the race, with the understanding that eventually it would be every man for himself.

The world does not attach a huge amount of value to the U.S. national title, but when I crossed the line first, it was a win that meant more to me than many others. Not just the honor of wearing my country's colors, but based on the decisions I'd made over the past year, and where I won it. It was my last race of the season, and it was a final message to myself that my new path was the right one.

In October 2006, Discovery Channel signed Italian Ivan Basso, a perennial contender in the grand tours, but someone with a past very much like the rest of ours. I saw it as a clear sign that the team was not going to embrace my approach, but return to the status quo of past eras. I decided I wanted out. The only problem was that I was under contract for another year, but I wanted to explore the possibility of racing with like-minded guys.

I e-mailed Bob Stapleton, the man in charge of the T-Mobile squad for which my good friend Michael Barry was riding. Stapleton ran his team on a platform of change. A savvy businessman who had made a fortune in the telecom industry, he knew marketing and how to read trends in business. He understood that cycling needed a new look and message, and was eager to be part of the next wave of success. I asked him in my first e-mail if he would be interested in my racing for him. His response was emphatic and direct: "Hell, yeah."

My e-mail to Bob centered on my belief in his vision of the sport, affirming how much I thought his idea of change was needed.

I told him I could be one of the leaders he felt should be impactful and influential. I knew my current team did not feel the way I did, and the chance to be part of a dramatic change in my sport had me excited.

I had no idea how to approach getting out of my contract, so I called Lance and asked his advice. After his initial shock, he said he'd talk to Bob Stapleton and Bart Knaggs, his business partners in the Discovery Channel team. I flew to Austin, where they all live and where their offices are located, for a special meeting. Once we were all together, I immediately felt uncomfortable and figured it was a big mistake. They asked me what they needed to do to get me on the team and to keep me happy. I didn't feel comfortable talking about being anti-doping, since I didn't know if Lance had ever confided in them the lengths to which we had gone. I felt extremely weird not knowing what they knew, so in the end, I made up something about how I wanted to be a true team leader and I knew I couldn't have that role on Discovery. In reality, with the signing of certain riders, I assumed the old methods were going to be used.

They were very clear in their response. The answer was no, based mainly on the fact that he and his partners felt it would be a PR nightmare. I'd be considered a traitor—an American going to a German team. I couldn't come out and say I didn't want to dope, and there wasn't a clear way to spin the real reason to the media. I wasn't going to press them, and in my usual nonconfrontational style, I thought to myself, Okay, well, you gave it your best shot. You wanted to leave, but it didn't work out. And that was it. I e-mailed Bob Stapleton back and said I hoped he'd keep me in mind next year, and I spent the off-season training and knowing I'd be in Discovery kit for another year.

BOB STAPLETON

George had expressed a serious desire to join us, and
even though I was reasonably sure he'd done some
things, I believed in his sincerity. I had taken an
open, interpretive view of who should be on the
team. I didn't think it was black-and-white. People
who had been through the experiences George had
still had valuable insight to give my young riders.
In my mind, George, and others like him, had tre-
mendous value because of it. I needed to educate
my riders on the good AND the bad, if I hoped
my group of twenty-five twentysomethings were
going to be successful. The potential to bring on
someone of George's caliber—with the inspirational
and genuine leadership role he could provide—was
too good to pass up. I was devastated when it didn't
work out for 2007.

CHAPTER 24

JOHAN BRUYNEEL HADN'T KNOWN I had met with Bob and Bart, so at training camp in Solvang, in January 2007, there were a few tense moments when he found out. I was never buddies with Johan, like Lance was. Our relationship was not personal; it was all business. He was not happy to learn I'd tried to leave his team, but after a few sarcastic comments, we settled back into our de facto relationship, and it seemed to be water under the bridge.

During the off-season, I'd confided in Rich and a few of my closest friends that I was done with my drug use. I told them all exactly what I felt, that I wasn't going to take any more risks, I was changing my ways, and I was looking forward to changing the sport. I was so happy, and a bit relieved—not one of the people I confided in asked questions. They simply said, "We support you 100 percent."

LANCE ARMSTRONG

George saw the sport evolving, and realized he'd taken risks for himself in the classics and for me in the Tour. We'd always been very conservative, but he felt it was the right time to change completely. When I found out about his decision, I had to respect him for his courage.

As I reconnected with my teammates in Southern California that January, they provided me with a huge amount of support for what I wanted to do. And even though I was nervous about the team's direction, I was resolute in my path.

My first race of the year was again the Tour of California. I'd spent a few weeks on the West Coast prior to the start, and for all intents and purposes, figured I would factor into the mix on a variety of stages. Instead, I withdrew on the second-to-last day, badly injured and wondering, What's next?

I had finished ninth in the prologue, eight seconds behind my teammate Levi Leipheimer. He had targeted the race, making no secret of his desire to win in his home state. My next best result came in the Stage 5 time trial, where I finished fifth, once again behind Levi, this time forty seconds in arrears. What this all meant was that in the pecking order of the traditional cycling hierarchy, I took the role of "team player." It was my job to make sure Levi was protected and assisted at all times.

On Stage 6, from Santa Barbara to Santa Clarita, our Discovery Channel squad went into a typical "prevent defense" mode. Levi held a twenty-one-second lead over Jens Voigt, who was racing for CSC, so our only objective was to control the race and mark Jens if he tried to cut into Levi's lead. Early on, my teammate Tony Cruz accidentally clipped my front wheel, and I went forcefully down on my left wrist. I immediately felt a shooting pain go up through my arm and thought, Oh, no, my wrist is totally fucked.

I went back to the medical car, and the doctor told me, "No, I think you can go on. You'll be okay."

I rode up to our team car, which Viatcheslav Ekimov, my old teammate, was driving in his new capacity as directeur sportif. I told him there was no way I could handle the pain, and I intended to drop out at the feed zone. I couldn't even hold on to the handlebars with my left hand, and even though I had been off the back for what seemed like an eternity, and had talked to numerous people as I sat up and got treated, as we entered the feeding area, I could see the back of the front group up ahead.

Now, my guilt took hold. The break was enough of a threat that theoretically, we could lose Levi's lead, and the jersey. I didn't want that on my conscience or record, so I decided to soldier on a little longer. Every bump I rode over, no matter how minuscule, brought tears to my eyes. Each jolt felt as if I was being stabbed in the wrist with a knife. Over the radio, I heard, "The gap's not coming down, we need to get to the front and close it."

So I went to the front and did what I did best: suffer in silence, and find a way to make the object of my focus a reality. By the end of the stage, I'd pulled the whole peloton most of the way into Santa Clarita and narrowed the gap to under a minute, which kept Levi in the leader's jersey.

With five hundred meters to go, I sat up and let the others contend for the glory. When I relaxed, and released my focus, a sea of pain filled my body. I looked down and didn't comprehend what I was looking at. My wrist was the size of a small Nerf football. They had to cut the glove off of my hand after I crossed the finish line. I went to the hospital immediately, wasn't able to start the last stage of the race, and had surgery on my wrist the next morning in Santa Monica.

The surgeon, Dr. Modabber, happened to be the same race doctor for the Tour of California who had told me I was okay to keep racing that day. He operated early the next morning so he could work the race's final stage, and he also arranged to have one of his family members pick me up at the hospital after surgery and take me to the race finish so I could watch the end of the race. The doctor has since become one of my closest friends.

RAMIN MODABBER, M.D.

Cyclists are a great group of athletes to care for: they are as dedicated to their trade as any group of athletes I take care of. They train long hours and make incredible sacrifices during their "work hours" and especially after hours—no different from me and my colleagues. George in particular has taught me a lot about pro cyclists and their unique psyche. Their mentality has incredible depth and complexity. So many words describe them: intense yet calm, regimented yet free-spirited, selfless yet selfish, explosive yet cool. Oftentimes, and certainly with George, all these words apply. George in general seems to be able to apply the right attribute at the right time, though not necessarily all the time (who does?). It is his guiding principle of "family first" that will keep him grounded, his fun-loving and boyish spirit that will keep him young, and his insecurity—a sense of almost being uncomfortable in his own skin—that will keep him hungry and striving to take care of those around him. He is more than just a patient I operated on; it is a pleasure to call him a friend.

Melanie and Julia had just left for Spain. After surgery, I called to tell them what had happened. I also broke the news that I needed them to get on the next plane home, and that I'd meet them in Greenville. They'd landed just two days before; now I needed them to head back to the airport.

MELANIE

The first day after flying back was always exhausting, because we had to get ready to "live" again in Spain. Cleaning, shopping, and making it a home. Our Internet was down, so I couldn't watch the race. When he called after the stage, I could tell from his sad voice that something was wrong. I felt incredibly bad that I was not there for him. The next morning, I talked with his surgeon after surgery, and even though everything had gone well, George was being stubborn about wanting to be taken to the finish of the race. He wouldn't relent. He'd already finished a stage with a broken hand, and now he had to be at the end for his teammates. It made me realize even more how dedicated he was to his team and his job. It was a short trip to Spain, but the experience made me so proud to be his wife.

RAMIN MODABBER, M.D.

He is still pissed at me for letting him ride more than a hundred miles with a broken wrist, but it really sums up who he is and how he is willing to put himself through pain or a monumental sacrifice to help others reach their goals—loyal lieutenant, greatest teammate ever, reluctant warrior, he's been called them all. They all fit.

I was home in South Carolina for six weeks. I missed the spring classics for only the second time in my career, having skipped them in 2003 due to complications from glandular fever. This time my cast made it more obvious to the general public why I wasn't doing my job. It was the last time in my pro career that I'd ever miss taking part in my favorite races. One of the feats of which I'm most proud is that in nineteen professional seasons, I only missed the spring stretch twice.

I got tired of the monotony of riding on my indoor trainer early on in my rehabilitation process, and asked Johan if I could compete in the Giro d'Italia in May to get some racing days in my legs. With the sudden withdrawal of one of the team's overall contenders, Johan was more than happy to have me fill up the vacated spot. I went to Italy with the understanding that I would race the first ten days, then exit and get ready for the Dauphiné. I loved racing in Italy, and it felt great to be back among the elite. It was hard to leave, but the plan was the plan.

In June, I actually ended up leaving the Dauphiné as well. I got sick with a stomach bug and dropped out. Getting a stomach virus can be the most devastating thing for a cyclist. The body is unable to absorb any nutrients, and eventually the caloric loss becomes insurmountable. With no fuel in the body, it begins to run on fumes, and even though I'd finished one-day races with a bad stomach, in a stage race, it becomes impossible to trick the math. As cyclists, we're already walking a fine line between calories taken in versus calories expended, and illness adds a wrinkle no one can smooth.

For the Tour de France, the team had options in 2007. Alberto Contador had signed with the team in January, showing excellent form in winning the Paris–Nice stage race in March. Levi's strong showing early in the season put his name on the list of favorites as well. I knew I'd be working for one of them, and that made my job easier. I didn't have the baggage of contender status I'd had the previous year, and that allowed me to focus on what I did best—get my leader(s) into position. Whether it was Alberto or Levi, the team knew they could count on me to slot into my normal service role once we rolled down the ramp in London, where the race kicked off that year. More important, Levi and Alberto knew I wouldn't pick favorites. It didn't matter to me who was the designated leader; I was going to do my job.

Alberto Contador ended up winning the 2007 Tour. The circumstances surrounding his victory were surprising, to say the least. Alberto was almost the polar opposite of Lance in how he led the team. The first time I'd ridden with Alberto was in June at the Dauphiné. Simply put, the way he led was by being the best on the road. Lance held us together with an iron fist and iron will, but Alberto was laid-back and wanted to be one of the boys. I got along with him fine. We often conversed in Spanish, which may have made him more comfortable with me. Ultimately, it was a twist of fate that decided the 2007 Tour title, not a battle on the road.

Rabobank's Michael Rasmussen looked to have the Tour wrapped up, but with only three days left, a shitstorm developed having to do with Rasmussen's whereabouts during the off-season and whether or not he had been truthful in declaring his location to drug testers. In a span of twelve hours, after Stage 16 and his summit win atop the Col d'Aubisque, Rasmussen went from leading the world's greatest bike race to being removed by his own team because too many questions remained unanswered. Just like that, what we all thought would be a casual ride into Paris for second place, became one final push to protect cycling's prime podium position.

Contador ended up winning the Tour by a mere twenty-three seconds ahead of Cadel Evans. I know exactly where those miscellaneous seconds came from.

Johan had told me to make sure I was in a position to help Alberto down the Col de Peyresourde, the last climb of the day on Stage 15. I was up the road, having made an earlier breakaway, but I held back and made sure to wait for Alberto. He caught me with about five hundred meters to go before the summit, and then once he locked onto my wheel, we bombed the descent. Along for the ride was Rasmussen, but what mattered most was distancing Cadel Evans, who'd been separated on the last climb. I'd been given my instructions—fly like the wind down toward the finish, and do everything I could to remove Rasmussen from our back wheel. I complied with all my energies, and even though I didn't dislodge "The Chicken," and we didn't know it on the day, we gained valuable seconds on Evans on that descent. By the time we crossed the line, we were nowhere near the winner, Alexander Vinokourov, but we'd gapped Cadel by forty-three seconds. No one circumstance or event wins the Tour, but descending with my usual aggressiveness on that day had gained us what would end up being *the difference* in winning the Tour.

I'd done my perennial job of leading another man to the finish line, but weirdly, the sensations I felt were different. It was only my second Tour de France without using any doping products, but the ride into Paris felt light-years away from the previous victories with Lance. I'd just been a part of my eighth Tour de France championship, and I couldn't have been more proud of doing it clean.

I knew my time with Johan and his crop of cohorts was limited. After being forced to stay with the team the previous fall, I'd been in negotiations during March and April to switch squads. While it didn't work out to move to Bob Stapleton's T-Mobile team for the 2007 season, we'd had a handshake agreement to make it work for 2008. It was an offer that came about based on great intentions, and with a minimal amount of negotiations.

Rich had taken over my representation for the 2007 season, more out of a desire to consolidate our business dealings within the family than anything else. I'd been with my previous agent, Clay Young, for seven years, and I was happy with everything he did. I simply got to the point where I felt that if someone was going to get paid to help me negotiate, why not my brother?

I wanted to be a vocal part of the change in my sport. Transparency was essential. From an organizational standpoint, that left only two options: Jonathan Vaughters's Slipstream squad or Bob Stapleton's T-Mobile team. Jonathan may have been one way as a rider, but he'd evolved into a man who believed racing clean was the only path for the future. Winning wasn't as essential as establishing the message. Jonathan talked to my brother, Rich, while I mainly talked to Christian Vande Velde and British rider David Millar, who were also on the Slipstream team. We quickly realized we all wanted the same thing.

JONATHAN VAUGHTERS

I knew we needed an anchor for the team. I knew George could perform clean. No one from his era was disadvantaged more by the culture than George. He never got the percentage bump in performance that guys he raced against did. It was simple math. Due to his naturally high hematocrit, which we'd both had tested when we were fifteen at the Olympic Training Center, I'd always known George did less enhancement than anyone.

He also had the experience we needed, and finally, we shared the same perspective on where the sport should go. We'd both helped mentor a young rider who was a perfect example of why we needed to change the culture.

Bob Stapleton flew in from France to meet Rich and me at an Atlanta airport hotel, and it was one of the most intense, awkward moments of my career.

RICH

Bob said he needed George as the face of his new team. George was supernervous during the meeting. For all his success on the bike, he'd never been in a negotiating environment, so he was out of his comfort zone. Bob, who's a very accomplished businessman, would make eye contact with George and not look away. Whether it was to intimidate him, I don't know, but George grew increasingly uncomfortable. We'd had our letter of intent, so this meeting was really to finalize the fine print. At one point, after asking us questions about our family, Bob, without saying a word, stared at us both for what seemed like an eternity. He finally exclaimed, "Guys, I gotta tell you, I don't like your body language." George blurts out faster than a kid confessing a crime, "No, no, we're fine!" I'm thinking, What the fuck? Where's Bob going with this?

During that meeting, I felt like a fish out of water. Slipstream had already agreed to our price, so that forced Bob to agree to it as well. Bob's businesslike approach was in stark contrast to Slipstream's laid-back style. Slipstream was a chance to ride with my friends, on an American team. As Bob ticked off everything he'd do for us, and met every demand, instead of being elated, I got more uncomfortable, realizing I was going to be forced to make a very tough decision.

Even though the meeting could not have gone better, I rushed to a bar with Rich afterward. I needed to calm my nerves, and I don't think I've ever consumed a glass (or maybe two) of red wine faster.

RICH

My biggest challenge was to get teams to understand that George's value wasn't based on winning.
It was the intangibles he brought to the table. My
sales pitch was: you can always find someone to win,
but it's harder to find someone to lead. That's why
George got paid well the last few years of his career.
His role morphed multiple times in a given day, race,
or season. He could be the field general or the calming influence, or provide the veteran experience.

BOB STAPLETON

Our team had had a rough spring. The sponsor (T-
Mobile) was disappointed. We started to question
whether we would be able to implement our ideas
and plan. George's signing was essential; it gave us
hope, and when it happened, we figured it would
fire up the team. I went to Mark Cavendish and told
him the news, and I'll never forget the look on his
face. This wry smile slowly spread from ear to ear.
His expression said it all, and as his eyes lit up, he
half questioned, half exclaimed, "Big George?!"

CRAIG LEWIS, FRIEND AND FORMER TEAMMATE

We call him Big George, and it's not for his size, it's
for the size of his heart. He gave, and continues to
give back, to cycling and those passionate about it.

MARK CAVENDISH

I grew up in the Lance era, and George was one of
the stars. Not only was he nice, but he also had a rep-

utation of being one of the most consistent riders ever. I'd heard from guys on my team how great a person he was too. If you were young, and you liked the cobbles, you pretended to be him. He was the man.

As 2007 drew to a close and I was finally able to sever ties with Discovery Channel, I knew I was on the right path. It had been a decade since I'd had to take a leap of faith and be part of a new team. It forced me to test the limits of my comfort zone. As with most of the changes I had experienced in my life, I was enlivened by the challenge.

CHAPTER 25

WE HAD TWO TEAM-BUILDING trips at the end of 2007. The first included our wives and/or girlfriends, when we all traveled to Cologne, Germany, for a retreat. It was near the T-Mobile headquarters in Bonn, and the T-Mobile people went out of their way to make us all feel welcome.

BOB STAPLETON

We were all a little nervous about the media's reaction to an American being on Germany's team, especially the guy who was integral in Lance beating Jan Ullrich all those years. Telekom (the parent company of T-Mobile) employed almost a quarter of a million people, the German government was part owner, and the company put cycling on the map for a nation of eighty million. To them, Jan Ullrich was bigger than Lance. But I had complete control over the roster, and I told the rest of management they had to trust me on George. I was viewed as a maverick manager, and I trusted my gut. I just knew it would work.

BRIAN HOLM, FORMER DIRECTEUR SPORTIF AT T-MOBILE/HIGHROAD

George brought some class to the team when he arrived. He was a star. Bob thought it would be good for our image, and so did I. From the very beginning there was respect for him because he let his legs do the talking, instead of his mouth.

It was a great introduction to the staff and structure of the new team. I was excited by the possibilities, and everything I saw reaffirmed I'd made the right step in deciding to come here. It had been a calculated business decision to separate my past self from my new vision. Now, it just felt right.

MELANIE

I'd been so nauseous and dizzy at the Atlanta airport, I had to sit on the floor while we were waiting to check in. After I ate a huge breakfast I felt better, but I slept through the whole flight except for the meals. We had an amazing hotel room on the main street in Cologne, and after his meetings, George had to force me out of bed to come down and eat lunch. The wine during meals made me want to throw up. Afterward, I told him I'd just go up and get a jacket before we walked around the town. I went back to bed until dinner. George was so mad.

We later found out she was pregnant with our second child, our son, Enzo, who would end up being born in June 2008. Chalk one up to male insensitivity.

MELANIE

I'd had a feeling I might be pregnant during our time
in Germany, so I made George stop on the way home
from the airport. I lied and told him I needed Tylenol,
when in fact I bought a pregnancy test. When we got
home, it was positive, and I rushed out into the garage
to tell George, who was unpacking his bike. He was
so happy, he hugged me right away, and he couldn't
stop apologizing for how he had acted.

The next team trip was in December to Mallorca, an island in
the Mediterranean off the coast of Spain. This was the first real opportunity for me to ride with my new teammates and get a handle
on their habits, on and off the bike. I was assigned to room with
Mark Cavendish, the mercurial sprinter who was making waves
wherever he raced. He was so fast, so passionate, and so flamboyant. Part of my job was to mentor Mark and guide him, since at
twenty-two, he was only beginning what clearly was going to be
an illustrious career.

Our first day at training camp was like someone's first day at
college. Mark got to the room in our nonglamorous hotel first, so
when I arrived, it was all set up with his gear. I thought, Oh, man,
this is going to be a long ten days. As with any relationship, it took
time. After a couple of awkward days, we began to feel comfortable
around each other, and instead of asking the usual superficial questions, we really started to bond.

Mark was into the history of the sport, the Tour de France in
particular. His passion also extended into style and fashion, which
only solidified in my mind that cycling was for him. He wanted me
to tell him Tour stories, and what it was like to ride with Lance.
I was surprised by how well versed he was in Tour history, and
genuinely impressed. This wasn't a guy who just wanted to win; he

wanted to put his name among those of the greats he'd read about in the history books.

We both knew why we'd been roomed together. He was a fire-cracker, the new guy with limitless potential. I was the laid-back veteran, the one to help him chart his path, giving texture and meaning to the experiences that lay ahead. It was a case of yin and yang if there ever was one. We joked about it nonstop, and I couldn't have been happier getting to know him.

That camp in Mallorca was a quick introduction into Bob Stapleton's philosophy—we were going to train to be prepared for every race, and to win.

BOB STAPLETON

The year 2007 was tough. We were caught in a firestorm of controversy that predated our management. The best way to garner publicity, get the sponsors on our side, and drive home our message was to win. George was the key ingredient that was missing, the field general with the depth of experience. He was the man that could accelerate the learning curve of my young squad. We were building a clean and competitive team, but no one would notice unless we won. We needed success to make not only our own athletes but others believe.

Bob's strategy was simple and left little room for error. Surprisingly, our band of merry men seized hold of its essence and never wavered. André Greipel, the big German sprinter, who would later go on to win multiple grand tour stages, had come into our Mallorcan camp in top form. He was getting ready for the Tour Down Under and was riding so well, it was never a question of *whether* I would get dropped on the training rides, it was merely a matter of *when*. It was the most structured, and most serious, camp I'd attended. Whether it was team time trial training or intervals, we were expected to perform at 100 percent.

By the time our first camp of 2008 rolled around, we were all incredibly fit and connected. Between the trips to Cologne and Mallorca, I felt I really knew my teammates and what their personalities and roles would be in a race situation. The February camp took place in Pismo Beach, California, before we raced the Tour of California. It was the final chance for us to work out the kinks and a final opportunity to define our message.

BOB STAPLETON

T-Mobile had left as the title sponsor of the team, I hadn't found a replacement, so at this point, we were simply known as Team Highroad. To most of us, the meaning was obvious. We were going to be a new team with a new attitude—we would take the high road in everything we did, in every way we conducted ourselves. I wanted to have the camp in Pismo Beach as a way to introduce the team to the U.S. media, but also send a message to my own guys. Now that T-Mobile was no longer the sponsor, we weren't tied to the past and could cleanly move into the future. George had shown great leadership, and the guys had gravitated to him in the first camp. Now I just prayed it would translate in the midst of a race.

MARK CAVENDISH

George brought unity to the team. In 2007, it was the Germans and the non-Germans. In 2008, we were more cohesive. That was due to George.

The 2008 Tour of California brought a whole slew of frustrations and challenges. I crashed and suffered a concussion in Stage
1. As we sped into Santa Rosa, I was leading out one of our young,
talented German sprinters, Gerald Ciolek, and as I peeled off to
the side, Belgium's Tom Boonen ran me over. I landed headfirst
and was definitely dazed as I struggled to get up and cross the line.
Ciolek would end up finishing second, and it was a second day of
frustration following Bradley Wiggins's runner-up placing the day
before in the prologue.

Two days later, Stage 4 ended in San Luis Obispo, Bob's hometown. As a team, we wanted to win as a thank-you gesture to Bob
for all the work he'd put into our success. In cycling, nothing is ever
easy. Stage 4 tested my resolve as nothing had before. In nearly two
decades of professional racing, it was the coldest day I ever spent on
the bike.

The day began in Seaside, and the steady rain and whipping
winds only increased in volume and intensity for the full seven
hours we were in the saddle. In one day, we paid back the karmic
gods for the two years of near-perfect weather we'd enjoyed while
racing the California roads. I trembled the whole day, nothing I put
on seemed to help warm my core, and it was such a struggle to eat
or drink, I had to force food down my throat. My body wanted to
shut itself off in order to not have to deal with the elements.

Guys were stopping and simply getting off their bikes. For most
of the world's best, dropping out of the race was never an easier
decision. But for our team, it was different. We were motivated by
a greater good, and as I looked at my breakaway companions, I was
driven to not let Bob down. Sizing up the competition is easier on
the toughest days. Guys telegraph their condition and their intentions with less subterfuge. As I looked around, I liked my chances.
Most of the men surrounding me were guys I knew who I was
confident I could beat. I started to think, I've got this.

With about fifteen kilometers to go, our whittled-down bunch regrouped, and after some gamesmanship, Canadian Dominique Rollin (Toyota-United) pulled through and didn't look back. I cockily thought to myself, I'll just let him dangle off the front for a while; he'll tire himself out, and then I'll close the gap. But five kilometers later, after I decided to surge and bring him back, it was very clear the gap was not coming down, and in fact was increasing. Control quickly became panic as I asked my body for more, and there was nothing for it to give. I didn't know Rollin was a Quebecois and used to racing in less than ideal conditions. I also had no clue he was a former Canadian time trial and road race champion. As frustrating as it was, I had to give Rollin credit for outsmarting us all. He simply rode away from us and eventually won by around twenty seconds. I finished second, but my disappointment was overshadowed by Bob's—he really wanted to win going into his hometown. That may have been his first experience that drove home the point that cycling isn't like business, where results can be calculated and tweaked to a desired outcome. The one silver lining? On a day when the racing world was sent reeling by the conditions, we did not have one person drop out. We'd passed a test of commitment to a cause that counted as much as a stage win.

I got my chance to make amends a few days later, on Stage 7, Santa Clarita to Pasadena. It was the last chance for the team to break through our bedeviling bad luck.

The day before, Mark Cavendish seemed to have won the stage into Santa Clarita, but the race officials decided to penalize him when he was deemed to have returned to the peloton too quickly after a crash and bike change with about five kilometers to go. Needless to say, we were all a bit fired up, and fueled with the desire for redemption, as we took the line for the final day of the race.

MARK CAVENDISH

Bob hadn't been happy with the relegation, or how we had performed as a team. He sat the managers down and made it clear we'd almost run out of chances. That message was passed on to the riders, and in typical George fashion, he took matters into his own hands to motivate through example.

Conditions were moderately miserable again. It wasn't certain that we'd be able to get through the San Gabriel Mountains via the race route, but eventually Millcreek Summit was deemed passable, and away we went. I made the selection again, and was determined to deliver our first win on American soil. Once we got into Pasadena and onto the four 7.2-kilometer circuits, I found out afterward, both Bob and directeur sportif Allan Peiper questioned whether I should continue to work with the break or sit up and conserve energy, wait for the catch, and help Cav go for the final win. They were waffling as to the best use of resources, and which gamble of the team's ambitions gave them a greater chance of success. Bob and Allan were nervous I'd expended too much energy and depleted my resources a few days before.

BRIAN HOLM

I first met George in 1994, when he won a race in the Tour of Luxembourg. I was immediately impressed by his talent, but it wasn't until I saw him on our team that I realized there was so much more. He taught me how important it was to have a great "road captain" on the team—a rider who could always be a dark horse for the win, but also keep everyone on the squad focused and motivated. George was able to look out for the entire group's interests, while being one of the best at making difficult in-the-moment decisions.

I was happy they chose me. I didn't feel any pressure, I just calculated the possibilities as I looked around at the other four men in the front. Unlike in Stage 4, I knew all these guys well. Jason McCartney and Michael Creed were former teammates. McCartney was more of a climber. I knew I could beat him in a sprint. Creed could do everything, but he'd already done a lot of work. I also was confident I could catch, match, and outmuscle Rory Sutherland, a strong overall rider, but not known for speed. The wild card was Tom Zirbel. I had to make sure to not let him get too far in front, since his time trialing skills were legendary.

Fate finally smiled on our squad. Zirbel played the role of rabbit, and provided the carrot for most of our time on the circuits. Then, when it mattered most, my legs had enough left to seal the deal. After so many frustrating second-place finishes, fruition felt sweet.

BOB STAPLETON

After our incredible run of bad luck and near misses, George winning that last stage was motivational for the team. It showed our guys you never give up. If you come every day to race, maybe you'll get lucky and good things will come. It was a hugely symbolic victory. After George's win in Pasadena, the success started flowing.

I settled into my usual spring mode, and enjoyed some relative success. Top five in Flanders and top ten in Roubaix showed my fitness was on par with past seasons. Bob Stapleton looked to me to set the tone, on and off the bike.

I had a perfect chance to help my teammates at the Tour of Georgia. Belarusian rider Kanstantsin Siutsou had tons of talent but hadn't yet put it all together at the right time. He'd been training incredibly well, and as a climber, he was in a perfect position to take the race lead on the critical stage to Brasstown Bald. I shepherded him throughout the day, making sure he knew when to attack on the final climb. Everyone's attention was on Levi Leipheimer and Trent Lowe, but as a former under-twenty-three world champion, Kanstantsin, we knew, could climb just as well. He ended up winning the stage, and taking the race lead with one flat stage to go.

BOB STAPLETON

Every race George was in, the confidence factor went through the roof. He improved not only the plan, but also the execution. Kanstantsin had listened to George on Brasstown, but we still had a one-hundred-kilometer circuit race the next day to ensure the overall victory. Kanstantsin was not a good bike handler, and he was scared to death. There was no certainty we could keep the lead.

George wouldn't hear any talk of losing. He told everyone, "This is my neck of the woods. We're going to do a one-hundred-K team time trial if we have to. We can ride at the front all day if need be." And that's what we did. Siutsou never got into any trouble, and he won the first stage race of his career. George orchestrated it. As a bonus, one of our sprinters, Greg Henderson, won the final stage too.

A real change came with my preparation for that summer's Tour de France. It was a new frontier, or at least a return to the realm

I hadn't concentrated on in ages. In 2008, my lieutenant role re-
volved around Mark Cavendish's quest to win stages, and the green
jersey, in July. He got his coveted first Tour win on Stage 5, in
Châteauroux. At over 220 kilometers (134 miles), it was the longest
stage of that year's Tour, and our leadout worked to perfection.
Celebrating his milestone victory, I had no idea I'd be thrown into
a world of turmoil just two days later.

Aside from Cav's win, we found ourselves protecting the yellow
jersey, which was on the shoulders of Kim Kirchen, the Luxembourg rider who moved into the lead on Stage 6, after Gerolsteiner's Stefan Schumacher crashed heading up to Super Besse. Stage
7 was incredibly windy and hard. I was depressed and unhappy
with myself that I was not able to do the work asked of me. I had
been saved for the end, to do the lion's share of the work up the last
climb, Saint-Jean-de-Donne. In my mind, I had failed miserably,
dropping off the pace almost immediately after the road turned up.
The team needed me to go further and deeper into the climb so we
had the numbers all the way to the finish to assure Kim stayed safe.
By the end, even though Kim had kept yellow, when I got onto the
team bus, all I wanted to do was apologize and erase the bad day
from my memory. Instead, a simple phone call sent me into an even
faster tailspin.

My son, Enzo, had been born on June 20. It nearly destroyed
me to have to leave him, Mel, and Julia for the start of my biggest
race of the year. He was so tiny, and I felt an aching tug on my heart
each day I was away. I had tried Mel's cell phone a few times the
morning of Stage 7, but there had been no answer, which was odd.
After the stage, the message was simple: "Enzo's got a fever. We are
in the hospital." I frantically dialed the numbers, and my excitement to hear Mel's voice was immediately replaced by a crushing
weight in my chest.

"I'm in the hospital. Enzo's not good."

Her voice was cracking as she said those few words, and then she started to cry.

MELANIE

We were in a no-frills hospital in Girona. Enzo had been sick, but I didn't want to tell George, since there was nothing he could do while racing in France. It destroyed me to hear Enzo screaming as they tried to take his blood. Since they didn't know what was wrong, Julia couldn't stay in the room with me. And since Enzo wasn't even three weeks old, they wouldn't give him Tylenol, so he was constantly given ice baths to try to cool him down. We ended up staying in the hospital for close to six days, and thankfully my father was able to take care of Julia.

I sat in the bus, and it took everything I had to keep it together and in check. No matter what the pain, I was never one to cry at the Tour. I was not someone who showed his emotions in public. Roughly an hour later, when I entered the food room at the hotel, my directeurs, Brian Holm and Allan Peiper, asked me how I was doing. They had seen how upset with myself I was after getting off the bike, but they had no idea what I was dealing with now.

Like a pressure valve being released, my façade came crashing down instantly, and the tears tumbled toward the floor. I told them about Enzo, and how I didn't know if my son would live until I got home. Both men looked me square in the eyes as Brian said, "George, go home. Nothing is as important as family."

BRIAN HOLM

George was hurting and "on his knees" with the
news of little Enzo being sick. I'd never seen him
like that. Of course he could have left the Tour.
Family is the most important thing in life. He said
he would call and wait until the next day to make
any decisions. It was a rough night.

I called Mel and said I was coming home. She implored me to
stay, going so far as to say, "I don't want you to come back, there's
nothing you can do." That didn't matter to me. I *wanted* to be there.
I *needed* to be with my family. I wouldn't let myself think of the
worst-case scenario, but I didn't have to. It was obvious. Mel's mom
called me a few minutes later to tell me she would be with her
daughter and implored me to finish the Tour, insisting she'd help
Mel with any needs. Reluctantly, I relented to her wishes.

One man who came to our rescue was Pedro Celaya, my friend
and doctor from the U.S. Postal/Discovery Channel years. He's
become embroiled in the drug story, by some painted as a Dr. Evil–
type guy, but back then, he'd always instructed us to take less and
train harder in order to achieve our results. He was always super-
nice. He worked with us on our mental state, always looking for a
positive way to motivate us. He cared about our health. And now
he called because he cared about my son's. Pedro wasn't at the Tour
that year, but home in Spain, and he dropped everything he was
doing to call the hospital to get the best care, and doctors, for Mel
and Enzo. He didn't have to do that; we weren't even on the same
team now. He just did it as a friend.

I didn't share any of the Enzo news with my teammates. I didn't
want to burden them with my problem, and I was more than happy
to have a small diversion in the day's events when, at dinner, the

talk at the table was that the French newspaper *L'Équipe* was reporting that Manuel "Triki" Beltrán had tested positive for EPO after the first stage of the Tour. Upon hearing the news, his team, Liquigas, sent him home immediately. Triki had been my teammate for the final three Lance wins, and I reflected with more than a little satisfaction that I was out of that game and racing clean.

Even though the racing continued (we helped Cav win a second time the next day in Toulouse, and helped Kim keep the yellow jersey for a couple more days), my concentration wavered wildly. I called to the hospital and home as often as I could, each time reassured by Mel, or her mom, that Enzo was improving and in good hands. Just as it began to sink in that my son's health was in the clear, I got another dose of good news when we celebrated Cav's Stage 12 win.

The day's joy soon became a nightmare in Narbonne.

Once I got back to the hotel, I received a call from a friend. He wanted to warn me that Floyd Landis was about to release a series of videos on YouTube detailing how we all doped during our years on U.S. Postal. My friend didn't know what Floyd's timetable was—in fact, no one did. He'd just threatened to do it, so I had to plan for the what-ifs. It was incredibly stressful, and I immediately went to inform Bob Stapleton. I told Bob everything I knew, and he simply sat there and soaked it all in. He asked me to keep him informed and told me he'd devise a plan if and when the videos surfaced. I called Lance. He didn't care, commenting that nobody would believe Floyd. I wasn't nearly as confident, but Floyd's tutorials never did appear.

My roller-coaster ride continued. We enjoyed more success the very next day when Cav won his fourth stage in Nîmes. With the win, he doubled Barry Hoban's previous record number of stage wins by a Briton in a single Tour, and then Cav decided to withdraw before Stage 15 in order to get ready for the Olympic Games in Beijing. With Mark gone, the pressure was off, but there was still the small detail of getting through the Alps before riding into Paris.

On Stage 17, which finished on top of legendary Alpe d'Huez, I was coming down another famous climb, the Col du Galibier, when my friend and fellow American Christian Vande Velde took me out when he cut to the right quickly. I went down and started sliding at over fifty miles per hour.

Wrecks, no matter when they happen, are weird. They take place in slow motion. Wheels touch. You see, then hit, the curb or the ground, hear the *snap,* and don't know whether it's your bike or your bones.

I felt my skin peeling off as I skidded across the asphalt. The heat caused by the friction was overpowering. I didn't feel any pain at first, but I knew I was going to be screwed up. While I was sliding, I kept thinking, I just hope it's not too bad. After coming to a stop, I prayed I could move, and when I did, I immediately started looking for my bike. My skin started to simmer and radiate enough heat to power a small appliance. Sweat dripped onto my wounds, and as each drop registered a bull's-eye, it was as if someone set a white-hot cinder on my skin. I still had over one hundred kilometers to go, and I suffered like a dog that day, eventually finishing more than twenty-four minutes behind CSC's Carlos Sastre, who not only won the stage but took over the yellow jersey, and in the process sealed his first and only Tour de France victory.

When it was all over, it was such a relief when Mel met me in Paris. Enzo was out of harm's way, so she left him and Julia with her parents in Dijon. Even though Cav had dropped out, we had a great party to commemorate his victories and Kim Kirchen's time in yellow. The team rented a boat on the Seine, and I was so happy to have the chance to share some time with Melanie.

Right after the Tour was over and I'd returned to Girona, I got an interesting call from Lance. He wanted to know what the Tour was like.

Was it harder? How'd I find the racing? Was the peloton cleaner? What teams were riding well?

In typical Lance fashion, all his questions were direct, and he expected direct answers. I didn't think about it at the time, but I'm sure I was the only person he trusted to give him honest answers as well as keep his questions confidential. I was probably the only guy in the world who'd keep this conversation a secret, and he knew it. Lance ended up calling me again at the very end of 2008, this time asking about Bob Stapleton and what it had been like to be on his squad. He was definitely plotting which team to join to make a comeback.

Looking back, for all the obvious reasons, going to Astana was probably the worst decision he could have made. He just didn't think it through. He was so eager to get back in the game that I think, for the first time in his life, his judgment was clouded.

I had one final goal for 2008. I thought I would only be racing for another year or two, so simply based on that circumstance, I sincerely thought that Beijing that year was going to be my last Olympics. The team in China was made up of seasoned pros— David Zabriskie, Jason McCartney, Christian Vande Velde, and Levi Leipheimer. Levi was the only automatic qualifier, as a result of a top-three finish in a UCI grand tour between July 1, 2007, and July 1, 2008. He placed third overall at the 2007 Tour de France, when he finished just thirty-one seconds off the pace of teammate Alberto Contador of Spain and eight seconds back from runner-up Cadel Evans of Australia. An Olympian in 2004, Levi was headed to his second Games. For Christian and Jason, it was their second Olympics as well—Jason had been on the team with us in 2004, and Christian had raced on the track in Sydney in 2000. Z-Man (Zabriskie) was going to his first Games, while I ended up setting a record as the first five-time U.S. Olympic cyclist. We had all raced countless times either with one another or against one another, so coming together for the Games was no big deal.

As was customary, almost all of us were coming off our July romp around France, and that year, Christian had placed a career high fifth overall as part of his Garmin squad. Levi's pro team, Astana, was not invited to compete that year, so after being on the podium in 2007, he had July of 2008 to rest up and focus on the road race in China. For those of us that had done the Tour, it was the yearly return to the battle and balancing act of recovering after three weeks of punishing our bodies daily. After the Tour, I never felt good. One of the hardest things to work through and negotiate is making sure to not overeat. My body would be so leached of nourishment, it would crave everything, but since I was racing a couple weeks later, mentally turning off that urge was always a Herculean task.

During the Tour, my body was in a state of shock, so if I could manage the weeks that followed, I would actually get leaner and stronger since I was resting. That was always the $100,000 question: What do I need to do in order to best recuperate my muscles and replenish my reserves? We all knew that the critical point of figuring out that formula didn't come until the 200-kilometer mark of a 250-kilometer race. That's what made it even more of a crapshoot. No one racing the Olympics would do a ride like that *before* the Games, so you looked for other, smaller signs that you might be ready.

Limiting time in the saddle was the easiest thing to control. I'd ride for about two hours, never pushing my pace. When I pushed on the pedals, if I felt pain or I could not push down hard, I needed to back off even more. It was a never-ending cycle of what could be done, or tried, to improve the formula and energy equation. Usually, I'd start to feel good a day or two before I left. The first and best indicator of my form returning was when my legs still hurt but my power numbers returned. I didn't like what I was feeling, but the math was there and told me more of the true story of my muscles. As an aside, before there were power meters, the easiest way to tell if I'd returned to normalcy was the gears on my crank set. If I was tired, I'd hit a hill and there would be no way I'd be able to shift into the big chain ring. Once my freshness was back, those bigger gears weren't a problem. It was a simple but substantial signal from my body.

There were only two weeks between the final day of the Tour, raced on the world's most famous boulevard, the Champs-Élysées, and race day at the Olympics. After the Tour ended, I first went to Dijon, France, and hung out with my family for a week. We had Enzo's baptism during that time, and I found plenty of things to distract me from my normal single-mindedness about riding. Then we went home to Girona. No one would have accused me of spending all my time getting ready for the Olympics.

CHRISTIAN VANDE VELDE

We were all old guys who had known each other for ages. We had a lot of fun, and basically laughed for four days straight. We lived in a three-bedroom apartment—I roomed with Jason McCartney, George and Dave Zabriskie were together, and Levi Leipheimer got the single. You needed thick skin to survive.

Jim Ochowicz was the manager-coach of the U.S. team again, and the goal was the same—podium. Bring home a medal for the

Red, White, and Blue. But by race day, even though I had begun to recover and have "good legs," I was never in the hunt. There would be no storybook ending to my Olympic career.

The thing I reflect on most about Beijing was how "manufactured" it all seemed. There was so much aside from the Athletes Village that I did not experience, and out on the course, it felt like the government shipped in people to cheer and support our sport. It didn't seem as if there were any real cycling fans there. The finish was out at one of the most majestic of world landmarks, the Great Wall, but because it took place one hundred kilometers away from the city, it was devoid of any real energy and lacked some of the soul of what the Games should be about.

I also regret leaving as quickly as I did. I had tickets to watch USA Basketball's latest version of the Dream Team play China, but because I missed Melanie and the kids so much, I skipped the game, went back to Europe immediately, picked up the family, and headed home to Greenville. It had been a long year, and even though my body was ready for a break, mentally I was refreshed and focused on what the future could hold. The change to Bob Stapleton's crew had been a gamble, and I gleefully looked back on twelve months of good times, good results, and a new crop of great friends.

CHAPTER 26

As DECEMBER 2008 DISAPPEARED and January's days jumped off the pages of the calendar, I was in great shape. I'd started my season training earlier than usual in order to be ready for my first trip to the Tour Down Under. My prep in Greenville had been great, and Australia was part of the plan to have me and the team ready for the Tour of California. In between the races, we rented a house on the coast in Malibu. I loved the weather, the riding terrain, and walking out onto the beach each evening.

Our name morphed again, into Team Columbia-Highroad, and we spent a few days together in Solvang before the race prologue start in Sacramento. It was always fun to see Bob in business mode. He loved to have State of the Union talks with us and give us progress reports on everything that was going on—not just individually, but with the team structure as well.

We joked that his go-to attire was a pair of jeans and a Columbia shirt, not a fancy European suit with a twenty-thousand-dollar watch. He didn't care about food or wine. So there was always a cautious optimism when we knew we'd be getting together as a group. Cyclists crave the flashier things in life, but Bob emphasized substance over style.

I played my team role during California, helping Mark Cavendish to two stage wins and the overall Sprint Classification green jersey. The big news was Lance's return to racing in the United States. He'd already competed in Australia, but this was a chance for fans in California to throw their support behind his comeback. He was riding for the Kazakhstan crew, Astana, and reunited with the man who helped create much of his magic, Johan Bruyneel.

I was overjoyed to not have to deal with the squabbling that was destined to arise in the Astana squad between Lance and Alberto Contador. Even though they were now teammates, both expected Johan to name them the team leader come July, and it was the worst-kept secret in the peloton that they didn't get along. I had my own job to do, and as cool as it was to see cycling get a media "bump" from Lance 2.0, it didn't affect me at all, or at least so I thought at the time.

The weeks ticked off, and Europe once again became my base. At Tirreno–Adriatico, I helped Cav to another stage win and Swede Thomas Lövkvist to a fourth overall. What I remember most about "The Race of the Two Seas" was Cav absolutely starving himself. He was so focused on getting lean because only four days after the race finished, we were going to attempt an upset at Milan–San Remo. Mark was motivated by the fact that the press gave him no chance to win, based on his perceived lack of climbing ability. He was losing every last ounce of excess weight to give himself the best shot at success. At Tirreno, we also engaged in a bit of subterfuge— Cav purposefully held back on the climbs to keep his rivals from knowing how well he was riding.

The one hundredth running of "La Classica di Primavera" was no different from the ninety-nine before. It usually comes down to the two final, critical climbs, the Cipressa and the Poggio, and whether or not anyone can crack the sprinters to prevent a bunch finish.

Cav made it up and over the Cipressa without much issue, but

2006 Paris–Roubaix. One of those moments when you think, "What the hell just happened, and why am I doing this?" *(Graham Watson)*

2006 Tour de France. Just lost the yellow jersey by one one hundreth of a second, one of the most disappointing moments of my career. *(Graham Watson)*

2006 TDF. My one and only yellow jersey. Time bonuses and tactical acumen paid off. *(Graham Watson)*

Tour de France, 2007, with Melanie at Stage 1 in London. One of the coolest cities to start a TDF I'd ever done.

2007 TDF. Left to right: Benjamin Noval, Alberto Contador, and me. Never got to know Alberto really well, but it was special to help him win the Tour. *(Graham Watson)*

2008 Critérium du Dauphiné. Was not the speediest guy in this sprint. It's not always the fastest legs—Lady Luck can play a part. *(Graham Watson)*

2008 TDF. Busy day protecting two jerseys. Thomas Lövkvist in white (best young rider) and Kim Kirchen in yellow. (Graham Watson)

Tour of Missouri 2008, winning Stage 1. Always special to win, no matter where or when. (John Pierce, PhotoSport International)

Me and Christian Vande Velde (left), one of my best friends in cycling, at the start of the 2009 Tour of Missouri. (John Pierce, PhotoSport International)

Me and Mark Cavendish at the 2009 Tour of Missouri. One of the best personalities in the sport. I admired and became very close with him. (John Pierce, PhotoSport International)

2009 Tour de France—
Annecy time trial. I'm
not sure if the look of
pain is from the effort,
or the lack of skin and
the broken collarbone
I had at that moment.
(*John Pierce, PhotoSport
International*)

2009 TDF Stage 21—final day heading into Paris. Left to right: Mark Renshaw,
Mark Cavendish, and me. The demeanor of this team kept me young. We were
always laughing. (*Graham Watson*)

2009 U.S. Pro, crossing the line. Nothing like winning in your hometown in front of your friends and family. (*John Pierce, PhotoSport International*)

On the podium, the anger I'd felt three weeks earlier when I lost my chance at the yellow jersey was quickly forgotten. (*John Pierce, PhotoSport International*)

2010 Tour de France, with Jim Ochowicz, manager of BMC. Started and ended my career with him. (*John Pierce, PhotoSport International*)

2011 TDF, start of the last stage. Left to right: Marcus Burghardt, me, Cadel Evans, and Steve Morabito. With all the turmoil surrounding the sport, I took pride in the fact I could still do my job with the best of them. (*Graham Watson*)

Last stage of the 2011 Tour de France. One of my favorite TDF winning teams. (*John Pierce, PhotoSport International*)

2011 USA Pro Challenge—winning the stage into Aspen. My good friend and the future of American cycling, Tejay van Garderen, finished right behind me. We'd ridden the stage just a few days before to learn the route. *(John Pierce, PhotoSport International)*

Doing what I did best. Pacing my leader, Tejay van Garderen, up a steep slope. So focused, we're oblivious to the craziness around us. *(John Pierce, PhotoSport International)*

Stage 15, 2012 TDF. Awful day for me, but worse for Cadel Evans. He was very appreciative that I waited for him, then helped him to the finish. His gesture as we crossed the line meant a lot. *(Graham Watson)*

Cadel Evans and me. He made a huge effort to travel around the world to see me off into retirement. *(Shane Orr, Chilkat Photography)*

2012 TDF. I left a lot of my skin on the roads of France over the course of my career. *(John Pierce, PhotoSport International)*

On the Champs-Élysées, last stage of my career. Excited to start a new life with my family.

had to hang on for dear life ascending the Poggio. I was ahead, but I heard my directeur, Valerio Piva, shouting into the radio, "He's still there! He's still there!"

In order to wait for Cav, for the first time ever, I went down the Poggio applying my brakes. I went backward as if I had an anchor attached. Mark was at the tail end of approximately fifty guys, and throughout the winding, twisting three-kilometer descent, I had to let them all drift by me. It was nerve-racking work. At speeds of close to sixty miles an hour, it's hard enough to avoid crashing, but staying out of the way of passing riders, all the while looking back for Mark, made it a memorable experience.

MARK CAVENDISH
George had to be the first rider in the history of Milan–San Remo to sit up and lose positions on the Poggio. Usually, any rider that finds himself in a lead group at that point decides to work for himself. He had gotten me into position before the climb, but I'd gotten swamped and lost places. As we descended, I could see him constantly looking back for me.

By the time we reached the bottom, and with only three kilometers to go until the finish, Cav found my wheel, and away we went! I passed people as if they were standing still. I rode with the strength of multiple men. I was possessed. I rode with such an adrenaline surge that Cav was barely hanging on. I'd done a lot in my career, but helping someone win a spring classic had never been a notch on my belt. I felt that day was special.

Whether it was my focus or simply the fast speeds we were traveling, it ended up being a blur how we actually got to the front, and with less than four hundred meters to go, for the first time I allowed myself to think, We've got this!

I heard the whizz of spinning gears just before I felt the whoosh of air blow by me. Heinrich Haussler rocketed past on our left, in an attempt to set up his teammate Thor Hushovd. Thor was too tired to hitch a ride, but Haussler had so much momentum, he decided to try to hang on for the win himself. I was cross-eyed from my effort to bring Cav to the front, so all I could do was will him to chase. I didn't have the energy to do anything but hope.

> ### MARK CAVENDISH
> He'd ridden his guts out for me. I pushed "all in" when Haussler went. Nobody gave me a chance, but I never race for second.

Cav burst from behind my wheel, and with only one hundred meters left, still had close to ten meters to make up. It wasn't until I heard the PA announcer scream that Cav had won, and I saw Mark raise his hands, that I realized we'd pulled off the near impossible. It was just me those last kilometers, and it gave me immense satisfaction that I'd helped Mark win his first monument. It was an incredibly fulfilling feeling.

Cav was quoted afterward: "When you win sprints you prove you're a great sprinter. When you win a great one-day race, you've proved you're a great rider." Being one of the most flashy practitioners of the "bling" lifestyle, Cav gave me a watch to commemorate the victory. It was special to share, and his declaration of "I love you, man" as we hugged after the line meant a lot, but it was the memories he gave me that were priceless.

> ### MARK CAVENDISH
> He's a hug man, so we shared that after the line. I would not have won without him. Anyone else

would have gone off on their own, but George helped me. I found out about a watch he wanted and got it for him. It was the first big gift I got for anybody, and it was the best way I could think of to say thank you.

March made its way into April, and I rolled into my classics campaign. At Gent–Wevelgem, Cav flatted almost immediately, then missed a critical break a couple of kilometers later. We had four men who made it, however: me, Edvald Boasson Hagen (EBH), Bernie Eisel, and Marcus Burghardt. It was a miserably cold, wet day with crosswinds to boot. I didn't feel great, and at only twenty-one years of age, EBH, the up-and-coming superstar, had been shuttling back and forth to the team car to keep me supplied with water bottles all day. Finally I said to him, "Dude, you have to stop working for me, work for yourself. You are looking great."

He promptly rode off and eventually won, and I was sincere in my happiness and praise. It didn't matter to me if I didn't win, as long as someone from the team did. The day had started with all eyes on Cav, and it ended with our jersey on the top step of the podium, just not the Columbia-Highroad rider everyone expected.

Amid all the success and positivity, Floyd found a way to be a fly in the ointment again right before Paris–Roubaix. He called Dave Zabriskie and told him to tell me that Floyd had called the cops and told them everything, and that they would be waiting for me right after I crossed the line in the velodrome.

Z first texted me and told me he needed to talk. Then, when we finally spoke, Dave sounded concerned as he explained he didn't know what to do—whether to call me or not—but if something did happen, and he hadn't let me know about it, he'd feel terrible and never forgive himself.

It had been almost a year since I'd thought about the video incident involving Floyd, and I found myself shaking my head at his agenda.

I felt sorry for him. We had once been friends and teammates. But I still had to deal with his threats.

I didn't have a restful night. I won't use stress as an excuse, but I'll simply say I didn't do as well as I would have hoped, finishing forty-fourth, over six and a half minutes back.

I'd learned a long time ago that if I wanted to have a long career, I'd better learn to focus forward and not dwell on things in the past. I took that approach as the eyes of the world eagerly awaited July. At the Tour, we were a force to be reckoned with. Every other team expected us to do the majority of the work on each stage, since we had the World's Fastest Man on our side. Mark Cavendish made it seem as if he won at will. But what no one saw was the painstaking preparation we did to get Cav into position during a race, or even away from the prying eyes of the press before race day. The pro peloton seemed resigned to the fact that Cav was unbeatable, hoping only that his team would get so tired from working on the front that someone else might have a shot to squeak into our protected zone. It was maddeningly frustrating, but at the same time, incredibly motivating. We used the conviction that it was us versus the world with great success.

MARK CAVENDISH

The biggest thing I learned from George was preparation. He called it the Regime. Nothing was done without purpose. He rarely, if ever, indulged in anything. His actions were driven by his need to become the best he could be. We roomed together that year at the Tour de Suisse. Every night the hotel

would put peppermints on our pillow, and every
night he would set them aside. I couldn't believe it.
He wouldn't even eat a little candy, because he knew
it didn't help him become a better cyclist. He was
totally dedicated to that goal.

There's a lot to say about the 2009 Tour de France. If you haven't
seen Jason Berry's award-winning documentary *Chasing Legends,* you
should. It's a perfect encapsulation of what we all went through in
those three weeks. I loved, and still love, every one of those guys. I'd
walk through fire for them.

We had a new sponsor again in cell phone manufacturer
HTC. Our jerseys might have looked different from the start of
the year, but one thing was the same: Mark Cavendish was our
epicenter. I was Mark's loyal servant, but I was merely one of a
few guys truly dedicated to Cav's leadout. He also had Swiss star
Bernie Eisel and Aussie Mark Renshaw at his disposal. It was up
to a couple of Germans, time-trialing freak Tony Martin and
quiet man Bert Grabsch, to keep the wattage wolves at bay. Belgian jack-of-all-trades Maxime Monfort was essential, as were
our GC contenders, Luxembourg's Kim Kirchen and Australia's Michael "Mick" Rogers. If my 1999 team had been the Bad
News Bears, in 2009, we were the New York Yankees. We were
a team where no expense was spared and only one result was ac-
ceptable: winning.

BRIAN HOLM
What a cast of characters!
MARK RENSHAW: Prince Harry (because he looked like him)
GEORGE: Captain America
CAV: The Missile

TONY MARTIN: Panzerwagen (when he started going, nobody could stop him)

BERNIE EISEL: Mr. Freestyle (he always found an imaginative solution)

KIM KIRCHEN: Kim de Lux (he was from Luxembourg)

BERT GRABSCH: Luftwaffe (sounded so beautiful in German)

MAXIME MONFORT: Max (simple, already his nickname)

MICHAEL ROGERS: Mick (already his nickname)

Monaco was an amazing backdrop for *le départ*. No matter how many times I took part in the Tour, every year it was special. Cav converted in his first attempt, a Stage 2 win in Brignoles. Our leadout worked to perfection. I took over with a little under a kilometer to go, then handed off to Mark Renshaw, who piloted Cav perfectly to 250 meters. At that point, it was a foregone conclusion. As close to a slam dunk as it gets in our sport.

JASON BERRY, DIRECTOR OF *CHASING LEGENDS*

Bob Stapleton had issued a directive: the guys were to give me and my crew access throughout the Tour. Initially, the riders weren't happy about it, but winning tends to help the team vibe. George was always happy after a stage win, but he positively beamed when his wife and family were around. He would light up like a Christmas tree.

Stage 3 resulted in another victory, but the circumstances leading up to the final kilometers were unique. Mind-melting heat and dead-flat roads had the whole peloton waiting for, and expecting, us to work. We'd been on the front controlling the break, but were looking for a moment of rest. We'd studied the road map extensively and knew there was the chance for crosswinds at a couple of junctures in the last part of the stage course. With just over thirty kilometers to go, Mick Rogers and I made a few critical split-second decisions that got our whole team, save Bert Grabsch, back to the front; called out for them to charge full gas; and eventually forced a split in the main group that left a number of important protagonists—including Astana's Alberto Contador—without the means to make back the lost ground.

It was an incredible show of force. Eight of our nine guys populated a split of only twenty-eight. Once we committed to the surge, the hard part became maintaining the momentum to catch the few remaining men up front. Among the group, and more than happy we'd done the initial work, was Lance. He had Astana mates Yaroslav Popovych and Haimar Zubeldia with him, and eventually those two put in a lot of work to help our group stay away.

Astana's drama was real, and a daily soap opera. With Contador left behind, Lance seized an opportunity to order his men to the front to gain precious seconds on his own teammate.

In the end, the headwinds at the finish didn't matter, and the reduced peloton probably didn't make a difference. We delivered Cav to the two-hundred-meter mark, and he crossed the line pointing to the "HTC" on his jersey, with his other hand pretending to hold a phone up to his ear. We had done everything *but* "phone it in" on the stage, and the reward was Cav "phoning home" that he had won.

After a seesaw struggle through the Pyrenees, we got back to work on the transitional stages heading toward the Alps. Stage 10 brought us another chance to put Cav on the podium. We timed our catch of the early break perfectly, passing the last of the brave breakaway artists with just over a kilometer to go. From there, autopilot locked in, and Mark made it a triple scoop of success.

The very next day, Stage 11's slightly uphill finish looked to not suit Cav. But we'd made a contingency plan. Instead of only a couple of us the last 1.5 kilometers, we knew we needed four guys to help pull the weight. And instead of Mark Renshaw dropping Cav off with just over two hundred meters to go, we knew we needed to have him closer to 150. It was getting to be a predictable script. Anywhere around fifty to sixty kilometers out, we were expected to move to the front and close down the break. We were so confident, and so blessed to have Cav as our closer, we were more than happy to oblige the fearful mind-set of the other teams. Stage 11 was no different.

By the time we reached Saint-Fargeau, the uphill finish might as well have been flat. Cav's acceleration caught all his rivals off guard, and for the second time in the Tour, he took back-to-back stage wins. For his efforts, Cav also wrested the green jersey off the shoulders of Norwegian Thor "God of Thunder" Hushovd. Everything seemed to be going our way. However, fate had other things in store.

CHAPTER 27

Before the start of Stage 14 into Besançon, we had no idea of the magnitude of the shock waves that were about to be unleashed on us. On paper, it was a flat stage, so we planned to have Cav in the mix if everything fell into our lap, but we were also aware that with the Alps on the horizon, it was a day for the opportunists, and a breakaway might stick.

At just fourteen kilometers, a brave bunch went off the front, and I found myself our lone representative. Once the peloton gave our odd mix the nod, the lead began to stretch out, and all thirteen of us took stock of one another and our own bodies. I was keenly aware of what all the guys brought to the table, but I figured we had enough firepower and leg strength to mount a decent challenge. A fan favorite, German Jens Voigt, was there—his famous line of "Shut up, legs!" all too appropriate at this point in the Tour. My old teammate Gerard Ciolek had made the split, as had Russian strongman Sergei Ivanov. The talented Irishman Nicolas Roche was present as well. After about sixty kilometers, we lost Jens to a puncture, and I was disappointed we'd lost his fortitude as well. We were now an even dozen.

As our advantage grew, we all became keenly aware that I was now the *maillot jaune virtuel*—the virtual leader of the Tour—based on our lead over the peloton and the fact I'd started the day five minutes and twenty-five seconds behind Ag2r's Rinaldo Nocentini. I cajoled and coaxed my fellow escapees to drive the pace, knowing full well that every second counted. I actually worked out a deal with the Liquigas guys, Daniele Bennati and Frederik Willems. Deals are done in a break every day during the Tour. Sometimes a guy wants mountain points, so he's allowed to crest a climb first. It didn't happen in this instance, but plenty of times in professional cycling a rider will take cash if offered. Bennati was a sprinter, and the fastest finisher in our group. No one wanted to go to the line with him because they knew they'd lose. I guaranteed I would work for Bennati to win the stage if he and Willems helped pull and keep our lead. I spoke to Bennati in Italian and Willems in English, and both acknowledged we had a deal.

At the 120-kilometer mark (only 80 kilometers to go), we hit our maximum lead, 8:50. Finally, Ag2r and, interestingly, Lance's team, Astana, came to the front of the peloton to drive the chase. At sixty kilometers to go, our advantage was still 8:30. With only twenty kilometers left, we had still managed to keep them at bay by a whopping 6:45. I tried to resist the urge, but I began to believe that for the second time in my career, I would put on the yellow jersey at the end of the day.

My legs felt lighter, my mind clearer, my heart steadier. It's weird to use the word *energized,* but after more than two weeks, and three and a half hours into the day's ride, adrenaline gave me a boost. But my euphoria didn't last long.

It had been one thing to hear over the radio that Ag2r was on the front. That made sense. They were protecting the lead of the Tour's yellow jersey. Astana on the front was confusing. Alberto and Lance were six and eight seconds back, respectively, from No-centini's lead. Nocentini was in their group, they were not going to gain any time on him, and since I was the next closest on GC, their efforts to close the gap looked like they were only trying to rob me of my chance at the leader's jersey. The really screwed-up part was that toward the end, Garmin-Slipstream put all their men on the front and started drilling the pace. And taking huge chunks of time out of our advantage.

BOB STAPLETON

I called Doug Ellis (chairman of Garmin) during the chase. I said it was good for all American teams if George was in yellow. He readily agreed and said he would try to reach JV.

BRIAN HOLM

My worst day ever as a directeur. Bruyneel and Lance didn't allow the break to go, and then Bjarne Riis (manager of SaxoBank) told me Garmin would screw George because they did not want him in yellow. I thought Riis was joking! Who would do something like that in cycling?

I was oblivious to any backroom dealings or directeur instructions. I just knew I had to ride hard to give myself a chance. Katusha's Sergei Ivanov attacked with eleven kilometers to go, and that spread chaos through our collective. He chose his moment well. I'd been busy trying to cover the accelerations to keep us as a unit, so I could fulfill my promise to Bennati. But I was too tired when Sergei shot off. Over the radio, I heard the seconds slipping away.

PHIL LIGGETT, CYCLING COMMENTATOR (FROM THE FILM *CHASING LEGENDS*)
It didn't make any sense. What was Garmin doing on the front? George was never one to make enemies, but they were riding like men possessed. There was no question they were riding to close the time gap.

By the finish, I'd given every ounce of energy I had. Our splintered group of eight finished sixteen seconds behind Ivanov, but the real countdown began after I crossed the line. Five minutes and twenty-five seconds. Three hundred and twenty-five ticks. Each one reverberated in my ears and brought into focus what was at stake. When I'd worn yellow in 2006, I never dreamed I'd have another chance.

I could barely stand, but I'd been asked to stay near the finish in case I was the new leader. My mood was tense, my emotions raw. Now that I could breathe, I tried to process everything I'd heard. Lance's team chasing me down? My friends on Garmin, some of my best friends in the sport, killing themselves to close the gap? I didn't want to believe any of it was true.

It seemed like an eternity. And then I felt as if I'd been cast into hell. The horde of remaining riders was led across the line by Cav, who had tried to hold back as long as possible before sprinting and protecting his green jersey lead. Five minutes and thirty-six seconds behind the winner. Five minutes and twenty seconds behind me. I'd lost the yellow jersey by five seconds.

PHIL LIGGETT
I'd never seen George so bitter; he was a broken man. In his mind, it was Astana, and his best friend, that had chased him down.

LANCE ARMSTRONG

Johan and Brian Holm had made a deal. We monitored the gap for quite a while, and it went up steadily to just under nine minutes. We couldn't let it get too high; otherwise, the French rider Christophe Le Mével (Française des Jeux), who was in the break with George and could climb, would be well ahead of me and Alberto and pose a potential risk.

BOB STAPLETON

I spoke with Jonathan Vaughters after the race. He claimed that he was not in the car but at a VIP wine-tasting event. I asked him who ran Slipstream, and who was making decisions? He would not tell me who was in the car, and was extremely defensive. He said that Highroad "had it in" for Garmin.

Dave Zabriskie later said that it was Garmin's president, Matt Johnson, driving the team car, along with the CMO of Garmin, who told him, "We can't have another American in yellow" (not on the Garmin team). Dave said the Garmin riders did not want to chase, and they were just "pawns in their game."

JONATHAN VAUGHTERS

I wasn't on-site, or in the car, but ultimately, it's my team, so I take responsibility. I've never gotten a straight answer from anyone as to how it transpired. Yes, there was a rivalry that had developed that year between our two teams, and that day became emotionally charged, which led to poor decision making. I don't think anyone in our organization is proud of that moment.

CHRISTIAN VANDE VELDE

We [the Garmin team] were ordered to go to the front and chase. There was no explanation, and nobody questioned it. As a team, we just did it. In the moment, you're just doing your job. We had total trust in Matt White, our directeur, and what he told us to do. There was frantic pushing and shoving to get to the front, and it was only after we crossed the line that things felt weird.

MARK CAVENDISH

I never understood it or got a satisfactory answer. I always went into a race to win, not to make somebody lose. Even though I needed the points for the green jersey, I tried to wait as long as possible to sprint at the end. We got to the front and tried to block the speed of the group. I basically freewheeled until seventy meters, and sprinted as slowly as possible. Afterward, it was the first time I'd ever seen George NOT talk to the team. He was devastated. When I saw him walk up to Mel and the kids, I started crying, it hurt me so much to know he'd lost the chance to share that with them.

I was crushed. I wanted to lash out at everyone. My family was there, so I had to control my emotions even more than I might have. I felt deceived. By my best friends, no less. Everyone said the right things; claimed it wasn't their fault, that it was out of their control. Bullshit. Chasing down a friend to make sure he doesn't embody the pinnacle of his sport? Never. No way. I would have told my directeur to fuck off if the roles had been reversed.

Lance tried to reach out on numerous occasions to explain his, and Astana's, side of the story, but I was so livid, I didn't talk to him for months.

LANCE ARMSTRONG

After the stage, I tried, but he wouldn't take my calls. I slept only about two hours that night. I felt bad, but it was very frustrating to not be able to plead my, and the team's, case because it was not our fault. It didn't help that Phil Liggett said what he did during the TV commentary (blaming me and Astana for chasing George down), but bottom line, George had missed out on an opportunity and it sickened me that he felt I had a hand in it.

The Garmin guys—Christian Vande Velde, Dave Zabriskie, Ryder Hesjedal, and Matt White—all came up to me at different times, individually, over the next year and apologized, but it was hard to accept. It wasn't just the act but the lying at the time that upset me.

JASON BERRY

George got caught in a political drama and a case of payback. Jonathan saw an opportunity to get back at the team, at Cav and Bob Stapleton. It could have been a great send-off for George as he wound down his career. Garmin didn't race to win that day; it was racing to do damage to another. And it crushed George. His whole family was there, and an opportunity was taken from him. I was in the car with

Bob Stapleton after the stage when he got the text.
He asked me to put down the camera and stop film-
ing because he was so upset and he did not want his
reaction recorded. The text from Jonathan read, "I'll
accept your apology now!"

Unbelievably, my bad day became infectious for the team. What
should have been Cav's putting more points between himself and
Thor became a ridiculous example of bad officiating. After the race
ended, Thor lodged a protest claiming that Cav had impeded him
in the sprint to the finish. Unbelievably, the commissars agreed,
citing him for "irregular sprinting." Cav was relegated to the back
of the pack, moving him from thirteenth to 154th. The decision
ended up costing Cav the green jersey.

Our mood on the bus, and in the hotel that evening, was despondent but also defiant. We forged an unbreakable resolve. We
had lost my chance at yellow, but we'd be damned if we were going
to lose our last two opportunities to help Cav win.

BRIAN HOLM

It was a very long evening, but we all knew we
needed to use our anger in the right way.

I am in no way a superstitious guy, but whatever I rubbed up
against before the start of the 2009 Tour, I don't ever want to come
in contact with it again. Three days after going through perhaps
the most mental anguish I'd ever experienced, I was thrust into a
physical hurt locker. On Stage 16, I went into a right-hand turn,
my wheel slid out from under me, and as I hit the pavement, I immediately knew something was wrong. I had felt something crack
in my right shoulder, the same one I'd broken years before in Paris–

Roubaix. I told the guys on the radio, and told myself to just block out the pain.

At the finish, I refused to go to the hospital. I kept telling myself, "You can get through this. You have to finish the Tour." I didn't want any doctor taking X-rays, whether it was our team guys or the local medics. What good would that do? I knew my shoulder was screwed up, but if I got confirmation there was a break, I might be forced out of the race.

"Just tape it up" was my final answer.

I might have been a mess, but I was a man on a mission.

JASON BERRY

We had cameras rolling on the team every step of the way. What encapsulated George perfectly was on the bus after the finish atop Ventoux, where Tony Martin came in second. Tony had the fitness to win that day, but a plethora of issues conspired against him: the fact that the red kite (one kilometer to go) banner blew down, he'd never been up the famous climb, and he had pulled out his earpiece midway up the mountain. As George made his way onto the bus, he noticed Tony was a bit despondent. George, barely able to stand, his mouth and face caked in salt, broken collarbone and all, immediately went over and gave him a huge one-armed bear hug while exclaiming, "I can't believe how good you are! I can't believe it! Do you know how good you are?" Tony's mood changed instantly. George's pride in him was an elixir. The whole time I was around him, George always put others first.

MARK CAVENDISH

Even when George was down, he wouldn't let it
affect others. He always wore a smile, and it was
incredibly uplifting.

Before Stage 19 in Aubenas, Cav implored us on the bus to stay
with him on the final climb and he'd do the rest, uphill finish be
damned. He was true to his word. It was his fifth victory of the
Tour, and it was the perfect remedy for our funk. The day before,
I'd been reinvigorated when my family showed up in Annecy at
the start of the time trial. Adrenaline always helps, but I felt every
bump and crevice in that fifty minutes of effort.

That left Paris. The most famous boulevard in the whole world
and the most precious place to win for a cyclist. The Champs-
Élysées is our Lambeau Field, Yankee Stadium, and Indianapolis
Speedway all rolled into one. It's Wembley, Wimbledon, and Wat-
kins Glen. We had a chance to prove our superiority one last time,
but the final victory of the Tour is a symbol for so much, every team
is willing to sacrifice and do whatever it takes.

After the obligatory celebrations involving the overall winner
(Alberto Contador, with the podium rounded out by Andy Schleck
and Lance), and the elation associated with just making it to the
Tour's end, it was back to business for the sprinters and anyone else
with designs on glory. Close to a month of work culminated with
eight laps around some of the world's most breathtaking icons. But
we only concentrated on the cobblestones. Paris's picturesque main
boulevard is bone jarring at best. I especially took note. My right
shoulder was an undeniable reminder of my surroundings and what
I was riding for.

The bell lap brings out the aggression and ramps up the adrenaline. Every team seemed to want to disrupt our leadout train, none

more so than Garmin. As we took the sweeping left-hand turn
around the Place de la Concorde, Garmin had three men on the
front. I was sitting fourth wheel, first in *our* triumvirate, which
included Mark Renshaw and behind him Mark Cavendish. Just
before the red kite, which always denotes one kilometer to go, I
swung to the left and put in a huge acceleration to pull even with,
then pass, all of the Garmin gang. Julian Dean, with Tyler Farrar on
his wheel, tried to swoop into our space, but they were a millisecond too late and a mile per hour too slow. I wasn't aware, but they
dropped behind Cav, hoping his scraps of speed would keep them
in contention. As we approached the final chicane, I put everything
into the pedals one last time, standing and nearly ripping my handlebars off with the force I was transferring via my leverage.

MARK CAVENDISH

Our goal had been to just stay together. When
George took off at the 1K banner, the speed changed
so quickly, I had to get out of the saddle to accelerate. I was on Mark Renshaw's wheel, and I almost
lost contact. Fuck, it was like in *Star Trek* when they
go to warp speed.

As I pulled off to the right, I almost crashed into a wall of
orange and blue. Dean and Farrar had taken a huge gamble and
cut the final right-hand corner dangerously close. At the speed
we were going, the angle they'd chosen not only put them in serious danger, but also endangered anyone in their vicinity. Their
trigonometric miscalculation ended up playing perfectly into our
hands. *They* had to scrub speed, while Mark Renshaw and Cav
used every last centimeter of real estate on the left side of the road
to keep their momentum. Renshaw stood and powered up his own

rockets before giving way to perhaps the greatest sprinter of all time.

With only daylight in front of him, Cav confirmed why he is known as the Manx Missile. It was only when I could watch the replays on television that I truly appreciated the devastation he had unleashed on his competitors. Cav didn't just win his sixth stage, he blew away any doubt of his supremacy. His speed was otherworldly.

BOB STAPLETON

We knew we needed George to win in Paris, having ridden all those stages with a broken collarbone. If George didn't suffer through those days, we had no chance on the Champs-Élysées. Even though the Garmin guys almost took out the peloton in the final corner, if George hadn't made the critical move with one kilometer to go, there's no way Renshaw and Cav would have been set up to go 1-2. I'll never forget Cav's emotion. His passion is etched in my brain. George made that possible.

BRIAN HOLM

We went over everything that morning in the meeting. I said we were here to win, and that when they grew old like me, they would look back and say this was the best time of their entire career. This team was something so special, and it would only happen once in a lifetime.

George rode from the red kite banner until the last corner. He used all his anger and frustrations in one four-hundred-meter pull. Imagine riding over those last cobbles with a broken collarbone . . . crazy!

George didn't let Julian Dean smack him in the last right corner. Not even a four-ton truck could have moved George that day. It's a bit scary that a fine gentleman can turn from Dr. Jekyll to Mr. Hyde that quickly, but that's why George was "Captain America," a good role model for all young kids who dream about becoming a pro cyclist. That's why I loved to work with George. He was always setting new standards for pain and discipline.

MARK CAVENDISH

We don't win like that without George. He made it impossible to lose. I said, "You wanted that" to him afterward and his reply was, "Yeah, I had fire in my eyes because it was Garmin!" I often referred to him as "the Guarantee." He could put anyone in the best position at any time.

My partying was put on hold for a while. The day after the Tour ended, I was in a doctor's office back home in Girona. He didn't believe me and was downright dumbfounded when I told him I'd broken it almost a week previously and that I'd been biking on it since then. I was sent home in a sling, with specific instructions to rest. I called Bob and told him I wouldn't be able to race the following week in Hamburg.

I'd been told to lay off the exercise, but to be honest, I was on the trainer right away. I had some unfinished business to attend to, and if I wasn't going to be allowed to race, I'd at least be damn sure I was ready when I got the chance. I lived like a monk, counted calories, and denied myself any excess. I'd checked the calendar: the U.S. National Championships were August 30. If I did everything right, I could heal in time to fulfill my plan. In my mind, I was destined to win another national title. I never doubted for an instant it was a foregone conclusion; I just needed the future to arrive and the race to happen.

I saw it as my fuck you to everyone who had taken the yellow jersey from me that day in Besançon. I know it's childish, but I was mad at everyone.

The race was held in my hometown of Greenville, South Carolina. On race day, I knew everyone expected me to either dictate the pace or do the work to bring back early escapees. It was my friend Dave Zabriskie who set off on an insanely brave solo effort at the start of the race. He rode alone for almost one hundred kilometers, nearly half the race. I bided my time in the group and waited until the last ascent up Paris Mountain, a climb that nine out of ten days is part of my training. Eventually, we formed a group of eight that agreed to an uneasy alliance. At one point, our inattentiveness allowed the chasers to get within ten seconds, but once we got into town and began the small finishing circuits, we were able to build back our advantage.

I knew I was a marked man. But no one else knew my motivation or how much it meant to me to win a third national title. Both were powerful propellants. At around three kilometers to go, friendships went out the window. Jeff Louder was first to take off, but I knew the undulations near the finish would rip the energy out of any of us. So I waited. Finally, I went off in pursuit, and Andrew Bajadali hitched a ride. We passed Louder with half a kilometer left, then Bajadali came around me with about three hundred meters to go. I found a final gear, fought back, and eventually passed him just 150 meters from the line. I held on, and got to hold my arms in the air once more as champion of the United States.

It was my third National Championships. They were all special, but this counted a little bit more. For one, it was in front of my fans in Greenville, but more important, it was a championship that no one would ever dispute. I knew what I'd done in the past, and even though all of my wins felt earned, there could never be any debate about 2009. Add in the extra motivation from what had happened in France a couple months before, and it's still a jersey that brings back strong emotions.

CHAPTER 28

THE YEAR 2010 BROUGHT major change.

The new year saw me join BMC Racing. It was a tough decision, but it was not taken lightly. I'd actually had my initial contract meetings right around the time of the classics back in 2009. Rich had set them up while I was racing in Belgium, and even though it was March, we felt the time was right to start planning for the following year.

RICH

We held the meetings in Kortrijk, near the hotel George always stayed in. We met first with Bob Stapleton. He wanted to cut George's salary in half, since he was having some money issues. Obviously, that was a hurdle. The next day, I met with Scott Sunderland from Sky. He explained they were going to be a new team, with a new philosophy, and they wanted George. I told him what it would take and he nearly threw up! I didn't budge, emphasizing that if he wanted someone to lead his team, my number was what it was going to take. Finally, we met with

Och [Jim Ochowicz], who was now with BMC
Racing. My dad was there with me; we had a few
bottles of wine while we caught up, and finally,
Och emphatically said, "We have to have George."
I looked him in the eye. "George gets paid a lot
of money." Och never lost my gaze. "How much?"
and then didn't even blink after hearing my answer.
"Send me a letter of intent, DONE."

JIM OCHOWICZ

We were only a pro continental team in 2009. I told
Andy [owner Andy Rihs] that if we wanted to get in
the Tour de France, we needed to make some strate-
gic moves. We had to have a cyclist with undeniable
credibility to attract other riders. We needed a guy
to commit to our project and allow us to use his
name. The best person that I knew to fill that role
was George. If the others found out he was on the
team, I just knew they would sign.

RICH

I did the letter, but I really thought there was no way
Och would agree to everything. Besides the money,
there was a generous travel package, George would
get to dictate his race schedule, we'd use Hincapie
Sportswear to outfit the team, and we also got to
bring another rider of our choosing onto the squad.
Five minutes after I sent him the letter, he called and
said, "You've got a deal. Have George sign it." Och is
a phone guy, and he must have called me two or three
times a day until that deal was completed. That's how
important George was to his overall plan.

Anyone who knows me will laugh at this—and I quickly admit, I'm not the best at making decisions—but even though Och had given us everything we'd asked for, I still had a tough time deciding to leave HTC. Mark Cavendish had become like a brother to me, and I felt a responsibility to him and to the success we'd built.

MARK CAVENDISH

When he told me he was leaving, I filled up. I couldn't feel anything but the tightness in my throat. I was gutted, and very emotional. I love him to bits. He's very much a big brother. On a personal level, I didn't want him to leave, and on a professional level, I freaked out a bit. I didn't know if I could win without him.

There was no guarantee BMC was going to be a great team. I was already on one, so I was rolling the dice by leaving.

MARK CAVENDISH

He should be known as the most famous domestique ever. There's no one in his league. He helped all types of riders win—GC, climbers, classics, sprinters, TT . . . It didn't matter the situation, he worked with the best in their discipline. He worked as their right-hand man.

BOB STAPLETON

He delivered everything he said he would and more. He wasn't a superstar, but someone who was quiet, calm, and showed what was possible.

But Och was also like family. And the chance to use Hincapie gear was a great opportunity for the company—an opportunity I knew might not come along again. To go to BMC was a big step, and really, a big leap of faith. We had no idea who was going to be on the team. Ultimately, I was motivated by a chance to do something new. Upon hearing the news in the fall of '09, most people felt I'd just switched so that I could slowly ride off into retirement, which only fueled me more.

Ten years before signing the BMC deal, my agent at the time had given me a Mont Blanc, telling me his father had always told him to make sure to have a nice pen with which to sign contracts. It was a meaningful gesture, and I still use that pen to this day. But before I signed, I went in to our office in Greenville one final time to weigh the decision I was about to make. Our Hincapie Sportswear office had filled a big chalkboard with a list of the pros and cons. I'd made up my mind, but it was fun to involve our office workers since their workload would greatly increase if I decided yes. Collectively, they wanted me to sign, and it was fun to see their enthusiasm.

RICH

I couldn't help but think that Och was repeating history. In 1980, he'd needed legendary speed skater Eric Heiden to get his fledgling cycling team, 7-Eleven, up and running. It was only through Heiden's agreement to be the figurehead and face of the team that sponsors jumped on board. Now, thirty years later, Och was using the same approach. This time, the lure and linchpin was George.

In the fall of 2009, we all traveled to Switzerland for our first team meet-and-greet. Cadel Evans had just won the World Championships in Mendrisio. Och had mentioned that Cadel was one of the guys he had targeted, but having just won the rainbow stripes, I figured there was no way Cadel would come ride for BMC. As world champion, he could dictate where he went and whatever team he joined. Before I boarded the plane, I called Och, and to my surprise, Och confirmed Cadel had called and said he was coming. That was to be my first indication, of many, of how different Cadel was from what I perceived him to be.

I stayed a couple days after the initial camp so that we could have a brief, somewhat clandestine, meeting with Cadel at one of Andy Rihs's hotels in Lachen. There as well were Andy, Och, and Dr. Max Testa. Since Cadel hadn't officially signed with the team, we wanted to wait until after the camp to meet with him. Cadel came in with a focus I hadn't expected but instantly admired. His demeanor was laid-back, but his approach toward the Tour was very much "been there, done that" in regards to the minor steps on the podium. He was choosing his next team based on the idea of winning it all. He made no secret that he felt my experience, leadership, and commitment to past leaders was the one ingredient he'd lacked in the past. The prospect of joining BMC and riding alongside me excited him because of the possibility to finally have all the pieces of the puzzle.

CADEL EVANS

George signing with BMC was the biggest sign that the team was serious. It instantly gave the team credibility, and further, eliminated my need to do much research. I knew he wouldn't go to a team if it wasn't professional and he wasn't confident they could win. I trusted George's judgment, and it made me see the team in a better light.

Once everyone had signed, Och, Andy, and our directeur sportif, John Lelangue, felt like we had a great shot at getting invited to the best races under the UCI's Wild Card status. We were enticing PR for any race organizer, having the world champ (Cadel), the U.S. champ (me), and international stars like Italian Alessandro Ballan (2008 world champion), German Marcus Burghardt (multiple stage winner of the Tour), and Norwegian Karsten Kroon (a classics specialist, also a stage winner of the Tour) on the squad. I was excited to have a number of good Americans on the roster as well, including Brent Bookwalter.

TEJAY VAN GARDEREN

Timing is everything. I had signed my contract to join HTC thinking George would be there. A couple days later, he calls and says, "Hey, if you haven't done anything, you should really think about coming to BMC." My whole goal in going to HTC was so that we could be teammates! He'd always been supportive and a source to rely on, and being on the same squad would have intensified our bond, but it wasn't meant to be . . . yet.

Right after New Year's, I was in Australia to do the Tour Down Under with Cadel. The crowds were insane—reminiscent of Lance's fans in their fervor and passion toward Cadel in his world champion's jersey. He was relaxed and easily able to balance his PR responsibilities with getting the days of racing into his legs. I was struck by how laid-back he was, and how different my perception had been. Cadel and I had always exchanged hellos, but it was never much more than that before our fall '09 meeting. We were all getting used to one another, as well as confirming, from an organizational standpoint, that we knew what we were doing. It was a feeling-out period, without any real margin for error. The learning curve went from the bottom all the way to the top.

CADEL EVANS

From the very beginning in Australia, I could see how the other riders looked up to him. They also looked to his mood and attitude to be the indicator. His calmness and consistency set the bar for us all.

Cycling was Och's passion, but day-to-day managing of a team was new to him. He'd been a consultant for Andy Rihs for a couple years, but now, even though he was always known for being organized, this was a whole different level. That year, at Het Volk in Belgium, we had a perfect storm of circumstances that highlighted the team's infancy.

Back in Girona, I'd been forced out of our apartment due to mold. I'd been sick, perhaps from (take your pick) training, the weather, and/or my living conditions. It was cold in Belgium, the race was hard, and when I flatted, due to so many groups strung out on the road, it took forever for our team car to reach me. I knew it would be a long shot to get back to the front. After chasing for over ten kilometers, it was clear that I wouldn't be rejoining the leaders. The conditions only got worse. The winds picked up, and on the horizon, the black clouds telegraphed there was a storm on the way.

Into the headwind, our small group had slowed to a crawl. All of a sudden, I noticed the broom wagon behind us. I got a burst of adrenaline, thinking, There's no way I'm getting in THAT! I proceeded to convince our whole group of about twenty riders that we were going to carry on. Matters only got worse. The temperature dropped ten to fifteen degrees as the black cloud encroached. As the wind kicked up, it began to rain sideways, and more than a couple guys started to voice their concern for our safety. Eventually, the moto assigned to stay with us said, "You're on your own!" and shot up the road.

Fabio Baldato, our race director, implored us: "Just make it to the feed zone, we'll take care of you there." When we got there, the feed zone had closed. There was no way we were going to make it to the finish. It might have only been afternoon, but the lack of light made it feel as if the sun had already set. When the hail started, I began to think we were goners. Pitch black, gale-force winds, near freezing temps—not exactly ideal conditions. All the other riders we'd been with had scurried into their team cars. The Gerolsteiner and Garmin guys practically left their bikes on the road in their haste. My Swiss teammate Martin Kohler was with me, and he started looking at me with real fear in his eyes. Even though he was outwardly doing his best to show strength, his eyes gave away that he was really freaking out. I did a quick assessment and realized our team car was nowhere to be found.

Just as I was about to cross over into full panic mode, a Belgian family drove up alongside us and the father said in a thick accent, "George! We love you! Can you sign my kid's hat?" I found myself saying out loud, "I'll give you my bike if we can get in your car!" Just as we were figuring out how to fit two freezing humans and twenty kilos of cold carbon into his vehicle, a PR car and a minivan driven by a man named Gunter pulled up. The minivan was completely empty and became our lifesaving chariot for the ride to the finish line. I am still indebted to all those kind Belgian fans.

Even though we got left for dead at the feed zone, I didn't hold any ill will toward the staff. It was just part of the team's growing pains in those initial months. We learned together, and it bonded us even tighter. It was a new adventure. We were all professionals, but we had to learn one another's mannerisms, idiosyncrasies, and patterns.

Spring came and went. The classics were good to me, but I still didn't land on the top step. It really didn't matter; that wasn't why I was riding. Don't get me wrong, I always wanted to win, but Cadel's commitment to me, and the role he needed me to play in July, had skewed my interest and my focus. May was to be the month I truly tested my form.

Even before the Tour of California, I had known about Floyd's e-mail exchanges and meetings with the race organizer, Andrew Messick. This was the third year in a row I was now dealing with a Floyd issue—2008 was the videos, '09 brought the Paris–Roubaix phone call, and now, in 2010, he was threatening to reveal our past again. It didn't take a rocket scientist to see that the scenarios were escalating. At the press conference before the race, Lance informed me, Levi Leipheimer, and Dave Zabriskie that he had the room on lockdown, and had hired extra security.

In retrospect, all of these events may have left me concentrating on my job less than 100 percent. At the start, I was happy to be in great shape, but then immediately pissed off when I crashed on my head in Stage 1. It seems now like an obvious omen. As in, the universe was telling me to use my head. Days later, after Stage 5, checking my messages on the bus in Bakersfield changed my life.

In all the preparation for what might happen, I was always most concerned with the media, and how Floyd's message would affect my *daily* interaction. I never, in a million years, expected it to escalate to the level it did. Upon hearing Jeff Novitzky's voice, I was 100 percent surprised, and completely adrift.

Floyd was the devil I knew. The feds represented the unknown. Floyd brought the wrath of the media and possible suspension from the sport I loved. I wasn't exactly sure what the government's involvement brought to the table, but I was now dealing with something I had never imagined. *Jail* became not just a four-letter word, but a fuzzy, frightening scenario that crippled me with fear.

DAVID ZABRISKIE

That night in the hallway, we were just trying to figure things out. I didn't understand what was happening, but because we were friends, I tried to help him make sense of it. I was placed really well in the race, and I remember one or two nights after being with George, deciding I was going to go to USADA and tell them everything. His situation gave me the idea that some major powers were getting involved. It made me realize that the time was right, and it was smart for me to talk. George's predicament gave me the strength to face up to my past, even though it was still a time when guys who spoke up could get destroyed for doing so.

The phone call from the feds added a ton of tension, but it also added work. I felt fortunate I had such accomplished, influential friends I could call for advice. I knew I needed to reach out to people smarter and more removed from the situation than me. They all knew how to deal with high-stress situations, and advised the first step was to get legal representation. They all offered to help as well.

Within hours, I told Och, and while being supportive (basically telling me I would still have a job), he made sure to distance himself and emphasize this was *not* a BMC issue due to the time frame in question.

I never called Novitzky. I called a friend in Los Angeles, who was an entertainment lawyer, and he agreed to help with the initial phases. We set up a timetable, and then he handled all contact with the government.

The next day, I did what I had always done when something was wrong, or bothering me. I went hard on the bike. Ever since I had learned to ride, if something was not right at school, with a girl, or in any aspect of my life, the bike was my sanctuary. It was my answer to anything, the one thing I could do that would make everything else melt away. In this case, I didn't know what the future held.

Stage 6 could be my last day of racing, ever. I was determined to make it into a breakaway. The harder the overall conditions, the better my chances, and leaving Pasadena toward Big Bear, the day started off with countless, almost crippling attacks. With every leg-draining surge, every yo-yoing of the pack and subsequent catch, my confidence grew. Finally, I pounced, and put myself among the group that stuck.

Being in a breakaway never complicated a race; it always made it easier, and that day the mission was even simpler. My mind was filled with daydreams of winning the stage and using the podium as part pulpit, declaring to the world, "Test my hair, test my urine, test my blood, and freeze it for fifty years! You're not going to find a fucking thing! Ever!"

Winning was my way to prove I was clean and that I could win now. Fuck the phone call and all that the future might hold. I never left the sport. I didn't run and hide. I chose to stay and try to change it. I set out to be influential in my own way and on my own terms. I wanted to win so I could say, "Cycling is my life. I can still win. I am still one of the best. And I'm clean."

I never got the chance. The break got caught. Peter Sagan won again. The desire to lash out still burned inside me, so I purposefully took the time trial easy the next day in order to rest for the final stage, a circuit in and around the Westlake Village/Thousand Oaks area, which included four times up a famous Los Angeles climb called Rock Store. It was similar to the Paris Mountain climb I did back home, and once again, I planned on enlightening everyone from the podium at the end of the day. Once again, I came close, but no platform for my rant was provided. Ryder Hesjedal ended up winning after bridging up to our break, and I took second. No shame in the result, but no satisfaction in a lost chance to make my opinion heard.

Oddly enough, the same day I got my phone call, Lance had abandoned the race. He fell early in the stage, and after riding a bit longer, he left. He texted me afterward and said he was thinking of not doing the Tour de France. I didn't tell him about my phone call, but I was sincere when I replied, "You can't quit now! Cycling's changed; go try to win the Tour!" Lance didn't believe the Floyd stuff was serious, but a certain message on my cell phone was evidence to the contrary. I told him he should take it all seriously.

The Monday after the race, my lawyer called Jeff Novitzky and began the process of agreeing to meet. Our main request (we couldn't call it a stipulation, since really I had no bargaining power) was that I testify after racing the Tour. Graciously, the feds were okay with that.

I talked to my lawyer at least a few times a week, and he was always very frank. I had to meet with Novitzky's people. I shouldn't leave anything out. If I lied, I'd be in serious trouble. I didn't know until a couple days before I left to race the Tour de Suisse that it had been arranged for me to meet with the government's reps after the Tour de France. It was never a question of if, it was always a matter of when, and after our request for more time was granted, I packed and got ready to race the 2010 Tour. The two stages toward the end of the Tour of California had been good for my state of mind. In the midst of all the uncertainty, and perhaps chaos, of my future, I wanted to prove I could still contend. My results gave me a clear indication I could.

The year 2010 was a tough one for the Hincapie men. Right after Paris–Roubaix, my brother's marriage of thirteen years came to an end. The day after I left to race the Tour of California, my father fell and shattered his right hip. He would end up being hospitalized for weeks. When I heard the news and insisted I immediately come home, both my father and brother told me, "No, you can't come home"; my racing was more important, and there was nothing I could do sitting in a hospital room. It showed me a whole new level of my family's commitment to my success. And as most superstitious people will tell you, bad things show up in threes—it was my phone call from the feds that completed the Hat Trick of Dire Circumstances.

Once I arrived in Rotterdam for the Tour's *grand départ,* most of my angst evaporated. BMC was to contest its first ever Tour de France, wearing Hincapie Sportswear, and I was tapped to aid and protect the reigning world champion, Cadel Evans, in his quest to win his first Tour title. We were an inexperienced squad, as shown when Mathias Frank crashed out in the prologue, his Tour over just as it began. It ended up being a three-week learning-the-ropes type of Tour.

JIM OCHOWICZ

George was well respected by the peloton, and for the generation that was just starting to transition, he provided a link. On a simpler level, due to the respect he was given, if he made a move, people gave us space. Prior to George being on the team, we weren't given that leeway. In the peloton's eyes, we hadn't earned it. George changed everything in the way we interacted as a whole with the other riders. George coming to BMC was critical.

Our introductory excursion had a major positive. Cadel wore yellow after Stage 8. And in a further testament to his toughness, we all discovered later that he'd actually broken his elbow in a fall he took early in the stage, then ridden all day controlling the pain while responding to the race.

CADEL EVANS

It was only one day, but I was proud I got to wear yellow over the rainbow stripes of world champion, with the Hincapie name on the jersey.

We'd gotten our feet wet, and in the process learned valuable lessons we'd apply in the future. Cadel's runner-up position in 2010's Giro d'Italia, combined with his performance in July, confirmed Cadel had the skills to win the Tour de France another year. We now had the knowledge, and the experience as a team, to do it.

BRENT BOOKWALTER, BMC TEAMMATE
2010-2012

After riding with him in the Tour, I had to constantly remind myself that while I could strive and aspire to be like George, I shouldn't beat myself up when I couldn't do the seemingly miraculous moves he could. He was always so good in race situations. He lived at the front, at the hardest part of the race; and at the most crucial, hardest, and important times, he delivered.

After the Tour, I was physically drained. Mentally, I had to rally to face the feds. I met with them in mid-August, in Los Angeles, ironically, in a building located along the time trial course I had raced months earlier. Before I flew to L.A., I went to New York to meet with my new law firm and be prepped for my deposition with the feds. I'd switched based on a referral from a friend. My new lawyer was a former bike racer, who was sympathetic to what I was going through and had a firm grasp on the type of law needed.

I arrived in NYC and was whisked into a boardroom with four or five people, and all I could think was, How the hell did I end up here?

I was peppered with what seemed like a thousand questions, and reminded over one hundred times to tell the truth. Each time, the caveat was "even if you have to throw people under the bus!" The grilling lasted more than five hours, but eventually everyone was satisfied that we were all armed with the same information and we had a plan.

I spent the night with a friend in the city, and the next day flew out to Los Angeles with my lawyer. In L.A., we headed straight to the courthouse, where we were ushered in a back door to avoid any press who might have gotten wind of something. A DEA agent met us at security in order to escort us. As we went through the metal detector, my stress level grew with every second. I began pulling my metallic items—mainly electronics—out of my pockets. I hadn't thought about it beforehand, but my "normal" was to carry a number of cell phones. I pulled out my team phone, then my personal phone, then my European phone, and finally my Hincapie company phone. I nervously looked over at the DEA agent, who had a look on his face that read, Who the fuck is *this* guy, a drug dealer?

I did my best to telepathically apologize while chastising myself for being so stupid as to bring so many phones. Since we'd come in the back way, we had an extended walk through the corridors and hallways. With each step, one major question rattled inside my head: How is it possible, with everything I've done in my career, that it's come to this?

Since I'd signed an agreement not to be deposed in front of the grand jury, we all met in a room, where I was finally face-to-face with a number of serious individuals.

Originally, they'd wanted me to meet right after racing in France. But I needed to decompress after my three weeks on the bike. I'd provided them with a one-sheet of information before the Tour, confirming most of the basic information, and that bought me some time. It didn't matter when I went in, but I knew I'd be exhausted after the Tour, so I wanted to delay the process as much as possible.

Jeff Novitzky was the most intimidating presence before the meeting got under way. I knew of his reputation, plus his physical characteristics, mainly his six-foot-six height, and it all added up to a scary aura. Once he introduced himself, however, he couldn't have been nicer. There were a total of seven or eight people present: aside from Novitzky, prosecutor Doug Miller, an FBI agent, a couple of court reporters, my attorney, and a young assistant for the government who was the gruff one of the bunch.

The room was no bigger than a classroom. There were no windows; there was nothing on the white walls. An unattractive brown plastic table was in the center, with uncomfortable plastic chairs. As I sat down, immediately my first thought was of the phone call I'd received from Jim Ochowicz seventeen years earlier, asking me to become a professional cyclist, and I remembered how excited I had been. Now, I was afraid. The seating arrangement broke down along company lines. They were on one side; we were on the other.

Once the proceedings began, I was hammered with questions.

They wanted to know about my conversations with other cyclists. Timetables of when things occurred. They knew about my whole life. It was a very awkward and disconcerting feeling. It scared me that they could know so much, and actually, at times, they reminded me of things I had completely forgotten.

The first question they asked was, "Did you get stopped for drugs in the Charlotte Airport in 1996?"

I hadn't thought about that incident in fourteen years! My attorney immediately looked at me and said, "You didn't tell me about this!" We'd prepared for the deposition meticulously, but I hadn't even remembered it then.

As the hours went by, it was all a blur. Throughout the process, I kept remembering a video one of my buddies sent me of Marion Jones being interviewed by Oprah. In it, Jones talked about how she'd thought for a second about how to answer one question in her deposition, and that, of course, was the answer that eventually landed her in jail. My buddy's line attached to the e-mail and video was simple: "Don't let this be you." So, I made sure not to. I answered everything truthfully.

When it was over, Novitzky and Co. told me I'd probably have to come back for some follow-up questions, but they were very appreciative of me taking the time to come in and expressed what seemed like genuine empathy, noting that it must have been hard for me.

As we walked out, my lawyer tried to soothe my frayed nerves. "You did a good job. I know it was hard. You're safe. You told the truth. I know you felt bad talking about other people, but that was the only option."

I was supposed to travel directly to a friend's to prepare for the Tour of Utah, but I was so mentally cracked that I needed to return to Greenville to be with my family. I changed my ticket to return

on the red-eye, and was willing to forgo my usual total commitment to race preparation in order to be with Melanie and decompress for a few days. Upon recounting what I'd been through, she
was a bit shocked but happy that I was home and that the process
had finally started. At least we knew there weren't going to be any
legal ramifications. I told her the toughest part was talking about all
the people, places, and events, and the eagerness of the government
to place blame on the people, rather than on the *sport*. I felt that was
the wrong approach.

I couldn't help but think how hypocritical it all seemed. There
was a monument on Mont Ventoux to Britain's Tom Simpson, who
died during the 1967 Tour because he took amphetamines. In some
ways, his drug use was a precursor, and also a direct link, to the escalating drug "arms race" that had gone on throughout the history
of our sport, the never-ending quest to get better by any means.
He gets immortalized. We get prosecuted. I didn't see the fairness.

JONATHAN VAUGHTERS
Ethically, did Merckx, Fignon, or Anquetil do anything different than George? No.

I never saw the feds again. Even though they scheduled other
sessions multiple times, the meeting kept getting moved or shifted
to another date. There were trickling media reports throughout the
months, so my lawyer would call to confirm facts, but the experience shifted into the background of my life. The last attempt the
government made to meet was penciled in for January 2011. They
canceled.

I ended up crashing out of the Tour of Utah in August 2010,
hurting my knee on one of the final stages. It caused me to take
time off the bike, limiting my preparation for the U.S. National

Championships in Greenville, where I ended up finishing fifth,
behind the winner Ben King, who'd had a phenomenal ride off
the front for most of the day, but whose result was aided by too
many teams expecting our BMC squad, along with Garmin and
RadioShack, to do all the work to bring back a break that at one
point had been nineteen minutes in front. I wasn't anywhere near
my best, but the competition that year wasn't about defending the
jersey. It was about making a point: I felt I was as good as anyone
in the peloton. I wasn't the best that day in my hometown, so I was
still very motivated to prove I was.

2010 drew to a close with races in Canada, a family vacation
afterward, moving into a new house, and noticeable growth in our
business. My father was recovering from his fall. Life was good.
Amid it all, my optimism made me firmly believe the best was yet
to come.

CHAPTER 29

I HAD A GREAT OFF-SEASON of training bridging 2010 into 2011. The winter weather wasn't bad in Greenville, averaging around fifty degrees, with less than normal rain. I was healthy and I felt good. I approached the season with a newfound desire to prove I could still race at the highest level in the professional ranks. I was as good as anybody, and I was as good as I'd ever been.

I started the season off at Montepaschi Strade Bianche (now called Strade Bianche), the Italian race in Tuscany that adds a unique gravel element and is considered a warmer alternative to the Northern classics. Two of my teammates finished in the top ten. I ended up fifteenth, but left feeling good about my form and fitness.

I headed north to gorge on my usual spring suffer-fest.

The Tour of Flanders is unlike any other bike race in the world. It is, without question, the hardest one-day bike race ever created. What seems like a million corners, combined with twenty to thirty steep pitches and narrow roads, none of which go the same direction for more than a mile, all mix together to make it war on a bike. There isn't a race in North America that compares. Flanders may as well be a different sport.

I finished sixth, five seconds behind winner Nick Nuyens. I'd been in the lead group with Fabian Cancellara, Tom Boonen, teammate Alessandro Ballan, and Sylvain Chavanel, but I didn't react at the right time, and the split second of indecision cost me valuable seconds at the line.

At Paris–Roubaix, untimely punctures and crashes took me out of contention, but in a definite sign of my shifting priorities, I came out of the classics that year satisfied and labeling them successful because I wasn't hurt. Nothing broken in my body was a tangible yardstick.

May brought the Tour of California and—surprise, surprise—a renewed sense of drama. In 2010, I had been targeted only as part of a large group. But in 2011, Tyler Hamilton was interviewed on *60 Minutes,* and CBS focused on me in its promotion of the show. My lawyer and I knew it was coming. *60 Minutes* had been calling him trying to work out a deal: in exchange for me commenting, the producers would keep my name out of the story. In order to drum up PR, CBS aired part of Tyler's interview on Thursday, May 19. The next night on the *CBS Evening News,* they aired a segment dealing with me. The onslaught of attention began. It was worldwide news. Google it today and close to forty thousand results will appear. Phone calls, interview requests, people at the race: everyone wanted a comment.

I released a statement via my attorney.

"I can confirm to you that I never spoke with *60 Minutes.* I have no idea where they got their information."

I also gave a quote to the Associated Press at the race in Solvang. I declined to talk specifically about the *60 Minutes* piece, but added: "It's unfortunate that that's all people want to talk about. . . . I'm not going to partake in any cycling-bashing. I have done everything to be the best I can be. . . . I want the focus on the future of the sport, what it's done to clean itself up. I believe in cycling and want to support it."

Everyone knew the information in the CBS story was leaked from my testimony to the investigators. I was pissed off because I was on the start line with other guys who had testified, but they weren't getting dragged through the mud. But I certainly wasn't going to dog them out. Jonathan Vaughters knew about the story as well. He'd talked to CBS in order to keep his guys out of the report. I didn't fault him for protecting his riders, but at the same time, I didn't like being the sole target. I was getting crushed on social media sites, but in person, people were vocal in their support.

For the second year in a row, the Tour of California became more than a bike race. It was hard to stay focused. I wanted to drop out, but my attorneys implored me not to, saying it would be a PR nightmare. Thankfully, the day the news broke, a great friend happened to be at the race. He's a highly successful businessman and public figure, a smart guy at the top of his field. He reached out, so we got together and talked. Just hearing he still supported me, and judged me not by my past but on the person he knew, was very helpful.

At the time, and throughout the process since then, I've had my haters, but I'm thankful I haven't lost one friend. I'm incredibly appreciative of the group of people in my life, and how they have never wavered.

Just a week later, the U.S. National Championships were back in Greenville, and with them came an added incentive. The media storm after the *60 Minutes* story was unrelenting. A friend of mine who worked for a local TV station kept asking me to do an interview, promising that she wouldn't ask any questions about the swirling revelations and accusations. I finally agreed, and on live television, the first question out of her mouth was "Did you dope?"

The race proved to be more straightforward, but no less frustrating. My mantra, once again, centered on my insistence that the world knew I was riding clean. I didn't care how I was tested, and whether or not the samples were held for eternity, no banned substances would ever show up. There weren't any. And I wanted every single person on the face of the earth to know. I thought I had the race won. I took off with about three hundred meters to go, sprinting around RadioShack's Matt Busche and thinking there was no way he could catch me. For the first time in my life, however, I got leg cramps, and there was nothing I could do except try to hang on. A quarter of the diameter of a wheel ended up being the difference. I came in second to Busche.

There would be no speech, no shouting at the rafters, just more time to mull over how I could make my message stick. Losing that year mattered more because I didn't get to say what I wanted. I didn't care about the jersey; I cared about being heard, being believed, restoring faith in the sport that defined my life.

It was time to focus on the Tour de France, which meant a mandatory prep race in June, so off to the Tour de Suisse I went. Afterward, I traveled with a number of guys on the BMC squad, as well as my family, to Livigno, Italy, for altitude training. It was a ten-day camp to get ready for the Tour, and I loved every minute of it. The riding was excellent, my family had a great time, the food was fantastic, and the people were incredibly friendly. We were in a tiny apartment, but it was such a good atmosphere for family and training, it prepared me perfectly, mentally and physically, for my job in July.

As we arrived on the west coast of France for the start of the ninety-eighth edition of the Tour, we knew Cadel was riding extremely well. Och had been to his altitude camp in June and reported that he could tell by the way Cadel was climbing that he was lean and motivated, and his power numbers were better than ever. We knew he could win, but we also knew it would be hard work.

Stage 2, the team time trial, was an immediate test. We finished a close second to Garmin, but ultimately it worked in our favor. Thor Hushovd ended up being in yellow for a week, and that meant we didn't have to work to control the race. We only had to work to keep Cadel protected.

After the team time trial, Och's favorite event, he was extremely happy. He had bought wine at dinner, and the whole team was enjoying the evening. Och had a habit of coming to the guys' rooms and shooting the shit after a good result. I was rooming with Marcus Burghardt, and a third person in our tiny Campanile Hotel room made it a tad overcrowded. But Och wasn't going to leave until he imparted his wisdom. He said, "Guys, we're in a good position. Good result today, but listen. All you have to do is . . . do not fuck this up!" I started laughing, but Marcus, being the staid German, was shocked. It became our funny mantra for the rest of the Tour.

Don't fuck it up.

It was all-hands-on-deck in Stage 4 as we raced into Mûr-de-Bretagne. The roads were extremely narrow in that part of France, and it was a constant fight the whole day to stay out of trouble on the rolling pathways. Toward the end, Manuel Quinziato and Marcus Burghardt helped me keep Cadel out of harm's way. I led him out until eight hundred meters to go, and then his instincts took over.

CADEL EVANS

With only thirteen kilometers to go, I had a mechanical, a problem with my derailleur, and needed to decide whether or not to make a bike change.

George very coolly said, "Do it now." He took control of the decision making and marshaled everyone
into line so that they could work to get me back into
position. The roads were narrow, and after some
nervousness and a bit of panic, he had gotten me
into the right spot, in time for the last climb. He was
the last teammate I saw before taking matters into
my own hands. I went from almost losing the Tour
to winning on the day because of his demeanor.

It was a surprise win, and it buoyed our whole team. Our squad
wasn't made up of the best climbers, so we had to take advantage
when we could. We made a habit that year of pressing our advantage in less than ideal conditions and situations. We took advantage
of the dicey stages.

BRENT BOOKWALTER

I played a very different role than George, but he
was masterful at reining me in. I was always so eager
to ride hard once I was given the opportunity to be
at the front, but he never lost sight of the long-term
goal. He was a calming and grounding force amid
the overall chaos, and his humble confidence was
contagious.

John Lelangue was the directeur, but I enjoyed a more vocal
role on the team. I liked being able to help with more than my
legs. On the road, I was the eyes and ears for the group, telling
them when to pay attention and where to switch their focus. Cadel
was laid-back and would rely on me to make the calls. He knew
where he needed to be and trusted me to get him in position. Even

though Cadel's conditioning was as good as ever, we never forgot for a moment that it would take a little luck to make it all work out.

One such instance was a gut feeling I had in Stage 9. Team Europcar's Thomas Voeckler went in a breakaway with eventual winner Luis León Sánchez. The day was marred by a couple of horrific crashes. One, on the descent of the Col de Peyrol, took out, among others, Alexander Vinokourov and David Zabriskie. Then, near the finish, a French TV car hit two of the five men in the break—Juan Antonio Flecha and Johnny Hoogerland. Because the peloton held up upon learning so many riders had gone down in the Peyrol crash, at one point, the break was up to almost eight minutes, so we decided we needed to close the deficit and not give Voeckler such a cushion. That small decision turned out to be huge by the end, but in the moment, it was just a call based on experience.

Cadel was an excellent bike handler and a master at studying the route. He was a freak about detail. He would know every corner, even which way the wind was going to blow. On Stage 16, we knew it would be a tricky descent into Gap. We got word over the radio that the descent was not dry, which provided us with an opportunity. Before I'd hit a descent, I always had to be in front. It's like setting up to be in a good position before hitting the cobbles.

CADEL EVANS

George had two great qualities as my teammate. First, I always knew he was looking out for my best interests. Second, he would only insert himself into a situation when he knew I needed him. He was not only great about tactically getting everyone in the proper position, but then he became the "insurance policy," hanging back in case something went wrong.

The break was already established, and with the miserable weather, we knew riders would be a little off their game, and not as decisive or willing to react. Typically, riders hope you never have to race downhill. It's nerve-racking enough to descend without the added pressure.

If you wait until someone else goes, you're fucked. You have to take the initiative. When we went, it pissed people off, wondering why we had upped the ante and started to race, but we had to use our strength. For the most part, we were all classics riders, bike handlers and rouleurs, not climbers. My senses were always amplified on a descent, but when you add in wet roads and the high-stakes game we'd committed to, it was an almost out-of-body experience. I felt like I was floating above myself, watching as I took risks, calculated moves, and smoothly strung out the group.

There were rules I lived by going downhill. I'd always look to see who was in my space. I'd never ride next to someone I didn't know or trust, especially if they looked like they weren't good at bike handling. It's easy to find the proven descenders in the bunch: they seamlessly move to the front. I'd always be in the first five to ten guys, to make sure I had time to react. The farther back you are, the more dangerous and harder it is to descend. A lot more water gets kicked up, visibility drops, and you're at the mercy of other riders' decisions.

We knew how good Cadel was in adverse conditions, and it made us much more motivated to go for it. It was never a call that John Lelangue made, it was just a feeling we had. Once I set the tone, I expected guys to follow, but I was continually looking back to make sure Cadel was with us. I can see the wheel behind me by looking underneath my bike, and can judge circumstance based on computing the surrounding factors.

Every rider learns how to read their tires, especially in the wet, so you can know what the tires can handle. That was essential. We increased the speed so quickly that the peloton stretched out for almost three kilometers behind us.

We didn't care what happened behind us. The goal was to keep Cadel in position all the way until the slopes of the Category 2 Col de Manse, the final climb of the day, and then go as hard and as deep into the climb as we could, until we couldn't any longer. Alberto Contador unleashed multiple attacks, which ended our attempts at control, and then it was up to Cadel to follow. As they crested the summit, Contador's efforts had cracked the Schleck brothers as well as Voeckler, and along with Cadel and Sammy Sánchez, he'd gained a gap of eighteen seconds.

Their return into Gap ended up deciding the Tour. Cadel utilized all his mountain-biking skills as he ferociously attacked the decline. With every twist in the road, he extended his advantage on Contador and Sánchez, and more important, the Schleck brothers and Voeckler. He showed no mercy and no fear, eventually gaining three seconds on Contador, twenty-one on Voeckler and Fränk Schleck, and a whopping one minute and nine seconds on Andy Schleck.

Two days later, Stage 18 brought its own drama. Andy Schleck went on a solo flyer that rivaled the best rides in Tour history. Unfortunately, I was of little use to Cadel and the team, as I had what inevitably happens in each Tour, a bad day. I was hugely disappointed, but at dinner I felt better as we recounted Cadel's heroic chase, and I was buoyed by how relaxed and confident he seemed. Cadel was fired up from the day's success, but we all knew the next day was crucial. I left dinner emboldened by Cadel's aura. He was in the Zone.

Stage 19. Three brutal climbs, all-out from the start, finishing on the legendary Alpe d'Huez. The day couldn't have started off worse for us: Cadel had a mechanical problem on the climb up the Télégraphe, eventually had to have two bike changes, and then found himself virtually alone—behind the main contenders, but ahead of the main field. I immediately got on the radio and told him to wait for us. It was much better to lose a little time initially in order to then let us gain it back for him later. It was better for us to crush ourselves in an all-out effort to get him back into position than it was for him to fight on with no teammates.

A decision like that went against everything we're hardwired to do, but Cadel smartly listened. I told our guys to just make it to the top of the Télégraphe as fast as they could, and we'd regroup there. Once together, we hammered the descent and transition to the Galibier, where we'd go up the opposite side from the day before. I told Manuel Quinziato, "I need everything," and we proceeded to bring our leader back to the contenders.

I ended up producing my best hour of power of the year that day.

I'd decided that Cadel would need Steve Morabito and Amaël Moinard the most, so I had instructed those two guys to stay on my wheel the whole time until I blew up. We needed those two guys to try to stay with Cadel and protect him once I was gone. I pulled as long as I could up the Galibier, and once my body gave out, focused on making my own way to the finish, praying that I'd hear good news on the radio along the way.

CADEL EVANS

It was a crucial moment, but in the Tour, there are countless moments like that that add up. But, yeah, that day was almost unimaginable. The one day I get in the front group, but then to have to switch bikes, and make the team kill themselves to bring me back into contact . . . George got everyone to rally around me, in the most efficient and smartest way possible.

Cadel got some help over the Galibier and toward Alpe d'Huez from a few French riders who were perhaps a little jealous of Thomas Voeckler's time in yellow. And once on the Alpe, it became a battle: Cadel reacted time and time again as the Schlecks tried to deliver blow after blow. Cadel showed the world what I'd seen the night before.

He was in his Zone. Like a prizefighter who methodically jabs and counterpunches, he was not overly fluid, but perfectly powerful. I'd seen his face so often as he climbed the Tour's most legendary hairpins. Focused. All muscle. Cringing with each effort. But never willing to give in.

At the finish, he had to watch Andy Schleck pull on the yellow jersey, but we could all sense it was Cadel who had the upper hand. Andy was not known as a time trial expert, but it was one of Cadel's specialties. Cadel had stayed within fifty-seven seconds with the final time trial less than twenty-four hours away. It wasn't a foregone conclusion by any means, but a betting man would have felt pretty good placing his money on Cadel.

JIM OCHOWICZ

George calmly got the team to reassess (not easy to do with eight other guys), slow down, wait, and regroup. He not only organized the chase, but was the main contributor of effort until Cadel closed himself. He saved the Tour that day.

At dinner, Cadel was serene again. My Tour was over. The time trial was meaningless to me, so I could celebrate. Cadel shared a glass of wine with us all, and to see him that calm was memorable. He said he'd done all the work, knew the course, and would ride it again in the morning. It was soothing to see him that way. He was physically with us, but his mind was on a positive future.

In Grenoble, Cadel clinched his Tour title in fitting fashion, by crushing Andy Schleck in the time trial and *almost* beating Tony Martin for the stage win. We all watched in the team bus, screaming and hugging each other throughout his ride, as he easily ate into Andy's lead. Toward the end, John Lelangue got so nervous that Cadel might crash that he purposefully lied to Cadel about his time—telling him he was twenty seconds off the stage win, when in fact he was much closer—just so he wouldn't take unnecessary risks.

When he finally crossed the line, pandemonium broke out on our bus. No one left to go back to the hotel. It took well over an hour for Cadel to come back after the podium presentation and interviews, and we were all there to greet him as he walked on wearing the most coveted color in our sport.

CADEL

I walked into the bus and George and I did a fist-pump. That was our thing. We'd done it all Tour.
It was just a small way we bonded in big moments.

Cadel wasn't the type to make speeches, so that night at dinner, Och did it for him. The wine flowed. The stories were unending. I couldn't help but think it had been four years since I had led Alberto Contador down the Col de Peyresourde in Stage 15, and on that day, I'd helped Contador gain forty-three seconds on Cadel. Cadel ended up losing that Tour by only twenty-three seconds. It made me feel good that now I'd helped *him* win a Tour title in a similar fashion. Most of the team stayed up that night, reminiscing in the common room of our hotel, dining on hamburgers and wine. Nothing ever tasted better.

TEJAY VAN GARDEREN

I learned a lot from George that Tour, especially how to stay calm. That's his greatest attribute. After I lost the white jersey earlier in the race, he came up to me and said matter-of-factly, "It's a three-week race. You've got the TT coming up. Just keep kicking ass, because people are going to start cracking." Before learning from George, I tended to sweat the small stuff, but he always knew what to say to relax me.

The next day we flew from Grenoble to Paris, as the final processional stage started in Créteil. It was particularly fun to board the chartered plane and sit in first class with the rest of the BMC squad, and watch all the other riders and managers have to go back into coach. A final perk from the organizers for Cadel and the squad that got him there. I had a lot of friends and family come to Paris, and I found it surreal that I was part of a ninth winning team. It was comforting to know I was still there at an elite level; I was still part of the best team; I was still the athlete I'd always been. And I'd been completely clean for five years.

BRENT BOOKWALTER

It was one of the highlights of my career to get to ride into Paris with George, and see how excited he was. It was my first Tour win, and at number nine, he was as giddy, relieved, and emotional as I was.

JIM OCHOWICZ

Cadel would have had a hard time, if not an impossible one, winning the Tour without George. George decided when and where to use energy. Not just his own, but for Cadel and the whole group. Finding the right way to react is a day-to-day occurrence. Hell, it's not just one moment. That's what defines the Tour. Cadel won the Tour in the TT, and in his ability to stay with Alberto and Andy at the end of the climbs, but George protected him every pedal stroke until those critical moments. George made sure Cadel only had to think when it mattered and George expended the MENTAL energy all the other times. It was the million moments that Cadel didn't have to think that allowed him to use his energy at the right time.

CADEL EVANS

I don't think I would have won the Tour without George. Actually, I'd hate to think about the result we would have gotten without him. I considered it our victory. The team had done so much work. I came to BMC to be with guys who would do whatever was necessary, but George's commitment, and our bond, was on a whole different level. He was an extra set of eyes for me. I never thought I'd be able to have complete trust in another person. With George, it was even more. It was complete faith, and it was special. The biggest contribution he gave me that July was to create an aura of reassurance around me and the team. It was an air of conviction.

I was happy for Cadel, and I appreciated everything he had endured to get to this point. But it was a forced happiness, for all the festivities. I was relieved the Tour was over, but the shit had hit the fan before we left, and it was time to return.

In the United States, I'd constantly been hounded after the *60 Minutes* story, but in Europe it was a nonissue. The journalists just cared about the race. I knew I was headed back into the eye of the storm, and I was worried. I didn't know when my official testimony would be released; it was the black cloud on the horizon, one that was going to burst.

I had a great fall, highlighted by some good racing at the USA Pro Cycling Challenge in Colorado. I'd spent a few days beforehand in Aspen with Tejay Van Garderen, and we'd ridden the course for Stage 2, the "Queen Stage," as a training day. Heading over the two highest passes in Colorado, Cottonwood and Independence, it was not an easy day—when we did recon on it, or when we raced. I was psyched the day we did it in training because Tejay cracked before I did: he told me to go ahead with five kilometers to go to the summit of Independence, but with around one kilometer to go to the top, I, too, succumbed to the conditions.

When we both got there, we were dead. Completely drained. Starving.

A fan walked up and asked us if he could take a photo, and we agreed, on one condition—he had to give us whatever food he had. He got the photo; we each got half a tasty Clif Bar. Refueled, we headed down into town, but once there, we split off to go to our respective hotels.

Three days later we were racing. Tejay took off with about two kilometers to go to the Independence summit, and I thought, I just need to stay close. I knew I could catch him, and the others in front, on the descent. I got in a groove as I picked people off right and left; the weather conditions helped as other racers' hesitancy cost them valuable seconds. I passed Levi Leipheimer, Christian Vande Velde, and a host of others. Finally, a group of five formed at the front with me, Tejay, and Tom Danielson among them. It had been hot going up the mountain, now the thermometer swung the other way; it was bitter cold, and the rain made conditions even worse. From my recon ride with Tejay, I knew the descent, and when I saw an opportunity to weave through the riders, I decided to take a risk and go for the win.

As we headed into town, I had a sudden thought. *Tejay, that little fucker, didn't show me the finish!* He knew the area well and eventually led out the sprint, but I was able to come around him for my first win since my 2009 National Road Race title. It was fun, and funny, that we'd ridden most of the course together only days before, and now we finished one-two for the stage. Tejay was able to take over the race leader's jersey for his efforts. On the podium, I saw Lance, and we exchanged hellos, but nothing more. It was extremely awkward.

Cadel had come to Colorado as well. As Tour champion, it was great for the sport for him to be at the inaugural race in the Centennial State.

CADEL EVANS

George's win in Aspen made me appreciate what he meant to the sport. Seeing the fans' response when he won struck a chord. They didn't just cheer for the victory; they cheered passionately for him as a person. It really resonated with me how delighted the crowd was and how much respect he had earned. It was an example to me that doing your best and being a good person are just as important as winning races.

I ended up fifth in the overall classification, and I got to share some great days of racing with great friends. I knew I was winding down my career, and that week's success allowed me to appreciate it all even more.

CHAPTER 30

I'D HONESTLY THOUGHT I'D be done racing after my contract with Highroad, Columbia-Highroad, and HTC Columbia ran out, but Och had convinced me to hang on. I'd wanted to do a one-year contract, but he insisted on two. In 2011, we agreed to a one-year renewal with an option for 2013. Thus, 2012 started with a BMC training camp in Spain, but it was weeks later that the big news came on the Friday before the Super Bowl. The feds had dropped the case against Lance Armstrong. For the first time in years, I thought my testimony might not come out. I'd be lying if I didn't admit I felt a twinge of optimism at the possibility of my testimony never becoming public knowledge.

I never felt that the focus on past doping was good for cycling. I believed we had done more than any other sport behind the scenes to change the culture, and the media attention was only detrimental. We'd changed the mentality of the riders already by offering alternatives to the doping culture of the past. There were teams and organizations that were dedicated to the clean path, and offered a choice besides walking away and quitting. I felt, and still feel, that leaving the sport, then turning around and assigning blame years later, helps no one. The media had become so focused on just the wrongs we had done, without considering the "rights."

The spring wasn't notable for any racing reasons. I'd tweaked my diet a bit in January, and noticed I wasn't able to maintain my fitness later in races, which had been my strong suit throughout my career. I changed back right before Paris–Roubaix, and even though I felt better, it didn't matter. Flats and other race situations kept me out of contention. I rode around most of the early months of the year not enjoying my job as much as I should have. My results weren't stellar, and so I questioned myself. Och was already asking me to come back for 2013. He wanted me to come to the decision on my own, but was keen to have me in the squad for another year.

Fast-forward to the Tour of California, and a couple days before the start of the event. I was feeling great. I was happy, healthy, and motivated, so I said, "Fuck it, I'll ride one more year!" I loved the team; I got to make my own schedule and only race when I wanted. Riders work their whole careers to get to the point I'd reached, so it was very hard to leave.

I signed my contract to race for BMC in 2013 on the first day of the race, but the Stage 5 time trial in Bakersfield changed everything. It was a miserably hot day on the course, and as I drove back to the hotel, I checked my phone. I had a text and e-mail from my lawyer asking if I could talk. Even though I'd heard nothing since February, immediately I knew the drug story was back in play.

My lawyer told me USADA (the U.S. Anti-Doping Agency) had called, they were moving forward with the case against Lance, and they needed to talk to me as a witness. He further said that he had to call them back and that he'd keep me informed. It came down to a choice, or really an ultimatum. Either I agreed to talk to USADA or my racing days were over.

I spent the week in between the Tour of California and the

National Championships on the phone with my lawyer as he negotiated how and when I'd testify. Throughout those days, I vacillated
constantly as to what was the right decision. My friend and teammate Tejay Van Garderen was staying at my house, and I'm sure he
sensed something was amiss, as I had to leave dinners, or evening
get-togethers, to go talk on the phone at all hours of the night.

> ### TEJAY VAN GARDEREN
> I could tell something was going on. There would
> be subtle shifts in his personality, and eventually
> he shared what he was dealing with. The amazing
> thing was that once we got to the races, you couldn't
> tell anything was the matter. He'd already processed
> the "Oh shit!" and turned it into "It is what it is." He
> could turn it all off or separate it so well.

I didn't have to talk to USADA, but because they governed
my sport, if I wanted to keep riding professionally, they held all
the power. We finally agreed that I would talk to them right after
Nationals. I almost told them to fuck off, and decided to retire. I
called my brother and told him that was my plan. I was tired of
fighting. I just wanted it over. But then I realized if I did do that—if
I thumbed my nose at them, issued a press release, admitted my
doping past, and said my sorrys—nobody would have believed I
cared about the sport or tried to change anything.

If I stayed in, as painful as it would be, I could still race and still
be part of the change. I would send a message—I'm still here doing
what I've always done, and that's help the best.

> ### CHRISTIAN VANDE VELDE
> I feel the biggest change was from the inside, and
> it happened long before 2012—which is a compli-

ment to teams like Slipstream and Highroad. Those teams, we gave people an opportunity AND an organization to go to. The hardest pill to swallow is that we'd done a majority of the work to clean up the sport before the investigation.

We showed riders, and the public, that it was possible to race clean. If I hadn't done it, I would not have believed it was possible. It was a turning point mentally, and therefore physically, for the sport.

At Nationals, my focus was not on the road in front of me, but on the metaphorical path I'd committed to take, and the upcoming phone call. Roughly forty-eight hours after crossing the finish line in Greenville, I was on a conference call with Travis Tygart and his USADA team. With that call, I felt I went against everything I had stood for my whole career. I had been the "loyal lieutenant," the one guy people could count on. It's what had defined me, and now I was being forced to turn on my teammates, friends, and associates.

After that phone call, I struggled. I knew that I was the last pawn they needed. Once they got me, it was all over. They'd promised a reduced suspension and a statement saying I was part of the change in the sport. Their validation counted for nothing. I'd already been part of the change way before they'd come along.

It crushed me. My sleep suffered, and so did my relationships. But I slowly started to realize I needed to focus on the positives: my family and friends. Enzo's birthday was around the corner, and that helped me prioritize what I should appreciate. I did my best to find enthusiasm in racing, but there were many days I'd get out on the bike and cry. Not because of what I'd had to do, but because of the manner in which I'd been forced to do it and the knowledge I'd hurt people I cared about.

JONATHAN VAUGHTERS

Drugs have always been part of our sport, but the drugs that came about during George's era dramatically changed the landscape. It went from types of drugs that helped your performance by 1 percent to drugs that increased it by 10 percent. You can't overcome that with talent alone. Physiologically, there's no question he would have won more if doping didn't exist. In a fair world, he would have accomplished a lot more, not less. It's scientific fact. Doping allowed others a larger advantage than him.

At the Critérium du Dauphiné, our June prep race for the Tour de France, Cadel Evans and Tejay Van Garderen were both in the top ten after Stage 6, when I walked into Och's room and told him I was done—that I wanted to opt out of my contract for 2013. It had been eating at me since I testified, and when I knew the suspension was going to take place in the fall, I took it all as a sign that my time had come to an end. Och was shocked but didn't try to talk me out of it.

On the team bus after the last stage, without making a fuss, I informed Cadel and John LeLangue of my plans, then headed to the airport in Geneva with Jeremiah Renegar, my soigneur, who'd also become a great friend, and Tejay. I struggled with how I would break the news to these two, who in a relatively short time had become integral parts of my life.

Upon arriving at our nondescript hotel, we made our way to some bar stools, and over burgers and beer, I quickly dispensed with the small talk by dropping the bombshell that only three others already knew. After we got back to our cramped quarters—two beds in a room barely wide enough to open a suitcase—it was Tejay who wouldn't let the night end, declaring, "We should get some good wine to celebrate!" Room service brought one, then eventually two, of their best bottles. Amid the bonding, they helped me craft an e-mail to my closest friends explaining my reasons, and telling them it was time for me to leave the sport. I explained I'd finally had enough, and was tired of dealing with the grind of being a professional. I also typed up the press release I planned to send before flying back to the United States the next day.

TEJAY

He told me he was done and that it was his last season. I kept trying to convince him to go another year, but he was committed to his decision. We had ordered burgers and beers, but then decided to celebrate with some wine. We knew we'd have to get back to "Full Regime" starting in the morning, but this was a moment we wanted to share together. He sent the e-mail to his close friends, and wrote the draft to send to the press the next day. It was fun to play a small part.

I'd decided I'd hit "send" when I got into my seat on the plane. That way, I'd get some uninterrupted peace during the flight home. When I landed in the United States, I didn't have any regrets and received no negativity via e-mail. Everyone was supportive, and some were disappointed my career was coming to a close, but I was excited to start a new phase of my life. It was the first time in my career I came back to the United States after my June prep race, and it helped me immensely. My family only had to spend two weeks in Europe, not two months; I got to train on familiar roads, and I left for the Tour only days before the start.

On June 12, 2012, USADA publicly announced it was moving ahead with the case against Lance and five others, including Johan Bruyneel. It was a chaotic time, but I was relieved my role in the drama was drawing to a close. The Monday before the start of the Tour, I flew to Belgium and got ready for my seventeenth and final time around France. I tried not to attach too much significance to it all. But others did. At the team press conference, I was given a custom BMC bike commemorating the milestone of being the person to start the most Tours. Teammates, press, and other riders all wanted to express their support and their wishes as I counted down the days. All I cared about was doing my job. Being there for the team. I was over what was required to do the sport at the top level. I was tired, and I was looking forward to not having to worry about being fit every second of the day. I'd always had to be conscious of my image for my teams and sponsors; now, I wanted my life to quiet down.

TEJAY VAN GARDEREN

A perfect example of George's focus was that I only heard him talk about his retirement twice. The first day, before the prologue, he said, "Wow, I can't believe this is my seventeenth prologue. Okay, time to get to work." Then, on the last day, basically the same thing: "Wow, I can't believe this is my last time on the Champs-Élysées." All those days in between, it wasn't about him; it was about the team. He wasn't on a victory lap around France; he was trying to help us all win. The exact same attitude he'd had at his first Tour.

As for the racing, it wasn't Cadel's best year. We did everything we could to make sure he stayed in contention for as long as possible. The revelation of the race was Tejay, who had an epic Tour, wearing the white jersey as Best Young Rider for all but a couple of stages, and eventually becoming only the third American to win it. He and I roomed together, and before the start, I'd sworn off reading the cycling press. I just felt it was better to focus on my role, and not see anything that might take my mind off of my job.

Before the start of Stage 6 in Épernay, I woke up after him and enthusiastically said it was time to get ready for the day. Tejay knew about my reading ban, and very calmly said, "Dude, you may want to read the Internet."

TEJAY VAN GARDEREN

That was a bad morning. I was always waking up earlier than George in that Tour. I didn't want to wake him, so I would just lie in bed and browse the Internet, and this story was all over. He woke up not knowing that this bomb had been dropped on the world, and I didn't want to be the one to tell him. So we went to breakfast, everything was normal, and then we went back to our room to pack our bags. As we were about to leave I said, "Have you checked your phone today?" He said no, so I told him to turn it on, and the phone just blew up. I hated to be the one to break it to him that he was about to have a hell of a day, but I felt he probably needed to prepare himself for what was coming up.

The day before, the names of five of us who had testified in the USADA case had been leaked: Jonathan Vaughters, Christian Vande Velde, Dave Zabriskie, Levi Leipheimer, and me. We all knew the press would have to react, but I was fine with it all, actually more relaxed than ever. Why? Because I'd known for ages that these guys had testified, and now I wasn't going to be the only one dealing with the crap. My attitude was "Bring it." Safety in numbers.

The days flew by, and before I knew it, it was time to ride into Paris. There'd been a rumor about me leading the peloton onto the Champs-Élysées, but I did not want to do it. Having the eyes of the world on me is not my style, but as we drew closer to the City of Lights, first my old teammate and friend Bernie Eisel, then Mark Cavendish, then others started to pull up alongside me and confirm it was what the peloton wanted. The winner of the Tour, Team Sky's Bradley Wiggins, rolled up and said, "George, you have to do this. We all respect you." So I relented. I decided, Okay, what could it hurt?

Within seconds, Levi and Andreas Klöden slid beside me and asked, "Did you hear what Chris Horner's going to do?" My confusion betrayed that I had not. So they warned, "If you lead us out, he's going to chase you down." It took me a moment to process what I'd just heard. I'd had riders coming up to me all day, congratulating me and urging me to honor them and the race by leading into Paris. They represented the old guard and the new breed. I felt they respected me because I was not only the bridge between the generations, but I was still there, with them, performing. All except one guy.

I rode up to Chris and asked if he was really going to chase me down. I asked him, "What would you have done?" and said he was just lucky he didn't have to testify. His parting shot was "You don't deserve this honor. I'm chasing you down."

As we came around the Place de la Concorde and approached the Champs-Élysées, Team Sky slowed just enough to allow me to move to the front, and after some coaxing, I obliged. It could have been a final moment to savor, but instead, Horner kept his word, accelerating onto my wheel and eventually passing me to stage his one-man protest.

It was the maddest I'd ever gotten in my career. We had very different personalities, and I couldn't fathom being motivated to do such a thing. I didn't enjoy the last laps much because I was so furious.

TEJAY VAN GARDEREN

Team Sky, having the yellow jersey, wanted to honor him by letting him cross through first. I thought, Wow, Horner just stole his moment. I didn't feel good about it. I was pissed at Chris for fucking with my friend.

This was such a clear indication to me how fucked up our sport was—I was ostracized less for doping than for being honest.

After I crossed the line, my anger strangely melted away and my focus turned to the moment, my family, my friends, and everyone who had helped me along the way.

TEJAY VAN GARDEREN

He'd dealt with so much, but at races? Cool. Whatever came out, he just seemed to block it out. His attitude was "I've got a job to do. I'm going to do it the same until my last day." He could put it all aside and find something within the race to concentrate on. If you didn't know him, you would NEVER have known he was dealing with so much.

As we took our victory lap, oddly I found myself thinking, Don't crash! I tried to let the atmosphere soak in; this would be the last time I rode my bicycle on the Champs-Élysées. I thought back to when I'd first started, and how I'd never imagined I'd get to ride in the Tour once, let alone seventeen times. I remembered the good and the bad, and everything I'd gone through. Yes, I'd made some fucked-up decisions along the way. Yes, I felt bad for the handful of guys who felt they had to leave the sport because of doping. What I did was wrong, I realize that. But the sport needed to take responsibility for how fucked up it was too.

> ### TEJAY VAN GARDEREN
> I was overwhelmed as we took our victory lap. I was so happy to be able to share it with George. He shocked me, however, when he turned to me and said, "Remember this time, because one day, you'll be on the top step." George doesn't BS anyone. It meant so much to me for him to not only say that but also to believe it.

I relaxed, a lot, after July. I had one more major goal for my career, and that was to help Tejay win the USA Pro Challenge in Colorado, but I couldn't help it: instead of fighting against the natural letdown that always happened after the Tour, I embraced it. That meant I wasn't as prepared as I should have been. And I paid for it. It's a magnificent stage race, but as a rider, it turns you inside out, mainly due to the altitude.

Instead of racing the Tour of Utah and spending the week after in Colorado acclimating, I just went straight to the Pro Challenge. I remember thinking multiple times during the race, Thank goodness I don't ever have to suffer like this again!

It was worth it, however. Tejay battled throughout the week, wearing the leader's jersey for three days and finishing second overall, twenty-one seconds behind Christian Vande Velde.

> ### TEJAY VAN GARDEREN
> The time I spent at his house changed my life. He taught me the lifestyle of a cyclist. He opened my

eyes to what it took to be truly dedicated. I realized,
This is the life I have to live if I want to be great. I
vowed to be like him.

As crestfallen as I was for Tejay, I was happy for Christian when
he got the win. More than anything else, I was glad my days of
riding professionally had come to an end.

TEJAY VAN GARDEREN

I've never felt so bad after a race. He was my soldier.
Riding into Boulder, I thought, This is the last time
I'll ever be riding on his wheel. That can't be possible! I ended up losing the jersey. I really wanted to
send him home on the plane with the winner's jersey
from his last race. That was part of the reason why
I was so emotional on the final podium. I wanted
to dedicate the win to him, and I felt horrible I'd
screwed up the opportunity.

CADEL EVANS

It meant a lot to me to be at his last race, the USA
Pro Challenge. I was in the team car. Technically
I was George's mechanic(!), and afterward, to see
him take his number off for the last time was sad,
but special. I'm glad I got to witness and share that
with him.

I had a lot of fun with a few friends that night—Tejay and Christian among them. It was a low-key affair, and it seemed appropriate,
and fit my personality perfectly, that there wasn't a big send-off or
function.

Retirement wasn't restful. Every weekend I had somewhere

to be—a camp, an appearance, a charity ride. On top of that, Rich and I were organizing our first Gran Fondo ride, which was a main focus for the company, and for us, to give back to the community.

In the meantime, USADA's "reasoned decision" had been scheduled to be released right after the USA Pro Challenge, but they kept putting it off. My lawyer kept getting notified of delay after delay. It was incredibly frustrating and made me incredibly anxious. My inner circle was set—attorney, PR people, family—they all knew it was coming, but I was worried how the public would react.

We finally got word when it was to be released. That night, I was at a camp in Tennessee, and I decided to take an informal poll as a test run. There were about thirty campers, all with a cycling-centric mentality. Without giving them tons of detail, I did a Q&A session where I told them there would be some news coming out about me and others from cycling's past era. That small sampling of opinion was mostly favorable, but the next day, the reactions from some of the general public were more what I expected. The haters came out in force. I was appreciative of the supporters, but I was more sensitive to those angered by the news and who took personal aim not just at me, but at my wife and family.

We'd planned on putting out my statement before USADA released their reasoned decision. Before driving home from Tennessee, I texted my lawyer telling him to send it out, and within minutes my phone was buzzing nonstop. I wasn't really in any condition to drive, but I was anxious to get home. Between the phone and my imaginings about how the events of the day would affect me and my family, the whole trip home was a blur.

The day after the news broke and everyone was heralding me as the final straw, the pivotal witness to break open the case against Lance, I was blown away when Lance actually called and left a message. We hadn't had any contact since a brief hello in August 2011, and now he was checking in to see how I was holding up and to make sure I was okay. Calculated move or caring gesture, it didn't matter. It meant something to me.

I stopped reading all the press after a day or two. I was worried for my family. People were calling the house at all hours. Reporters had camped out at the front gate to our community. Thankfully, nobody ever made it to the house or said anything to Julia at school. I had to travel the next weekend to Charleston, South Carolina, to a charity event. Originally, I wasn't going to go, but my PR people insisted I had to be out in public and not seem like I was running away. Over two hundred people were there, and not one person had anything negative to say. It was incredibly uplifting to see all the support.

Our first ever Gran Fondo doubled as my official retirement party. We had over twelve hundred people there, many of whom had flown in just to wish me well. Cadel Evans flew in from Switzerland, on his way to Australia, to give me his best, and it was incredibly humbling to see a number of high-level business professionals whom I had met and befriended over the years show up to support the event.

CADEL EVANS

I forget how many flights it took, but there was no way I was going to miss his Gran Fondo. I could say thanks a million times, but making the effort to be there was the best way I could show him how much he meant to me.

The mass congregation wasn't just for my retirement. The weekend was a fund-raiser for our local chapter of Meals on Wheels, and the ride was a perfect opportunity to showcase the area around Greenville, which I would argue offers some of the best bike riding in the world. I'm a firm believer in the Fondo philosophy: the more people exposed to cycling through a well-organized, festive ride and in a setting like Greenville, the better for the sport. Most people who tried it that weekend, I still see out on the roads today.

JARED EMERSON, FRIEND
I'm an artist, and while I first heard of cycling because of Lance, I became a cyclist, and have stayed on my bike, because of George. After I got to know him, his work ethic, dedication, and discipline became contagious. He made me want to be better at what I did. I call him the Great Encourager. He makes others work harder and makes them better. I want to make George proud by proving to him I can strive to be as great at my craft as he has been at his.

The only time I had to relax was toward the end of the year. I'd promised Melanie the honeymoon I'd never been able to give her due to my schedule. I told her she could pick anywhere in the world, and she chose the Polynesian island of Bora Bora. We planned eight luxurious days—nothing but sand, sun, and relaxation. Melanie is able to actually *be on vacation*. I try, but I can never totally kick back. I always have to work out or find something to do.

In Bora Bora, Mother Nature conspired to make us bond. Indoors. It rained every single day we were there. The one day we tried to do an activity, we had booked an excursion to go swim with the sharks. But out on the water, an unrelenting tempest raged. We huddled underneath a big towel, freezing, while we got tossed back and forth in the swells. After that, we spent the rest of the time watching movies and Skyping the kids. They missed us so much that we felt guilty and came home early.

TEJAY VAN GARDEREN
Seeing his balance was the catalyst for me to want the same thing for myself. He had a lot to do with me and Jessica starting a family.

CHAPTER 31

JANUARY 8, 2013. I flew to New York City in the morning to meet Bill Bock and Travis Tygart from USADA along with my attorney. It was the first time I met Bock and Tygart face-to-face, and it was strange. As we sat in my attorney's large conference room and gazed out over the New York skyline, I got the impression Tygart and Bock just wanted to look me in the eye, to personalize the situation a bit more. They also wanted to prepare me for the Johan Bruyneel, Pepe Martí, and Pedro Celaya arbitration hearing that would be coming up at any time.

I thought the two hours were a colossal waste of time, and I was confused as to exactly why they were so adamantly going after guys who did not live in America and were clearly not ever going to work in the cycling industry again. Bock and Tygart wanted to clarify information and make sure I was ready to be cross-examined.

What *I* wanted was an explanation as to why the U.S. Postal team had been accused of having the "most sophisticated, professionalized and successful doping program that sport has ever seen." I didn't, and still don't, feel USADA looked at any other cycling teams, let alone other professional sports teams, the way they looked at ours. I understood Tygart was on a mission and doing what he felt best, but I think his view of the playing field was limited. To him it was black-and-white. To those of us who lived through that part of the sport's history and effected change from within, it was a different color. I never got my answer, other than a flippant, "Well, we were told you Americanized doping."

My day-to-day life seemed to only get busier in retirement. As a rider, I could always shut everything out and concentrate on what I could control. Everything was set. Sure, it *hurt,* but it was known and planned. Now, working with my company, I had to learn how to adapt to business situations and plan for contingencies. As an athlete, I got approached with deals. Now, with the development team, I approached others for sponsorship. My years as an athlete gave me insight into what companies wanted, but I still pounded the pavement to get money commitments for our team. When I first stopped riding, I knew I wanted to turn my attention to a few things: Hincapie Sportswear, our development team, and adapting to the new rhythm of my life. I loved not having to focus on my diet, and I loved having a less regimented lifestyle. Everything didn't have to be so controlled; I didn't have to live by the numbers—calories, watts, or speed.

I've read books about athletes retiring, and how unhappy they were, or how they couldn't find their place in life again. I never felt like that. I was really good about setting up my transition. For several years before I retired, I was always in tune with our company from afar, and the events the development team was doing. I went straight into the set of new challenges knowing it was with my family and the support network we'd been building throughout our lives.

As the calendar moved into spring 2013, it was a little strange to watch my old teammates start the season, but it was very nice not to have to worry about my weight or fitness level. And I definitely had not missed freezing my ass off during training all winter. I rode when I wanted to, as far as I wanted to. That was a great feeling.

In March I went skiing in Aspen. I originally hesitated to contact Lance, but eventually felt guilty and called to tell him I was there. He immediately got back to me and suggested we have dinner.

At first, it was awkward. It was the first time we'd been face-to-face since we'd stood onstage together at the USA Pro Challenge finish in Aspen back in 2011, and the first real conversation we'd had since May 2010. I was apprehensive about meeting again.

Lance picked up Mel and me and drove us to his house for drinks with his girlfriend, Anna, and then to a restaurant in town. I asked if he knew I was never out to hurt him, and told him I hoped he didn't hold it against me. He acknowledged it was hard, but that he understood.

That night felt like old times. I was relieved; dinner seemed to reset our normalcy a bit.

LANCE ARMSTRONG

The call, dinner at Cache Cache, and days we spent skiing helped get the relationship back to where it had been. But it never should have gotten to that point. We never should have had to reconnect. What really broke the ice was our competitive nature coming out on the slopes. We are both subpar skiers, but we challenged each other on the NASTAR course, and that rekindled the fun we used to have together.

It was interesting to see how Lance interacted with the public. People still wanted to come up and take pictures with him, and no one had anything negative to say. I couldn't help but notice he wasn't the same Lance, though; he seemed beaten down, more human. I couldn't help but wonder how much of a role I played in that transformation.

LANCE ARMSTRONG
I'd be in a better place if I'd had more of George's wisdom.

In April, the unbridled expressions and emotions were there for all to see. Shock. Joy. Fatigue. Triumph. Our Hincapie Sportswear Development Team swept the podium of Stage 3 of the Joe Martin Stage Race, and the photo of them with arms raised in victory as they crossed the line was validation of all the hard work we had put in over the years. Our guys had just beaten the best racers in the United States, and they'd made a statement in the process.

I'd always planned on giving back to the sport of cycling. I was fortunate to have opportunities presented to me at a young age, and I want to make sure I give back in the same way. It's also been a chance to pass on my decades of experience, while making sure no one is ever faced with the decisions I had to confront.

BRENT BOOKWALTER
I'm glad George went through what he did so I didn't have to. I'm appreciative and fortunate that my time came after the sport had turned the page and moved on. George, and his generation, started the change.

I figured when I was racing, the best way to honor the sport I loved was to commit every ounce of myself to being the best.

Cycling puts your body and mind through a rare hell, equally able
to elevate or crush your soul. It demands everything you have, and
then asks for just a little bit more. It also makes demands on anyone
around you. My brother, Rich, and I witnessed how expensive cycling can be, and we figured it was time to give our athletes a real
opportunity to see how good they could become.

Even before I retired, I'd been working with our development
team when I could, doing more or less what I was paid to do with
BMC Racing the last few years of my professional career: mentor
riders and lead by example. Now that my days on the bike are vol-
untary, not mandatory, my primary focus is passing on my racing
acumen and providing a sounding board for the myriad of questions
and situations that arise in a young rider's life.

RICH

Now that George is retired, his knowledge is instrumental in getting these guys to the next level, and as
you can see by their results, this year it seems to work.
George's real value, in my opinion, and why he was
paid like a leader, is not because he won tons of races.
I negotiated his contracts for his last eight years or so,
and had to sell people on a non–Tour winner making a
Tour winner salary: some people got that, many didn't.
George's real value is his leadership skills without being
an in-your-face leader. He's calm, funny, knowledgeable, and has a knack for inspiring people to try to be
like him. Guys like Lance, Cadel, Contador, and even
the younger generation would all look to George in the
bus for guidance and to calm them down. He made
his team his family and gave people a sense of worth,
which is what you see now in our development pro-

gram. His skill set was often more valuable than a big
engine. Thankfully for George, he had both.

The Joe Martin Stage Race victory made for a beautiful
memory, but it was a natural step toward what we've planned on
doing all along. We've already graduated riders to the Pro Tour,
cycling's highest level, but eventually, I'd like to see *our* team racing
on the Pro Tour. When I was on the bike, I embraced the ideal
that success does not happen overnight. It's been easy to apply that
approach in my role with our team.

I see the eagerness in the faces of our guys, and it reminds me
of myself. Our team is built on all the same cornerstones I used as a
professional athlete, paramount among which is the importance of
how each individual fits into the team concept and how the right
person can always make the group stronger. It's a simple message:
focus on the work.

MARK HOLOWESKO, PARTNER, HINCAPIE DEVELOPMENT TEAM

I choose to sponsor the team because I love cycling;
I admire what George has done; and I want to help
him give back to the sport. I also believe helping the
development team is a way for George to right some
wrongs in his past. If I can help him do this, it would
be huge for me, because it helps show others his
true character, despite all past issues. George Hincapie stands for dignity, humility, incredible loyalty,
family, success, and achievement.

One of our responsibilities is to constantly search for new, young
talent, and between Rich, myself, and our team network, it's a scouting

process that's rewarding. We take recommendations, follow race results, and often get to see potential team members race in person. Then, once they are with us, the nurturing begins. We've accomplished some great things this year, but there's so much more beyond the horizon and I'm dreaming big. While I understand that my dad's emotional investment in our cycling careers had a lot to do with the fact that we were his sons, I'm really understanding the pleasure that comes with creating the ideal conditions for young riders to be successful.

MARK HOLOWESKO

When it's all said and done, I'd like to see us create people in the mold of George Hincapie, to teach them values, teamwork, professionalism, persever-ance, and an incredible work ethic, so that they will be successful beyond cycling.

July. For the first time in nearly two decades, the month was my own. I was home in Greenville when the Tour began, and I followed the early parts of the race online. If a friend or former teammate was doing well in the stage, I'd turn on the TV. Instead of committing five to six hours a day, I invested thirty minutes to an hour. We visited Mel's parents in France, and I had some BMC appearances that brought me within arm's length of the Tour route, but I didn't feel comfortable being around the team or encroaching on their experience. I knew all too well their mind-set, and mine was steadfastly content in retirement. I didn't miss the pain, the crashes, the traveling, the hours in the bus, or the shitty hotels. I only missed the camaraderie.

TEJAY VAN GARDEREN

George was the one big personality everyone turned to, and he was sorely missed. He was the integral link between management and the riders. The most glaring example of his absence was in meetings. With him gone, they took forever. When George was with us, we all knew he'd ask the important questions, so everyone else would be quiet.

BRENT BOOKWALTER
I felt a void without him around this year. He was a grounding force we could have used. He knew how to reinforce the big moments, and when he spoke, everyone listened.

CADEL EVANS
George's greatest legacy is that he mentored others to follow in his footsteps. Just on our team, he looked at Manuel Quinziato, Marcus Burghardt, and Michael Schär as his apprentices, and instructed them on how to fill his shoes, and perform his role, once he was gone. George set the standard for my career, but he passed on his knowledge in the hopes that others can fill the void.

I was supposed to ride in the team car on Stage 20, which began in Annecy, but I left early. I didn't want to be one of those guys perceived to be hanging on, or overly reminiscing. I wanted to watch as a fan, not from the inside.

I walked onto the Champs-Élysées the morning the Tour was scheduled to finish in Paris. It was 8 a.m., and the riders wouldn't arrive for another twelve hours. The crowds were lined up four- to five-deep along the route. I was dressed in jeans, a T-shirt, and sunglasses, so nobody recognized me. The anonymity was comforting.

I'd never experienced this type of energy—from *this* side of the equation. Everywhere I turned, I could hear and see the excitement. Plenty of skeletons had come out of the closet in the past year, but still, the fans were there. It reinforced what had hooked me so many years ago—the power of cycling. I'd spent seventeen years riding on this boulevard, and as I turned to walk away and blend into the anticipatory mass of humanity, I smiled. I didn't know what the next chapter of my life would bring, but I was at peace with what I'd given to this one.

EPILOGUE

MY MEETING BACK IN January 2013 with Travis Tygart and his crew had left me unfulfilled. Not because I didn't share information they requested, but because of a question I hadn't had an answer for at the time, but that I finally came to be able to articulate over the course of the subsequent months.

In that meeting, the last thing Tygart asked, very pointedly, almost condescendingly, was, "What would you say to your daughter?" At that moment, an answer didn't appear. Now, I have one.

I've always tried to live honorably. First, by following in my father's, and brother's, footsteps. Then, once I discovered my passion for cycling and was given the means to pursue it, I honored the sport by working harder than anyone else I knew. Eventually, I felt duty-bound to show younger riders the proper path, to provide a blueprint of what to do and, at times, what not to do.

As I grew older and grasped my family's unusual commitment to each other, I vowed that loyalty would have an equal part in my motivation. I don't know any other way to be. Friends are part of my family. We've all heard the saying "Keep it simple, stupid"— and that's how I've approached my life to a certain degree. By simplifying my goals, my focus, and my energies, I've found success.

Bike racing was good to me, long before I met Lance, long before I took drugs, and thankfully, long after I gave them up. But as hard as others may try, I don't define myself as only a cyclist. I see myself as a person who found a passion to which he was suited, and who eventually strived to be a better man, husband, and father. That's what I want my kids to know and remember, not my athletic accomplishments.

Julia, your entry into the world changed me. It made me redefine my goals and realize what was important in life. While I would never want you, or Enzo, to make the same decisions I made, I would want you to dedicate yourself to something the way I did. Also, know that even though you can make wrong decisions along the way, you always have the chance to right them.

Ultimately, I wanted to leave the sport a better one than when I arrived on the scene.

I'd hope my family is a stronger one because of me, and I've never stopped trying to prove to them I'm deserving of their love and trust.

I never planned on riding off into the sunset, just to keep on riding.

ACKNOWLEDGMENTS

I THOUGHT ABOUT WRITING a book for years, and I went back and forth contemplating whether or not I should or would. There have been highs and lows in doing so, but ultimately my desire to tell my family story and show readers what events and experiences shaped and motivated me throughout the last thirty years of racing bicycles was the biggest factor in telling my story. I am aware that coming out and telling my story in recent years disappointed many, and I am truly sorry to those I disappointed. Hopefully this book offers not an excuse but a deeper context of why things were done. I have moved on to the next chapter of my life with a great passion to move the sport of cycling forward in a positive direction. My successes and mistakes of the past can hopefully contribute to showing young promising cyclists a modern new era of cycling.

I would like to express my gratitude to the many people who saw me through my nineteen-year career as a professional cyclist and helped me form the script of this book; to all those who provided support, talked things over, read, wrote, offered comments, allowed me to quote their remarks, and assisted in the editing, proofreading, and design. I truly thank you.

I would like to thank my sister, Clara, for teaching me how to ride a bike. My brother, Rich, for being my confidant and partner. Mark Holowesko, for being a great supporter of cycling and especially for believing and advising me along the way. Tim Hockey for his support and advice. Peter Gilgan for being a great friend and a great mentor. Bob Stapleton for taking me on a team that paved the way to changing our sport. Jim Ochowicz for all you have done for cycling and my family. Cadel Evans for allowing me to be part of one of my proudest tour victories. Mark Cavendish for bringing the joy of racing back to my life, and making it fun. My attorney David Anders for guiding me through the complexities of a world I had never been exposed to. Craig Hummer, for spending every evening of the last year with me helping me write this book. To close friends Michael Barry, Christian Vande Velde, Jared Emerson, Darren Fuller, William Crowley, and Ramin Modabber, and a special thanks to all my family in Colombia.

Last and not least: I apologize to all those who have been with me over the course of the years and whose names I have failed to mention.

—GH

My part in this book started out as a random request in a random European town almost a decade ago. So, first and foremost, thank you to George and Rich for their memory, and, particularly, their faith in entrusting me to tell their story. Thank you as well to Melanie, Julia, and Enzo for welcoming me into their home. I'm indebted to Adam Korn, Rory Scarfe, Trish Daly, and Carole Tonkinson—my HarperCollins leadout team. Sincere thanks to my agent, Jennifer Unter, who probably took my initial phone call about this project as a favor. Thanks to my daughters, Madison, Daisy, and Tatum, for understanding when I missed the countless dinners and days together as I eked out time to dive into this project. And finally, to my wife, Jennifer, the real writer in the family. I'll never be able to repay you for your compassion, selflessness, and wisdom. You are the standard.

—CH

GEORGE HINCAPIE is one of the most recognised and respected cyclists in the world, with numerous professional victories to his credit. Since retiring from professional cycling, Hincapie has taken a more active role in family business interests, including Hincapie Sportswear. He lives with his family in Greenville, South Carolina.

www.georgehincapie.com

CRAIG HUMMER is an Emmy-nominated sports broadcaster who has been involved in the action/lifestyle sports world for over twenty years, first as a professional athlete in the sport of Ocean Ironman racing, now as a commentator, and has covered over fifty sports. A graduate of Kenyon College, where he was a seventeen-time All-American, he lives with his family in Manhattan Beach, California.

www.craighummer.com